NTC's

Beginner's Spanish and English Dictionary

Regina M. Qualls, BVM
L. Sánchez

NTC Publishing Group

Library of Congress Cataloging-in-Publication Data

Quallis, Regina M.
NTC's beginner's Spanish and English dictionary / Regina M. Quallis, L. Sánchez.
p. cm.
ISBN 0-8442-7698-7 (cloth)
ISBN 0-8442-7699-5 (paper)
1. Spanish language—Dictionaries—English. 2. English language—Dictionaries—Spanish. I. Sánchez, L. II. Title.
PC4640.Q3 1997b
463'.21—dc21 97-39061
CIP

Published by NTC Publishing Group
An imprint of NTC/Contemporary Publishing Group, Inc.
4255 West Touhy Avenue, Lincolnwood (Chicago), Illinois 60646-1975 U.S.A.

Printed in the United States of America
International Standard Book Number: 0-8442-7698-7 (cloth)
0-8442-7699-5 (paper)

25 24 23 22 21 20 19 18 17 16 15 14 13 12 11 10

Contents

Introduction	v
How to Use This Dictionary	v
The Entries	vi
Pronunciation	vii
Pronunciation Guide: Spanish-English	vii
Pronunciation Guide: English-Spanish	viii
Stress	ix
Capitalization	x
Spanish Grammar	x
Spanish-English Dictionary	1
Illustrations	259
English-Spanish Dictionary	277
Appendices	459
Spanish Names	459
Family Members	461
The Body	461
Countries / Nationalities	462
Foods	462
Sports	463
At the Zoo	463
Months of the Year	464
Days of the Week	464
Numbers	464
Temperature	465
Weights and Measures	465
Maps	467

Introduction

This Spanish-English bilingual dictionary is especially designed to help the English-speaking student learn basic Spanish and may also be used to help the Spanish-speaking student learn basic English. Approximately 3,500 main vocabulary entries have been compiled in this useful reference. To highlight idiomatic expressions and shades of meaning, the dictionary also contains hundreds of subentries.

Because beginning language students often need more than a simple translation, this dictionary also presents information on the correct usage of entry words. At least one example sentence (followed by a translation) demonstrates the use of each entry word in context. Verbs are listed in their infinitive form and irregular verbs are conjugated in the present tense within the entry.

The typography of this dictionary, also designed with beginning learners in mind, allows students to clearly distinguish the various parts of the entries. Entry words are in boldface type, while parts of speech and translated sentences are in italics.

Between the Spanish-English and English-Spanish portions of the dictionary, an 18-page section contains drawings illustrating 174 common words in 21 categories that include sports, birds, insects, food, transportation, and animals. Each drawing is labeled both in Spanish and English. At the back of the book, a series of appendices provides metric conversions and a quick reference to useful words like months, days of the week, parts of the body, and more.

How to Use This Dictionary

This dictionary provides more information than just the simple translation of a word. Entries will also tell you how to pronounce words, what parts of speech they are, and how to use them in a sentence. When a word has more than one possible translation, all the translations are given. When looking up a word, the entire entry should be read in order to determine the most appropriate translation.

The Entries

In the Spanish-English section of the dictionary, entries follow this format:

1. *Spanish word.* This is in boldface type, making it easy to spot. Whenever a masculine noun also has a feminine form, the feminine ending follows directly and the corresponding definite article appears in parentheses.
2. *Pronunciation.* To help say the entry word correctly, a simple pronunciation guide follows each entry. The "Pronunciation" section below explains the use of these guides.
3. *Part of Speech.* This label indicates whether the entry is a noun, verb, adjective, etc. Abbreviations used for parts of speech are: *n.*, noun; *pron., pronoun; v.*, verb; *adj.*, adjective; *adv.*, adverb, *prep.*, preposition; *interr.,* interrogative; *intj.,* interjection; *cont.,* contraction; *coll.,* colloquial; *m.*, masculine; *f.*, feminine; *pl.*, plural; *s.*, singular.
4. *Definition.* English definition(s) explain the meaning of the entry word.
5. *Conjugation.* If the entry word is a verb, it will be conjugated in the present tense.
6. *Subentries.* Sometimes there are subentries to explain the meaning of words or expressions derived from the entry word. As in main entries, these feature a label identifying the part of speech and an English definition.
7. *Spanish sentence(s).* This shows the correct use of the entry or subentry word. Where a word has various uses, more than one sentence is provided.
8. *English translation.* Every example sentence in Spanish is then translated into English.

The following is an example of an entry in the Spanish-English section:

caerse [ca ER say] *n.* • to fall down

yo	me caigo
tú	te caes
usted	se cae
él, ella	se cae
nosotros, as	nos caemos
vosotros, as	os caéis
ustedes	se caen
ellos, ellas	se caen

No me gusta patinar; siempre me caigo.
I don't like to skate; I always fall down.

The English-Spanish section follows the same format, except that verbs are not conjugated in the entries. Here is an example of an English-Spanish entry:

fall, to [FO̲L] *v.* • caerse
You're going to fall!
¡Te vas a caer!

Pronunciation

Pronunciation can sometimes be difficult for beginning language learners. For this reason, a pronunciation guide is included in each entry. They follow a phonetic system that imitates the way an English speaker would try to sound out Spanish words or the way a Spanish speaker would try to pronounce English words.

Pronunciation Guide: Spanish-English

Below is a description of the symbols used to represent Spanish sounds in the pronunciation guides, along with an explanation of how to pronounce the sounds.

Vowels

Symbol	*Pronunciation*
a	like the *a* in *father*
ay	like the *ay* in *say*

e	like the *e* in *bet*
ee	like the *ee* in *teeth*
i	like the *i* in *fight*
o	like the *o* in *over*
ow	like the *ow* in *now*
oy	like the *oy* in *boy*
u	like the *u* in *rude*
wa	like the *wo* in *wobble*
we	like the *we* in *welcome*

Consonants

b	like the *b* in *boy*
c	like the *c* in *call*
d	like the *d* in *did*
d̲	like the *th* in *mother*
g	like the *g* in *go*
h	like the *h* in *happy*
k	like the *k* in *key*
ks	like the *x* in *extra*
ny	like the *ny* in *canyon*
r	single flap of the tongue against the roof of the mouth
rr	strongly trilled
y	like the *y* in *yet*

Consonant symbols whose sounds are the same as in English are not listed here.

Pronunciation Guide English-Spanish

Below is a description of symbols used to represent English sounds in the pronunciation guides, along with an example word for each sound.

Vowels

Symbol	*Pronunciation*
ä	like the *a* in *about*
a	like the *a* in *father*
a̲	like *a* in *hat*
ai	like the *i* in *kite*

au	like the *ow* in *cow*
e	like the *e* in *let*
ë	like the second *e* in *letter*
ei	like the *ay* in *play*
i	like the *ee* in *feet*
i̱	like the *in* in *fin*
o	like the *o* in *sofa*
o̱	like the *o* in *longer*
oy	like the *oy* in *boy*
u	like the *oo* in *moon*
ü	like the *u* in *full*

Consonants

b	like the *b* in *boy*
c	like the *c* in *cat*
ch	like the *ch* in *chip*
g	like the *g* in *game*
g̱	like the *g* in *gym*
h	like the *h* in *happy*
ke, ki	like the *k* in *kind*
kw	like the *qu* in *quick*
ng	like the *ng* in *thing*
r	like the *r* in *red*
sh	like the *sh* in *shop*
th	like the *th* in *thing*
v	like the *v* in *visit*
w	like the *w* in *west*
x	like the *x* in *extra*
y	like the *y* in *young*
z	like the *z* in *zoo*

Consonant symbols that sound the same in Spanish and in English are not listed here.

Stress

You will notice that some Spanish words have a written accent. This is to show you which syllable to emphasize or stress. If a word does not have a written accent, you pronounce it by following these rules:

1. If the word ends in a vowel, n or s, you stress the next to the last syllable.
2. If the word ends in a consonant (other than n or s), you stress the last syllable.

In English, stress varies. In the pronunciation guides, the stressed syllable of each word is always in capital letters.

Sometimes a written accent will not affect pronunciation and will help differentiate two words with different meanings but the same spelling. For example, *el* means "the," but *él* means "he." And the word *este* means "this," but *éste* means "This one."

Capitalization

Capital letters are not used as often in Spanish as they are in English. The following types of words are *not* capitalized in Spanish except at the beginning of a sentence: days of the week, months of the year, nouns and adjectives of nationality, names of languages, and titles of address (*señor, señora, señorita, doctor*) except when they are abbreviated (*Sr., Sra., Srta., Dr.*). So, for example, the words *martes, enero,* and *inglés* are *not* capitalized in Spanish, while in English, "Tuesday," "January," and "English" are capitalized.

Spanish Grammar

Nouns

All Spanish nouns (words for people, places, things, or ideas) have a gender. That is, they are considered either masculine or feminine. Most of the time, gender has to be memorized. Nevertheless, there are some helpful patterns: Nouns ending in *-o* are usually masculine, while those ending in consonants, *-a, -d,* or *-ión* are usually feminine. Of course, words such as "boy" or "man" will be masculine, while words such as "mother" or "woman" will be feminine. Generally, the definite article (described below) also indicates whether a noun is masculine or feminine.

Some nouns have a masculine and feminine form. For example, a teacher may be a man (*maestro*) or a woman (*maestra*). You will find such words listed this way: **maestro, a (el, la)**. Other words, such as *agua*, are feminine, but use the definite article *el*. Such words are listed this way: **agua (el)** (f.).

Definite Articles

Definite articles come before nouns and indicate a definite person, place, or thing. Generally, they can be translated by the word "the." In Spanish, definite articles can be masculine or feminine, singular or plural, depending on the gender and number of the noun. In most cases, the gender of a noun can be determined by looking at the definite article. The following are the definite articles:

1. *El* is used with masculine singular nouns.
   Examples: *el libro, el coche, el sofá*
2. *La* is used with feminine singular nouns.
   Examples: *la hija, la lección, la clase*
3. *Los* is used with masculine plural nouns.
   Examples: *los libros, los coches, los sofás*
4. *Las* is used with feminine plural nouns.
   Examples: *las hijas, las lecciones, las clases*

The entries in this dictionary include the definite article with each noun.

Adjectives

Adjectives are words that describe people, places, things, or ideas (nouns). Adjectives in Spanish differ from adjectives in English in several ways.

First of all, Spanish adjectives usually follow, but sometimes come before the noun they describe.

Examples: *un libro grande, un gran libro*

As you study Spanish, you will learn the rules that determine whether an adjective goes before or after a noun.

Second, adjectives "agree" in gender and number with the nouns they describe. This means that the adjective will change form depending on whether the noun is masculine or feminine, singular or plural. If a noun is feminine and singular the adjective will end in *a*. For plural nouns, add an *s* to the adjective (masculine or feminine).

Examples:	masculine singular	el lápiz rojo
	feminine singular	la pluma negra
	masculine plural	los lápices rojos
	feminine plural	las plumas negras

There are some exceptions to this rule. Adjectives that end in consonants (for example, *azul* or an *e* (for example, *verde*) have the same form in masculine and feminine singular (*el cuaderno azul, la casa azul*). To form the plural of an adjective ending in *e*, add *-s*: *los ojos verdes, las hojas verdes*. To form the plural of an adjective ending in a consonant, add *-es*: *los cuadernos azules, las casas azules*.

Prepositions

Prepositions are words that indicate purpose, destination, direction, location, or time. They usually come before a noun or pronoun. Some English prepositions are: *to* (a), *for* (por), *at* (a), *with* (con), *from* (de), *in* (en), *on* (en), *of* (de), and *until* (hasta). Since there are many ways to use prepositions, this dictionary provides numerous examples to show you how to use them correctly, as well as examples of Spanish expressions in which prepositions appear.

Adverbs

An adverb is a word that describes a verb, an adjective, or another adverb. Unlike adjectives, adverbs do not change form to reflect gender and number. In most cases, the adverb follows the verb and precedes the adjective in a sentence.

Example: María es *muy* inteligente.

Verbs

A verb is an action word. The basic form of a verb is called an *infinitive*. In this dictionary, verbs are listed by their infinitives. Spanish, like English, has both *regular* and *irregular* verbs.

The regular verbs are divided into three groups, according to the endings of their infinitives. These groups are called the *-ar*, *-er*, and, *-ir* verbs. Here are infinitives belonging to each group: *hablar* (to talk), *comer* (to eat), and *escribir* (to write).

Verbs change forms to tell you *who* is performing an action. The forms of regular verbs follow consistent patterns, so that if you know how to conjugate one regular *-ar*, *-er* or *-ir* verb, you can *conjugate* (know the forms of) the others. However, when you look up an irregular verb in its infinitive form in this dictionary, you will find it conjugated in the entry. Because irregular verbs do not follow the consistent patterns that the regular verbs do, they must be learned individually.

To conjugate a regular verb, begin by removing the *-ar*, *-er*, or *-ir* ending. So, *hablar* (to speak) becomes *habl-*, *comer* (to eat) becomes *com-*, and *escribir* (to write) becomes *escrib-*. Next, add the correct ending to the verb. Notice the endings (shown here in italics) on conjugated Spanish verbs.

The conjugated forms of *hablar* are:

yo	habl*o*	(I speak)
tú	habl*as*	(you speak)
usted	habl*a*	(you speak)
él, ella	habl*a*	(he, she speaks)
nosotros, nosotras	habl*amos*	(we speak)
vosostros, vosotros	habl*áis*	(you speak)
ustedes	habl*an*	(you speak)
ellos, ellas	habl*an*	(they speak)

The conjugated forms of *comer* are:

yo	com*o*	(I eat)
tú	com*es*	(you eat)
usted	com*e*	(you eat)

él, ella come	com*e*	(he, she eats)
nosotros, nosotras	com*emos*	(we eat)
vosotros, vosotras	com*éis*	(you eat)
ustédes	com*en*	(you eat)
ellos, ellas	com*en*	(they eat)

And the conjugated forms of *escribir* are:

yo	escrib*o*	(I write)
tú	escrib*es*	(you write)
usted	escrib*e*	(you write)
él, ella	escrib*e*	(he, she writes)
nosotros, nosotras	escrib*imos*	(we write)
vosotros, vosotras	escrib*ís*	(you write)
ustedes	escrib*en*	(you write)
ellos, ellas	escrib*en*	(they write)

Some verbs are called *reflexive verbs*, because they describe an action that a subject does to himself or herself. These are conjugated with an object pronoun. For example, *lavarse* (to wash oneself) is conjugated

yo	me lavo	(I wash myself)
tú	te lavas	(you wash yourself)
usted	se lava	(you wash yourself)
él, ella	se lava	(he, she washes himself, herself)
nosotros, as	nos lavamos	(we wash ourselves)
vosotros, as	os laváis	(you wash yourselves)
ustedes	se lavan	(you wash yourselves)
ellos, ellas	se lavan	(they wash themselves)

Some verbs can be used either in their simple form or in the reflexive form. In those cases, the entries in the dictionary include both conjugations.

Spanish–English/*Español–Inglés*

A

a [A] *prep.* • to, at, for
a causa de • because of
a la derecha • to the right
a la izquierda • to the left
a la una • at one o'clock
a las dos • at two o'clock
a menudo • often
¿A qué hora? • At what time?
a tiempo • on time
a veces • sometimes
a ver • let's see

1. The preposition *a* always precedes an indirect object (a+noun)

Martha le explica la lección a José.
Martha explains the lesson to José.

2. For the specific time at which something happens

El programa empieza a la una.
The program begins at one o'clock.

3. Direction or goal

Yo voy a la playa.
I am going to the beach.

4. Proportional count

Las rosas se venden a tres dólares la docena.
Roses cost three dollars a dozen.

abajo [a BA ho] *adv.* • down, below, downstairs
Yo estoy arriba y él está abajo.
I am upstairs and he is downstairs.

abandonado, a [a ban do NA do] *adj.* • abandoned
Encontramos este gatito abandonado en el camino.
We found this little kitten abandoned on the road.

abandonar [a ban do NAR] *v.* • to abandon
Tuve que abandonar el proyecto.
I had to abandon the project.

abeja (la) [a BE ha] *n.* • bee
Las abejas producen miel.
Bees produce honey.

abierto, a [a BYER to] *adj.* • open
El banco está abierto de las nueve a las cinco.
The bank is open from nine to five.

abogado, a (el, la) [a bo GA do] *n.* • lawyer
Los abogados están debatiendo el caso.
The lawyers are debating the case.

abotonar [a bo to NAR] *v.* • to button
La niña abotona su abrigo.
The girl buttons her coat.

abrazo (el) [a BRA so] *n.* • hug
En Latinoamérica la gente se saluda con un abrazo.
In Latin America people greet each other with a hug.

abrelatas (el) [a bre LA tas] *n.* • can opener
El abrelatas está en la cocina.
The can opener is in the kitchen.

abrigo (el) [a BREE go] *n.* • coat
Elena tiene un abrigo nuevo.
Elena has a new coat.

abril [a BREEL] *n.* • April
Los tulipanes florecen en abril.
Tulips bloom in April.

abrir [a BREER] *v.* • to open
Lupe abre sus regalos de cumpleaños.
Lupe is opening her birthday presents.

abuelo (el) [a BWE lo] *n.* • grandfather
abuela (la) *n.* • grandmother
El abuelo de Carmen la visita todos los años.
Carmen's grandfather visits her every year.

aburrido, a [a bu RREE do] *adj.* • boring; bored
Esa película es muy aburrida.
That movie is very boring.

Alberto está aburrido sin sus amigos.
Alberto is bored without his friends.

aburrir [a bu RREER] *v.* • to bore
aburrirse *v.* • to get (be) bored
Es muy fácil aburrirse cuando no hay nada que hacer.
It is very easy to get bored when there is nothing to do.

acabar [a ca BAR] *v.* • to finish
acabar de *v.* • to have just finished doing something
Los niños están acabando su tarea.
The children are finishing their homework.

Mi madre acaba de regresar del mercado.
My mother has just returned from the market.

aceite (el) [a SAY te] *n.* • oil
Los españoles cocinan con aceite de oliva.
Spaniards cook with olive oil.

aceituna (la) [a say TU na] *n.* • olive
Las mejores aceitunas son de España.
The best olives are from Spain.

aceptar [a sep TAR] *v.* • to accept
Casi todos los países aceptan la importancia de los derechos humanos.
Almost all countries accept the importance of human rights.

acera (la) [a SE ra] *n.* • sidewalk
Juan nos espera en la acera cerca del teatro.
Juan is waiting for us on the sidewalk near the theater.

acero (el) [a SE ro] *n.* • steel
Los tenedores son de acero inoxidable.
The forks are stainless steel.

acompañar [a com pa NYAR] *v.* • to go along, to accompany
Acompañamos a mi tía en sus viajes a México.
We go along with my aunt on her trips to Mexico.

acordar [a cor DAR] *v.* • to agree
acordarse *v.* • to remember

yo	me	acuerdo
tú	te	acuerdas
usted	se	acuerda
él, ella	se	acuerda
nosotros, as	nos	acordamos
vosotros, as	os	acordáis
ustedes	se	acuerdan
ellos, ellas	se	acuerdan

Miguel y Juan acuerdan hacer el proyecto.
Miguel and Juan agree to do the project.

No me acuerdo de eso.
I don't remember that.

acordeón (el) [a cor de ON] *n.* • accordion
El acordeón es un instrumento que se usa para tocar polcas.
The accordion is an instrument used to play polkas.

acostarse [a cos TAR se] *v.* • to go to bed

yo	me acuesto
tú	te acuestas
usted	se acuesta
él, ella	se acuesta
nosotros, as	nos acostamos
vosotros, as	os acostáis
ustedes	se acuestan
ellos, ellas	se acuestan

Los futbolistas se acuestan temprano antes de un partido.
Soccer players go to bed early before a match.

actitud (la) [ac tee TUD] *n.* • attitude
La actitud de este político es interesante.
The attitude of this politician is interesting.

activo, a [ac TEE bo] *adj.* • active
Los niños de dos años son activos.
Two-year-old children are active.

acto (el) [AC to] *n.* • act
El drama tiene tres actos.
The play has three acts.

actor (el) [ac TOR] *n.* • actor
actriz (la) [ac TREES] *n.* • actress
Muchos actores y actrices sueñan con ganar un "Oscar".
Many actors and actresses dream of winning an "Oscar."

actual [ac TWAL] *adj.* • current
La tecnología actual es sorprendente.
Current technology is surprising.

acuario (el) [a CWA ryo] *n.* • fish tank, aquarium
El pasatiempo de Roberto es su acuario.
Roberto's hobby is his fish tank.

acuático, a [a CWA tee co] *adj.* • aquatic
Las ballenas son animales acuáticos.
Whales are aquatic animals.

acuerdo (el) [a CWER do] *n.* • agreement
El acuerdo es que no vemos más de dos horas de televisión.
The agreement is that we do not watch more than two hours of TV.

acumulación (la) [a cu mu la SYON] *n.* • accumulation
La acumulación de basura es un problema alarmante.
The accumulation of garbage is an alarming issue.

además [a de MAS] *adv.* • besides, in addition to
Además de aprender español, quiero aprender francés.
Besides learning Spanish, I want to learn French.

adentro [a DEN tro] *adv.* • inside
En invierno los niños juegan adentro.
In winter the children play inside.

adiós [a DYOS] *intj.* • good-bye
Es difícil decir adiós a los amigos.
It is hard to say good-bye to friends.

adivinanza (la) [a dee bee NAN sa] *n.* • riddle
Las adivinanzas son divertidas.
Riddles are amusing.

admirador, a (el, la) [ad mee ra DOR] *n.* • fan, admirer
El actor tiene un club de admiradores.
The actor has a fan club.

admirar [ad mee RAR] *v.* • to admire
Admiramos su talento.
We admire his talent.

¿adónde? [a DON de] *adv.* • where to?
¿Adónde vas?
Where are you going?

adornar [a dor NAR] *v.* • to decorate
Los chicas adornan el pelo con cintas de muchos colores.
Girls decorate their hair with ribbons of many colors.

adulto (el) [a DUL to] *n.* • adult
Los adultos tienen muchas responsabilidades.
Adults have many responsibilities.

aéreo, a [a E re o] *adj.* • air
el correo aéreo *n.* • airmail
la línea aérea *n.* • airline
Cuesta $2 mandar esa carta por correo aéreo.
It costs $2 to send that letter airmail.

aeromozo, a (el, la) [a e ro MO so] *n.* • flight attendant
Jason es un aeromozo muy amable.
Jason is a very friendly flight attendant.

aeropuerto (el) [a e ro PWER to] *n.* • airport
El taxi va al aeropuerto.
The taxi is going to the airport.

afeitar(se) [a fay TAR] *v.* • to shave (oneself)
Pedro usa la navaja para afeitarse.
Pedro uses the razor to shave himself.

afortunadamente [a for tu na da MEN te] *adv.* • fortunately
Afortunadamente estudiamos español.
Fortunately we are studying Spanish.

agencia (la) [a HEN sya] *n.* • agency
agencia de viajes *n.* • travel agency
Podemos conseguir billetes de tren en la agencia de viajes.
We can get train tickets at the travel agency.

agente (el, la) [a HEN te] *n.* • agent
Susana es agente de viajes.
Susana is a travel agent.

agilidad (la) [a hee lee DAD] *n.* • agility
El deporte desarrolla la agilidad.
Sports develop agility.

agosto [a GOS to] *n.* • August
En España tomamos las vacaciones en agosto.
In Spain we take vacations in August.

agradable [a gra DA ble] *adj.* • pleasant, agreeable
El clima en Cuernavaca es muy agradable.
The climate in Cuernavaca is very pleasant.

agricultor, a (el, la) [a gree cul TOR] *n.* • farmer
El agricultor compra semillas.
The farmer buys seeds.

agua (el) (f.) [A gwa] *n.* • water
El agua contaminada es peligrosa.
Contaminated water is dangerous.

aguacate (el) [a gwa CA te] *n.* • avocado
Los aguacates son deliciosos.
Avocados are delicious.

águila (el) (f.) [A gee la] *n.* • eagle
El águila es un símbolo de nuestro país.
The eagle is a symbol of our country.

aguja (la) [a GU ha] *n.* • needle
Cecilia cose con la aguja.
Cecilia sews with the needle.

agujero (el) [a gu HE ro] *n.* • hole
El ratón escapa por el agujero.
The mouse escapes through the hole.

ahijado (el) [a hee HA do] *n.* • godson
ahijada (la) *n.* • goddaughter
Laura es ahijada de Irene.
Laura is Irene's goddaughter.

ahora [a O ra] *adv.* • now
ahora mismo *adv.* • right now
Necesitamos empezar la tarea ahora mismo.
We need to start the homework right now.

ahorrar [a o RRAR] *v.* • to save (money, time, energy)
Estamos ahorrando dinero para comprar regalos.
We are saving money in order to buy gifts.

aire (el) [I re] *n.* • air
aire libre *n.* • outdoors
La contaminación del aire es un problema hoy día.
Air pollution is a problem nowadays.

ajedrez (el) [a he DRES] *n.* • chess
El tablero de ajedrez es de Antonio.
The chess board belongs to Antonio.

ají (el) [a HEE] *n.* • chili pepper
No me gusta la comida con ají.
I do not like food with chili pepper.

ajo (el) [A ho] *n.* • garlic
A mi mamá le gusta cocinar con ajo.
My mother likes to cook with garlic.

al [AL] *cont.* a + el (see *a*) • to the
Vamos al teatro.
We are going to the theater.

ala (el) (f.) [A la] *n.* • wing
Los pájaros tienen dos alas.
Birds have two wings.

alarma (la) [a LAR ma] *n.* • alarm
Es importante tener una alarma de incendios en su casa.
It's important to have a fire alarm in your house.

albaricoque (el) [al ba ree CO ke] *n.* • apricot
¿Hay albaricoques en el mercado?
Are there apricots at the market?

albóndiga (la) [al BON dee ga] *n.* • meatball
Pedro come albóndigas para la cena.
Pedro is eating meatballs for dinner.

álbum (el) [AL bum] *n.* • album
Roberto tiene un álbum filatélico.
Roberto has a stamp album.

alcalde (el) [al CAL de] *n.* • mayor
El alcalde tiene que asistir a muchas ceremonias oficiales.
The mayor has to attend many official functions.

alcoba (la) [al CO ba] *n.* • bedroom
Mi casa tiene cinco alcobas.
My house has five bedrooms.

alegre [a LE gre] *adj.* • happy, cheerful, glad
Guillermo es un tipo alegre.
Guillermo is a cheerful guy.

alejado, a [a le HA do] *adj.* • far, distant
El aeropuerto está muy alejado de la ciudad.
The airport is very far from the city.

alemán, a [a le MAN] *adj.* • German
alemán (el) *n.* • German (language)
alemán, a (el, la) *n.* • German (person)
Las muchachas alemanas que nos visitan son de Berlín.
The German girls who are visiting us are from Berlin.

alfabeto (el) [al fa BE to] *n.* • alphabet
El alfabeto ruso es muy diferente del nuestro.
The Russian alphabet is very different from our own.

alfombra (la) [al FOM bra] *n.* • rug
Las alfombras persas son famosas por sus diseños.
Persian rugs are famous for their designs.

algo [AL go] *pron.* • something
Necesito algo de la tienda.
I need something from the store.

algodón (el) [al go DON] *n.* • cotton
La blusa es de algodón.
The blouse is cotton.

alguien [AL gyen] *pron.* • someone
Alguien está en la puerta.
Someone is at the door.

algún, alguna [al GUN] *adj.* • some, any, a
Compro algunos regalos.
I am buying some gifts.

alma (el) (f.) [AL ma] *n.* • soul, spirit
No hay un alma aquí.
There isn't a soul around.

almacén (el) [al ma SEN] *n.* • department store
Los almacenes están en el centro.
The department stores are downtown.

almohada (la) [al mo A da] *n.* • pillow
El bebé duerme sin almohada.
The baby sleeps without a pillow.

almorzar [al mor SAR] v. • to have lunch

yo	almuerzo
tú	almuerzas
usted	almuerza
él, ella	almuerza
nosotros, as	almorzamos
vosotros, as	almorzáis
ustedes	almuerzan
ellos, ellas	almuerzan

¿Almuerzas al mediodía?
Do you have lunch at noon?

almuerzo (el) [al MWER so] *n.* • lunch
¿Qué comes para el almuerzo?
What do you eat for lunch?

alpinismo (el) [al pee NEES mo] *n.* • mountain climbing
El alpinismo es un deporte peligroso.
Mountain climbing is a dangerous sport.

alpinista (el, la) [al pee NEES ta] *n.* • mountain climber
Los alpinistas van a la montaña.
The mountain climbers are going to the mountain.

alquilar [al kee LAR] *v.* • to rent
Podemos alquilar un automóvil en México y visitar los parques nacionales.
We can rent a car in Mexico and visit the national parks.

alrededor [al re de DOR] *adv.* • around
alrededor de *prep.* • around, about
Plantamos rosales alrededor del patio.
We're planting rosebushes around the patio.

alto, a [AL to] *adj.* • tall, high
Mi primo Eduardo es muy alto.
My cousin Eduardo is very tall.

altura (la) [al TU ra] *n.* • height, altitude
La montaña tiene más de 15,000 pies de altura.
The mountain has an altitude of more than 15,000 feet.

alumno, a (el, la) [a LUM no] *n.* • pupil, student
Hay quinientos alumnos en esta escuela.
There are five hundred students in this school.

allá [a YA] *adv.* • over there
Hay unas sillas allá.
There are some chairs over there.

amable [a MA ble] *adj.* • kind, generous, friendly
Tu papá es muy amable.
Your father is very kind.

amar [a MAR] *v.* • to love
Te amo, Juan.
I love you, Juan.

amarillo, a [a ma REE yo] *adj.* • yellow
La bandera española es roja y amarilla.
The Spanish flag is red and yellow.

ambición (la) [am bee SYON] *n.* • ambition
Mi ambición es ser científica .
My ambition is to be a scientist.

ambulancia (la) [am bu LAN sya] *n.* • ambulance
Las ambulancias usan una sirena.
Ambulances use a siren.

americano, a [a me ree CA no] *adj.* • American (from the US or any other country in North, Central or South America)
americano, a (el, la) *n.* • American
Muchos americanos hablan inglés.
Many Americans speak English.

Ellas compran un carro americano.
They are buying an American car.

amigo, a (el, la) [a MEE go] *n.* • friend
Mi mejor amiga es mi vecina.
My best friend is my neighbor.

amor (el) [a MOR] *n.* • love
El amor es extraordinario.
Love is extraordinary.

anaranjado, a [a na ran HA do] *adj.* • orange
El color anaranjado es una combinación de rojo y amarillo.
The color orange is a combination of red and yellow.

ancho, a [AN cho] *adj.* • wide
El río es ancho.
The river is wide.

andar [an DAR] *v.* • to walk; to run (a machine)
andar a caballo • to ride a horse
andar en bicicleta • to ride a bicycle
Ando por el parque.
I walk through the park.

El reloj anda bien.
The watch runs well.

¿Prefieres andar a caballo o andar en bicicleta?
Do you prefer to ride a horse or to ride a bicycle?

ángel (el) [AN hel] *n.* • angel
Mi hermana hace el papel de un ángel en el espectáculo de la escuela.
My sister is an angel in the school play.

anillo (el) [a NEE yo] *n.* • ring
Mi anillo de compromiso tiene un zafiro
My engagement ring has a sapphire.

animal (el) [a nee MAL] *n.* • animal
El elefante es un animal grande.
The elephant is a big animal.

aniversario (el) [a nee ber SA ryo] *n.* • anniversary
El 4 de julio es el aniversario de la independencia de los Estados Unidos.
The 4th of July is the anniversary of the independence of the U.S.

anoche [a NO che] *adv.* • last night
Anoche vimos Orión y la Osa Mayor en el cielo.
Last night we saw Orion and the Big Dipper in the sky.

antena (la) [an TE na] *n.* • antenna
¿Crees que los marcianos tienen antenas?
Do you think Martians have antennas?

anteojos (los) [an te O hos] *n.* • eyeglasses
Prefiero usar anteojos a lentes de contacto.
I prefer eyeglasses to contact lenses.

antes [AN tes] *adv.* • before
antes de *prep.* • before
Él viene a las cinco, no antes.
He is coming at 5 o'clock, not before.

Estudiamos antes de un examen.
We study before a test.

antiguo, a [an TEE gwo] *adj.* • old, ancient
El Partenón es un edificio antiguo.
The Parthenon is an ancient building.

antipático, a [an tee PA tee co] *adj.* • not nice, unpleasant, disagreeable
Esa chica es muy antipática.
That girl is very unpleasant.

anunciar [a nun SYAR] *v.* • to announce
El director anuncia el horario de clases.
The principal is announcing the class schedule.

año (el) [A nyo] *n.* • year
El año escolar empieza en septiembre.
The school year begins in September.

apagar [a pa GAR] *v.* • to turn off, to switch off
Apaga la luz por favor.
Turn off the light, please.

apagón (el) [a pa GON] *n.* • blackout, power failure
Un apagón es muy peligroso en una ciudad grande.
A blackout is very dangerous in a big city.

apariencia (la) [a pa RYEN sya] *n.* • appearance
La apariencia física es importante.
Physical appearance is important.

apartamento (el) [a par ta MEN to] *n.* • apartment
Cecilia y Bob tienen un apartamento al oeste de la ciudad.
Cecilia and Bob have an apartment west of the city.

apellido (el) [a pe YEE do] *n.* • surname, last name
¿Cuál es tu apellido?
What is your last name?

apenas [a PE nas] *adv.* • scarcely, barely, hardly
Tomás apenas tiene cinco años.
Tomás is barely five years old.

apetito (el) [a pe TEE to] *n.* • appetite
Siempre que voy de excursión regreso a casa con mucho apetito.
Every time I go hiking, I come back home with a big appetite.

apio (el) [A pyo] *n.* • celery
Me gusta la ensalada de apio con manzanas y nueces.
I like celery salad with apples and nuts.

aplaudir [a plow DEER] *v.* • to applaud, to clap
Claudia aplaude a su hermano.
Claudia applauds her brother.

apreciar [a pre SYAR] *v.* • to appreciate, to value
Aprecio mucho a mi amiga Elena.
I appreciate my friend Elena a great deal.

aprender [a pren DER] *v.* • to learn
Hay personas que tienen facilidad para aprender idiomas.
There are people who have a facility for learning languages.

apretado, a [a pre TA do] *adj.* • tight
¡No me gustan esos zapatos apretados!
I don't like those tight shoes!

aquel, la [a KEL] *adj.* • that (in the distance)
aquellos, as [a KE yohs] *adj.* • those
Aquel avión es grande.
That airplane is big.

Aquellas velas son bonitas.
Those sails are pretty.

aquí [a KEE] *adv.* • here
Aquí tienes el disco que quieres.
Here is the record you want.

araña (la) [a RA nya] *n.* • spider
Tengo miedo a las arañas.
I'm afraid of spiders.

árbol (el) [AR bol] *n.* • tree
En el norte los árboles cambian de color en otoño.
In the north trees change color in the fall.

arco iris (el) [AR co EE rees] *n.* • rainbow
El arco iris tiene siete colores.
Rainbows have seven colors.

arduo, a [AR duo] *adj.* • hard, difficult
El trabajo en una granja es arduo.
Work on a farm is hard.

arena (la) [a RE na] *n.* • sand
Hacemos un castillo de arena en la playa.
We are making a sand castle on the beach.

arepa (la) [a RE pa] *n.* • corn flour cake (Venezuela)
La arepa es una comida típica de Venezuela.
Arepa is a typical Venezuelan food.

árido, a [A ree do] *adj.* • desolate, arid
La ecología de las zonas áridas es interesante.
The ecology of arid zones is interesting.

arma (el) (f.) [AR ma] *n.* • weapon
La venta de armas a otros países es un tema de interés político.
The sale of weapons to other countries is a topic of political interest.

armario (el) [ar MA ryo] *n.* • closet
El armario de mi abuela tiene un gran espejo.
My grandmother's closet has a big mirror.

arquitecto, a (el, la) [ar kee TEC to] *n.* • architect
El señor García es arquitecto.
Mr. García is an architect.

arreglar [a rre GLAR] *v.* • to arrange, to fix
Mi hermana me ayuda a arreglar mi automóvil.
My sister helps me fix my car.

arrestar [a rres TAR] *v.* • to arrest
La policía arresta al ladrón.
The police are arresting the thief.

arriba [a RREE ba] *adv.* • up, upstairs
Juan está arriba.
Juan is upstairs.

arroyo (el) [a RRO yo] *n.* • brook, stream
El arroyo desemboca en el río.
The stream flows into the river.

arroz (el) [a RROS] *n.* • rice
El menú tiene arroz con pollo.
The menu has chicken with rice.

arte (el) [AR te] *n.* • art
La ciudad tiene una galería de arte.
The city has an art gallery.

artículo (el) [ar TEE cu lo] *n.* • article
Escribo un artículo para el periódico estudiantil.
I'm writing an article for the student newspaper.

artista (el, la) [ar TEES ta] *n.* • artist
David quiere ser artista.
David wants to be an artist.

artístico, a [ar TEES tee co] *adj.* • artistic
Laura es muy artística.
Laura is very artistic.

asado, a [a SA d̲o] *adj.* • roast, roasted
Mi mamá prepara un pollo asado.
My mother is making roast chicken.

ascensor (el) [a sen SOR] *n.* • elevator
El ascensor es la invención del señor Otis.
The elevator is the invention of Mr. Otis.

así [a SEE] *adv.* • this way, so, thus
Jaime lo hace así.
Jaime does it this way.

así, así [a SEE a SEE] *adv.* • so-so
Antonio se siente así, así porque está resfriado.
Antonio feels so-so because he has a cold.

asiento (el) [a SYEN to] *n.* • seat
Me gusta tener el asiento junto a la ventana cuando vuelo.
I like to have the seat next to the window when I fly.

asistir (a) [a sees TEER] *v.* • to attend
Juan y Patricia asisten a la universidad.
Juan and Patricia attend the university.

aspiradora (la) [as pee ra D̲O ra] *n.* • vacuum cleaner
Es buena idea tener una aspiradora portátil para limpiar el automóvil.
It is a good idea to have a portable vacuum cleaner to clean the car.

astronauta (el, la) [as tro NOW ta] *n.* • astronaut
María quiere ser astronauta.
María wants to be an astronaut.

astuto, a [as TU to] *adj.* • astute, sharp, cunning
El zorro es un animal muy astuto.
The fox is a very cunning animal.

atención (la) [a ten SYON] *n.* • attention
¡Presta atención!
Pay attention!

atender [a ten DER] *v.* • to assist, to wait on

yo	atiendo
tú	atiendes
usted	atiende
él, ella	atiende
nosotros, as	atendemos
vosotros, as	atendéis
ustedes	atienden
ellos, ellas	atienden

El dependiente nos atiende.
The clerk is waiting on us.

atentamente [a ten ta MEN te] *adv.* • sincerely yours, yours truly, attentively
Una carta de negocios termina con "atentamente".
A business letter ends with "sincerely yours."

aterrizar [a te rree SAR] *v.* • to land
El avión aterriza ahora.
The plane is landing now.

ático (el) [A tee co] *n.* • attic
El ático de mi abuela está lleno de antigüedades y fotografías.
My grandmother's attic is full of antiques and photographs.

atleta (el, la) [at LE ta] *n.* • athlete
Martha es una buena atleta.
Martha is a good athlete.

atlético, a [at LE tee co] *adj.* • athletic
El comité atlético del estado viene a visitar la escuela mañana.
The state athletic committee is coming to visit the school tomorrow.

atún (el) [a TUN] *n.* • tuna fish
¿Quieres ensalada de atún?
Do you want tuna salad?

aun [a UN] *adv.* • even, yet
aún *adv.* • still
Los niños están enfermos aún.
The children are still sick.

ausente [ow SEN te] *adj.* • absent
Pablo está ausente del campeonato por razones de salud.
Pablo is absent from the championship for health reasons.

autobús (el) [ow to BUS] *n.* • bus
El autobús que lleva a los niños a la escuela viene a las siete de la mañana.
The bus that takes the children to school comes at 7 a.m.

autógrafo (el) [ow TO gra fo] *n.* • autograph
No me interesan los autógrafos de actores.
I am not interested in actors' autographs.

automóvil (el) [ow to MO beel] *n.* • car
auto de carrera *n.* • race car
¿Puedes prestarme tu automóvil?
Can you lend me your car?

autoridad (la) [ow to ree DAD] *n.* • authority, the police
La fiesta es muy ruidosa; la vecina va a llamar a la autoridad.
The party is very noisy; the neighbor is going to call the police.

auxiliar de vuelo (el, la) [ow ksee lee AR de BWE lo] *n.* • flight attendant
Jason es un auxiliar de vuelo muy amable.
Jason is a very friendly flight attendant.

auxilio (el) [ow KSEE lyo] *n.* • help, aid
¿Dónde está la clase de primeros auxilios?
Where is the first aid class?

ávaro, a [a BA ro] *adj.* • stingy
¡Qué viejo tan ávaro!
What a stingy old man!

ave (el) (f.) [A be] *n.* • bird
El halcón es un ave de rapiña.
The hawk is a bird of prey.

avena (la) [a BE na] *n.* • oats
A los caballos les gusta la avena.
Horses like oats.

avenida (la) [a be NEE da] *n.* • avenue
La avenida más ancha del mundo está en Buenos Aires.
The widest avenue in the world is in Buenos Aires.

aventura (la) [a ben TU ra] *n.* • adventure
Mark Twain es el autor de *Las aventuras de Huckleberry Finn.*
Mark Twain is the author of The Adventures of Huckleberry Finn.

avergonzarse (de) [a ber gon SAR se] *v.* • to be ashamed (of)

yo	me	avergüenzo
tú	te	avergüenzas
usted	se	avergüenza
él, ella	se	avergüenza
nosotros, as	nos	avergonzamos
vosotros, as	os	avergonzáis
ustedes	se	avergüenzan
ellos, ellas	se	avergüenzan

Me avergüenzo de admitir la verdad.
I'm ashamed to admit the truth.

avión (el) [a BYON] *n.* • airplane, plane
El avión para Madrid sale a las tres de la tarde.
The plane to Madrid leaves at three in the afternoon.

¡Ay! [I] *intj.* • oh dear!, oh my!, ouch!
¡Ay! Me duele el pie.
Ouch! My foot hurts.

ayer [a YER] *adv.* • yesterday
Hablamos con Martín ayer.
We talked to Martín yesterday.

ayudante (el, la) [a yu DAN te] *n.* • assistant
Mi hermano es el ayudante del profesor.
My brother is the professor's assistant.

ayudar [a yu DAR] *v.* • to help, to assist
Te prometo ayudar mañana.
I promise to help you tomorrow.

ayuntamiento (el) [a yun ta MYEN to] *n.* • city hall
El jefe de policía tiene oficina en el ayuntamiento.
The chief of police has an office in City Hall.

azteca [as TE ca] *adj.* • Aztec
azteca (el, la) *n.* • Aztec (person)
El calendario azteca es muy interesante.
The Aztec calendar is very interesting.

azúcar (el) [a SU car] *n.* • sugar
¿Cómo te gusta el café? - ¿con o sin azúcar?
How do you like your coffee, with or without sugar?

B

bacalao (el) [ba ca LAO] *n.* • cod
El bacalao es un plato tradicional de Nochevieja.
Cod is a traditional New Year's Eve dish.

bachillerato (el) [ba chee ye RA to] *n.* • high school diploma
Para trabajar en esta compañía necesita tener su bachillerato.
In order to work for this company you need your high school diploma.

bahía (la) [ba EE a] *n.* • bay
Se puede ver la bahía de aquí.
You can see the bay from here.

bailar [bi LAR] *v.* • to dance
No sé bailar.
I don't know how to dance.

bailarín, a (el, la) [bi la REEN] *n.* • dancer
La vida de un bailarín es muy emocionante.
A dancer's life is very exciting.

baile (el) [BI le] *n.* • dance
¿Vas al baile?
Are you going to the dance?

bajar [ba HAR] *v.* • to go down, to descend
Tina baja las escaleras ahora.
Tina is going down the stairs now.

bajo, a [BA ho] *adj.* • short (height), low
Yo soy más baja que mi hermana.
I am shorter than my sister.

balcón (el) [bal CON] *n.* • balcony
Las casas españolas siempre tienen balcones.
Spanish homes always have balconies.

baloncesto (el) [ba lon SES to] *n.* • basketball
El baloncesto es muy popular en los Estados Unidos.
Basketball is very popular in the United States.

ballena (la) [ba YE na] *n.* • whale
Las ballenas viven en el océano.
Whales live in the ocean.

banco (el) [BAN co] *n.* • bank; bench
El banco abre a las nueve.
The bank opens at nine.

banda (la) [BAN da] *n.* • band (musical or radio)
La banda escolar va al concurso nacional este año.
This year the school band is going to the national competition.

bandera (la) [ban DE ra] *n.* • flag
¿De qué color es la bandera española?
What color is the Spanish flag?

bañarse [ba NYAR se] *v.* • to take a bath
Me baño todos los días.
I take a bath everyday.

bañera (la) [ba NYE ra] *n.* • bathtub
Esta semana le toca a Ivette limpiar la bañera.
This week is Ivette's turn to clean the bathtub.

baño (el) [BA nyo] *n.* • bathroom; bath
El baño está arriba.
The bathroom is upstairs.

barato, a [ba RA to] *adj.* • cheap
Necesito comprar un carro barato.
I need to buy a cheap car.

barba (la) [BAR ba] *n.* • beard
Mi bisabuelo tiene barba.
My great-grandfather has a beard.

barbacoa (la) [bar ba CO a] *n.* • barbecue
Mark y Norma nos invitan a una barbacoa.
Mark and Norma are inviting us to a barbecue.

barbaridad (la) [bar ba ree DAD] *n.* • outrage, atrocity; amazing fact
Habla tres lenguas. ¡Qué barbaridad!
He speaks three languages. How amazing!

barbero (el) [bar BE ro] *n.* • barber
El padre de Ricardo es barbero.
Ricardo's father is a barber.

barco (el) [BAR co] *n.* • ship, boat
Me gusta viajar en barco.
I like to travel by ship.

barrer [ba RRER] *v.* • to sweep
Elisa tiene que barrer la cocina después de la comida.
Elisa has to sweep the kitchen after dinner.

barro (el) [BA rro] *n.* • mud, clay
La cerámica de Oaxaca está hecha de barro negro.
Pottery in Oaxaca is made with black clay.

básico, a [BA see co] *adj.* • basic
No puedo hablar español si no estudio las lecciones básicas.
I can't speak Spanish if I don't study the basic lessons.

basquetbol (el) [bas ket BOL] *n.* • basketball
El basquetbol es mi deporte favorito.
Basketball is my favorite sport.

bastón (el) [bas TON] *n.* • cane
Mis abuelos usan bastones.
My grandparents use canes.

basura (la) [ba SU ra] *n.* • garbage, litter, trash
¡Ponga la basura en su lugar!
Put litter in its place!

bata (la) [BA ta] *n.* • robe
Hace frío; ponte la bata
It's cold; put on your robe.

batalla (la) [ba TA ya] *n.* • battle
Gettysburg es una batalla famosa de la Guerra Civil.
Gettysburg is a famous Civil War battle.

bate (el) [BA te] *n.* • bat (baseball)
¿Dónde está mi bate de béisbol?
Where is my baseball bat?

batidora (la) [ba tee DO ra] *n.* • mixer
Voy a usar la batidora nueva.
I'm going to use the new mixer.

batir [ba TEER] *v.* • to beat (cooking), to mix
Tienes que batir la masa muy bien.
You have to mix the dough very well.

bebé (el) [be BE] *n.* • baby
Beth tiene fotos de su bebé.
Beth has pictures of her baby.

beber [be BER] *v.* • to drink
Necesitamos beber ocho vasos de agua cada día.
We need to drink eight glasses of water every day.

bebida (la) [be BEE da] *n.* • drink
Horchata es una bebida española de almendras.
Horchata is a Spanish drink with almonds.

becerro, a (el, la) [be SE rro] *n.* • calf
El becerro se llama "Gordito".
The calf's name is "Chubby."

béisbol (el) [BAYS bol] *n.* • baseball
El béisbol es también un deporte muy popular en el Caribe.
Baseball is also a very popular sport in the Caribbean.

belleza (la) [be YE sa] *n.* • beauty
Mi tía está en el salón de belleza.
My aunt is in the beauty shop.

bello, a [BE yo] *adj.* • beautiful
Todos los colores del arco iris son bellos.
All the colors of the rainbow are beautiful.

beso (el) [BE so] *n.* • kiss
Dame un beso.
Give me a kiss.

bestia (la) [BES tya] *n.* • beast
A mi sobrinita le gusta mucho el cuento de "La bella y la bestia".
My little niece likes the story of "The Beauty and the Beast" a lot.

biblioteca (la) [bee blyo TE ca] *n.* • library
Patricia estudia en la biblioteca.
Patricia is studying in the library.

bibliotecario, a (el, la) [bee blyo te CA ryo] *n.* • librarian
El bibliotecario organiza una serie de conferencias.
The librarian is organizing a series of lectures.

bicicleta (la) [bee see CLE ta] *n.* • bicycle, bike
Mis abuelos me compran una bicicleta nuevo.
My grandparents are buying me a new bike.

bien [BYEN] *adv.* • well
Jorge canta muy bien.
Jorge sings very well.

bilingüe [bee LEEN gwe] *adj.* • bilingual
Necesitamos una secretaria bilingüe.
We need a bilingual secretary.

billete (el) [bee YE te] *n.* • bill (money); ticket
No hay billetes de mil dólares.
There are no one-thousand dollar bills.

binoculares (los) [bee no cu LA res] *n.* • binoculars
¿Traes los binoculares a la corrida?
Are you bringing the binoculars to the bullfight?

bisabuelo (el) [bee sa BWE lo] *n.* • great-grandfather
bisabuela (la) *n.* • great-grandmother
Mi bisabuelo tiene 95 años.
My great-grandfather is 95 years old.

bistec (el) [bees TEC] *n.* • steak
¿Prefieres bistec o cordero?
Do you prefer steak or lamb?

blanco, a [BLAN co] *adj.* • white
La Casa Blanca está en Washington, D.C.
The White House is in Washington, D.C.

blando, a [BLAN do] *adj.* • soft
No duermo bien en una cama blanda.
I don't sleep well in a soft bed.

blusa (la) [BLU sa] *n.* • blouse
Tengo muchas faldas pero necesito blusas.
I have a lot of skirts but I need blouses.

boa (la) [BO a] *n.* • boa
Las boas son muy largas.
Boas are very long.

boca (la) [BO ca] *n.* • mouth
Por favor, come con la boca cerrada.
Please, eat with your mouth closed.

boina (la) [BOI na] *n.* • beret
En el norte de España los hombres llevan boinas.
In northern Spain men wear berets.

boleto (el) [bo LE to] *n.* • ticket
Los boletos de avión están en mi bolsa.
The plane tickets are in my purse.

bolígrafo (el) [bo LEE gra fo] *n.* • (ballpoint) pen
¿Puedes prestarme un bolígrafo?
Can you lend me a pen?

bolos (los) [BO los] *n.* • bowling
Me gusta jugar a los bolos.
I like to go bowling.

bolsa (la) [BOL sa] *n.* • bag, handbag
Tengo que comprar una bolsa.
I have to buy a handbag.

bolsillo (el) [bol SEE yo] *n.* • pocket
El problema con este saco es que no tiene bolsillos.
The problem with this jacket is that it does not have pockets.

bombero, a (el, la) [bom BE ro] *n.* • firefighter
Mi tío Pedro es bombero.
My Uncle Pedro is a firefighter.

bombilla (la) [bom BEE ya] *n.* • light bulb
Thomas Alva Edison inventó la bombilla.
Thomas Alva Edison invented the light bulb.

bondadoso, a [bon da DO so] *adj.* • kind
Roberto es un hombre bondadoso.
Roberto is a kind man.

bonito, a [bo NEE to] *adj.* • pretty
Cati es una chica bonita.
Cati is a pretty girl.

bordado, a [bor DA do] *adj.* • embroidered
bordado (el) *n.* • embroidery
María Luisa hace un mantel bordado.
María Luisa is making an embroidered tablecloth.

borrador (el) [bo rra DOR] *n.* • eraser
¿Tenemos que comprar un borrador especial para la clase de dibujo?
Do we have to buy a special eraser for drawing class?

borrar [bo RRAR] *v.* • to erase
Ayudo a borrar las pizarras después de la clase.
I help erase the boards after class.

bosque (el) [BOS ke] *n.* • forest
¿Te gusta caminar por el bosque?
Do you like to walk through the forest?

bota (la) [BO ta] *n.* • boot
Tengo ganas de comprarme unas botas de vaquero.
I really want to buy myself some cowboy boots.

bote (el) [BO te] *n.* • boat (small)
Mi padre va a comprar un bote.
My father is going to buy a boat.

botella (la) [bo TE ya] *n.* • bottle
Mi vecino tiene una colección de botellas.
My neighbor has a bottle collection.

botica (la) [bo TEE ca] *n.* • drugstore
¿Puedo comprar aspirina en la botica?
Can I buy aspirin in the drugstore?

botón (el) [bo TON] *n.* • button
Me falta el botón de este abrigo.
I'm missing the button from this coat.

boxeador (el) [bo ksey a DOR] *n.* • boxer
El boxeador se entrena para los Juegos Olímpicos
The boxer is training for the Olympic Games.

boxeo (el) [bo KSEY o] *n.* • boxing
Mi hermano tiene boletos para el campeonato de boxeo.
My brother has tickets for the boxing championship.

bravo, a [BRA bo] *adj.* • brave; angry
bravo! *intj.* • yeah! well done!
Los soldados de marina son muy bravos.
Marines are very brave.

¡Bravo, Manuel!
Well done, Manuel!

brazalete (el) [bra sa LE te] *n.* • bracelet
Leticia lleva un brazalete de perlas.
Leticia is wearing a pearl bracelet.

brazo (el) [BRA so] *n.* • arm
Mi hermano tiene el brazo roto.
My brother has a broken arm.

brillar [bree YAR] *v.* • to shine
¡Mira como brillan las estrellas!
Look how the stars shine!

brincar [breen CAR] *v.* • to skip, to leap, to jump, to spring
María brinca a la escuela.
María skips to school.

broma (la) [BRO ma] *n.* • joke
A Lourdes no le gustan las bromas de Guillermo.
Lourdes does not like Guillermo's jokes.

bronce (el) [BRON se] *n.* • bronze
El trofeo es de bronce.
The trophy is made of bronze.

bronceado, a [bron se A do] *adj.* • tanned
¡Mira qué bronceada estás, Lupe!
Look how tan you are Lupe!

brutalidad (la) [bru ta lee DAD] *n.* • brutality, cruelty
La brutalidad es un problema serio en nuestra sociedad.
Brutality is a serious problem in our society.

buceador, a (el, la) [bu se a DOR] *n.* • diver
El buceador busca tesoro bajo el mar.
The diver is looking for treasure under the sea.

bucear [bu se AR] *v.* • to dive
Tengo ganas de bucear en el Caribe.
I'd really like to dive in the Caribbean.

bueno, a [BWE no] *adj.* • good
¡buen provecho! • enjoy your meal!
¡buena suerte! • good luck!
buenas noches • good evening, night
buenas tardes • good afternoon
buenos días • good morning, day
La cosecha de este año produce muy buenos vinos.
This year's crop is producing very good wines.

búfalo, a (el, la) [BU fa lo] *n.* • buffalo
No hay muchos búfalos hoy día.
There aren't many buffalo these days.

bufanda (la) [bu FAN da] *n.* • muffler, scarf
Hace frío; lleva la bufanda.
It's cold; wear your muffler.

buitre (el) [BWEE tre] *n.* • vulture
Los buitres son aves muy grandes.
Vultures are huge birds.

burro (el) [BU rro] *n.* • donkey
Los burros son muy monos cuando son chiquitos.
Donkeys are very cute when they are small.

buscar [bus CAR] *v.* • to look for
¿Qué buscas?
What are you looking for?

buzón (el) [bu SON] *n.* • mailbox
Hay un buzón en la esquina.
There is a mailbox on the corner.

C

caballo (el) [ca BA yo] *n.* • horse (male)
Mi tío tiene caballos en su granja.
My uncle has horses on his farm.

cabello (el) [ca BE yo] *n.* • hair
El cabello de Teresa es rubio.
Teresa's hair is blonde.

cabeza (la) [ca BE sa] *n.* • head
¡Me duele la cabeza!
My head hurts!

cabra (la) [CA bra] *n.* • goat
Me gusta el queso de cabra.
I like goat cheese.

cacahuate (el) [ca ca WA te] *n.* • peanut
Vamos a comer pollo en salsa de cacahuate
We're going to eat chicken in peanut sauce.

cacería (la) [ca se REE a] *n.* • hunting, hunt
La cacería de águilas es ilegal.
Eagle hunting is illegal.

cacto (el) [CAC to] *n.* • cactus
El cacto es del desierto.
Cactus is from the desert.

cachorro, a (el, la) [ca CHO rro] *n.* • puppy
Nuestro cachorro se llama "Gordito."
Our puppy's name is "Chubby."

cada [CA da] *adj.* • each, every
Cada estudiante tiene tres libros.
Each student has three books.

cadena (la) [ca DE na] *n.* • chain
Rebeca compra la cadena pero no el dije.
Rebeca is buying the chain but not the charm.

cadera (la) [ca DE ra] *n.* • hip
Mi abuela tiene la cadera rota.
My grandmother has a broken hip.

caerse [ca ER se] *v.* • to fall down

yo	me	caigo
tú	te	caes
usted	se	cae
él, ella	se	cae
nosotros, as	nos	caemos
vosotros, as	os	caéis
ustedes	se	caen
ellos, ellas	se	caen

No me gusta patinar; siempre me caigo.
I don't like to skate; I always fall down.

café [ca FE] *adj.* • brown
café (el) *n.* • coffee
¿Quieres tu café con leche y azúcar?
Do you want your coffee with milk and sugar?

caída (la) [ca EE da] *n.* • fall
Leemos *La caída del imperio romano.*
We are reading The Fall of the Roman Empire.

caimán (el) [kai MAN] *n.* • alligator
Todavía hay unos caimanes en Florida.
There are still some alligators in Florida.

caja (la) [CA ha] *n.* • box
Necesito una caja para mis juguetes.
I need a box for my toys.

calabaza (la) [ca la BA sa] *n.* • pumpkin, squash
Las semillas de calabaza son deliciosas.
Pumpkin seeds are delicious.

calamidad (la) [ca la mee DAD] *n.* • calamity, disaster
Un huracán es una calamidad terrible.
A hurricane is a terrible calamity.

calavera (la) [ca la BE ra] *n.* • skull
La bandera pirata tiene una calavera.
The pirate flag has a skull.

calcetín (el) [cal se TEEN] *n.* • sock
Esos calcetines rojos no son mis favoritos.
Those red socks are not my favorites.

calculadora (la) [cal cu la DO ra] *n.* • calculator
¿Puedes hacer tu tarea de matemáticas sin una calculadora?
Can you do your math homework without a calculator?

caldo (el) [CAL do] *n.* • broth
El arroz sabe mejor con caldo de pollo.
Rice tastes better with chicken broth.

calefacción (la) [ca le faks SYON] *n.* • heat heating system
En Costa Rica las casas no necesitan calefacción.
In Costa Rica the houses do not need a heating system.

calendario (el) [ca len DA ryo] *n.* • calendar, schedule
El calendario maya consiste en dieciocho meses y cinco días.
The Mayan calendar consists of eighteen months and five days.

calentar [ca len TAR] *v.* • to heat (an object)
calentarse *v.* • to warm (oneself)

yo	me	caliento
tú	te	calientas
usted	se	calienta
él, ella	se	calienta
nosotros, as	nos	calentamos
vosotros, as	os	calentáis
ustedes	se	calientan
ellos, ellas	se	calientan

Por favor, calienta agua para el té.
Please heat some water for the tea.

El gato se calienta al lado del radiador.
The cat warms itself by the radiator.

calidad (la) [ca lee DAD] *n.* • quality
Esto es lo que yo llamo un producto de calidad.
This is what I call a quality product.

caliente [ca LYEN te] *adj.* • hot, warm
Cuando tengo catarro mi tía me prepara sopa caliente.
When I have a cold, my aunt fixes me warm soup.

calma (la) [CAL ma] *n.* • tranquility, calmness
Me gusta la calma de este lugar.
I like the tranquility of this place.

calor (el) [ca LOR] *n.* • heat
Hace calor. • It is hot.(weather)
Tengo calor. • I am hot.
Hace calor en el verano.
It's hot in the summer.

callado, a [ca YA d̲o] *adj.* • silent, quiet
Tienes que estar muy callada, Linda.
You have to be very quiet, Linda.

callarse [ca YAR se] *v.* to be quiet, to shut up
¿Puedes callarte por favor?
Can you be quiet please?

calle (la) [CA ye] *n.* • street
La preparatoria de Juan está en la calle Colombia.
Juan's high school is on Colombia Street.

cama (la) [CA ma] *n.* • bed
Tengo ganas de comprar una cama de agua.
I want to buy a water bed.

cámara (la) [CA ma ra] *n.* • camera
Mi cámara no es automática.
My camera is not automatic.

camarón (el) [ca ma RON] *n.* shrimp
Eloise es alérgica a los camarones.
Eloise is allergic to shrimp.

cambiar [cam BYAR] *v.* • to change, to exchange
cambiarse *v.* • to change clothes
Necesito cambiar la bombilla.
I need to change the light bulb.

cambio (el) [CAM byo] *n.* • change
Lo siento pero no tengo cambio para el teléfono.
Sorry, but I have no change for the phone.

camello (el) [ca ME yo] *n.* • camel
No es verdad que los camellos guardan agua en la joroba.
It is not true that camels keep water inside their hump.

camión (el) [ca MYON] *n.* • large truck; bus
El camión de la basura viene los jueves.
The garbage truck comes on Thursdays.

camioneta (la) [ca myo NE ta] *n.* • van; small truck
La Sra. Montes necesita una camioneta para transportar a sus nueve hijos.
Mrs. Montes needs a van to transport her nine children.

camisa (la) [ca MEE sa] *n.* • shirt
Los muchachos compran sus camisas en el centro.
The guys buy their shirts downtown.

camiseta (la) [ca mee SE ta] *n.* • T-shirt
Éstas son las camisetas para el equipo de fútbol americano.
These are the T-shirts for the football team.

campaña (la) [cam PA nya] *n.* • campaign
La campaña electoral empieza mañana.
The electoral campaign begins tomorrow.

campo (el) [CAM po] *n.* • field, country(side)
campo de recreo (el) *n.* • playground
Los padres de Joanna tienen una casa en el campo.
Joanna's parents have a house in the country.

canario, a (el, la) [ca NA ryo] *n.* • canary
La Sra. Sánchez tiene catorce canarios.
Mrs. Sánchez has fourteen canaries.

canasta (la) [ca NAS ta] *n.* • basket
Esta canasta es de un mercado en el Ecuador.
This basket is from a market in Ecuador.

canción (la) [can SYON] *n.* • song
Mi sobrino tiene una casete con canciones de niños.
My nephew has a cassette with children's songs.

canguro (el) [can GU ro] *n.* • kangaroo
El canguro es un marsupial australiano.
Kangaroos are Australian marsupials.

canica (la) [ca NEE ca] *n.* • marble (for playing)
Joseph siempre gana los juegos de canicas.
Joseph always wins the marble games.

canoa (la) [ca NO a] *n.* • canoe
Casi nunca usamos la canoa durante el invierno.
We seldom use the canoe during winter.

cansado, a [can SA d̲o] *adj.* • tired
Crissy está cansada después de trabajar en el jardín.
Crissy is tired after working in the garden.

cantante (el, la) [can TAN te] *n.* • singer
¿Quién es tu cantante favorito?
Who is your favorite singer?

cantar [can TAR] *v.* • to sing
Juan canta muy bien.
Juan sings very well.

cantidad (la) [can tee D̲AD] *n.* • quantity, amount
Tenemos una gran cantidad de tomates.
We have a large quantity of tomatoes.

caos (el) [CA os] *n.* • chaos, confusion
La teoría de caos en matemáticas es relativamente reciente.
The chaos theory in mathematics is relatively recent.

capital (la) [ca pee TAL] *n.* • capital (city)
capital (el) *n.* • capital (money)
La capital de Chile es Santiago.
Santiago is the capital of Chile.

capturar [cap tu RAR] *v.* • to capture, to catch
No pueden capturar ese ladrón.
They can't capture that thief.

cara (la) [CA ra] *n.* • face
No puedo dibujar caras.
I cannot draw faces.

caracol (el) [ca ra COL] *n.* • snail
Los caracoles viven en ambientes húmedos.
Snails live in humid environments.

carácter (el) [ca RAC ter] *n.* • character; nature
Rita es una mujer de carácter.
Rita is a woman of character.

¡Caramba! [ca RAM ba] *intj.* • Wow!, My goodness!
¡Caramba! ¡Bob ganó trescientos mil dólares en la lotería!
Wow! Bob won three hundred thousand dollars in the lottery!

caramelo (el) [ca ra ME lo] *n.* • candy, caramel
Yo hago los caramelos si tú haces el flan.
I'll make the candy if you make the custard.

cardinal [car dee NAL] *adj.* • cardinal (number, point)
Los puntos cardinales son norte, sur, este y oeste.
The cardinal points are North, South, East and West.

cariño (el) [ca REE nyo] *n.* • affection
Los padres necesitan mostrar mucho cariño a sus hijos.
Parents need to show a lot of affection to their children

carne (la) [CAR ne] *n.* • meat
Preferimos comprar la carne en el mercado local.
We prefer to buy meat at the local market.

carnicería (la) [car nee se REE a] *n.* butcher shop
Esta carnicería garantiza la frescura de la carne que vende.
This butcher shop guarantees the freshness of the meat it sells.

carnicero, a (el, la) [car nee SE ro] *n.* butcher
El carnicero corta la carne.
The butcher cuts the meat.

caro, a [CA ro] *adj.* • expensive
Los vestidos de diseñadores son muy caros
Designer dresses are very expensive.

carpintero, a (el, la) [car peen TE ro] *n.* • carpenter
Raúl quiere ser carpintero.
Raúl wants to be a carpenter.

carrera (la) [ca RRE ra] *n.* • career; race
Raquel tiene una gran carrera como historiadora.
Raquel has a great career as a historian.

carretera (la) [ca rre TE ra] *n.* • highway
Siempre tengo miedo de manejar en la carretera.
I'm always afraid to drive on the highway.

carro (el) [CA rro] *n.* • car; cart
El carro está muy sucio.
The car is very dirty.

carta (la) [CAR ta] *n.* • letter; menu
Tengo que contestar las cartas de mis amigos.
I have to answer the letters from my friends.

cartel (el) [car TEL] *n.* • poster
Me gustan los carteles en esa tienda.
I like the posters in that store.

cartera (la) [car TE ra] *n.* • wallet
Tengo cartera, ¡pero no tengo dinero!
I have a wallet, but I don't have any money!

cartero, a (el, la) [car TE ro] *n.* • mail carrier
El cartero viene a eso de las once.
The mail carrier comes around eleven.

casa (la) [CA sa] *n.* • house, home
Compramos la casa porque está cerca de la escuela.
We bought the house because it's near the school.

casamiento (el) [ca sa MYEN to] *n.* • marriage
Los padres ya no arreglan los casamientos.
Parents no longer arrange marriages.

casarse [ca SAR se] *v.* • to get married
¿Cuándo se casa George?
When is George getting married?

casco (el) [CAS co] *n.* • helmet
Necesito un casco para andar en bicicleta.
I need a helmet for bicycling.

casi [CA see] *adv.* • almost
Miguel tiene casi treinta años.
Miguel is almost 30 years old.

castaño, a [cas TA nyo] *adj.* • brown (hair)
Irene tiene el pelo castaño.
Irene has brown hair.

castigar [cas tee GAR] *v.* • to punish
Mi mamá castiga a Juanito por la ventana rota.
My mother is punishing Juanito because of the broken window.

castillo (el) [cas TEE yo] *n.* • castle
Hay muchos castillos en España.
There are a lot of castles in Spain.

catarata (la) [ca ta RA ta] *n.* • waterfall
Las cataratas de Iguazú están entre Brasil y Argentina.
The Iguazú waterfalls are between Brazil and Argentina.

cazador, a (el, la) [ca sa DOR] *n.* • hunter
Daniel Boone es un cazador famoso.
Daniel Boone is a famous hunter.

cazar [ca SAR] *v.* • to hunt
Está prohibido cazar en los parques nacionales.
It is forbidden to hunt in the national parks.

cazuela (la) [ca SWE la] *n.* • pan
La cazuela está en la mesa.
The pan is on the table.

cebolla (la) [se BO ya] *n.* • onion
Las cebollas me hacen llorar.
Onions make me cry.

cebra (la) [SE bra] *n.* • zebra
Las cebras son de África.
Zebras are from Africa.

ceja (la) [SE ha] *n.* • eyebrow
Ana tiene las cejas espesas.
Ana has thick eyebrows.

celebración (la) [se le bra SYON] *n.* • celebration
La celebración de la independencia mexicana es en septiembre.
The celebration of Mexican independence is in September.

celebrar [se le BRAR] *v.* • to celebrate
Los abuelos de Jim celebran su aniversario.
Jim's grandparents are celebrating their anniversary.

cena (la) [SE na] *n.* • dinner
Yo preparo la cena esta noche.
I'm preparing dinner tonight.

centavo (el) [sen TA bo] *n.* • cent
El periódico cuesta treinta y cinco centavos.
The newspaper costs thirty-five cents.

centro (el) [SEN tro] *n.* • downtown; center
¿Vas al centro conmigo?
Will you go downtown with me?

cepillar [se pee YAR] *v.* • to brush
Creo que necesito cepillar los dientes antes de salir.
I think I need to brush my teeth before I go out.

cepillo (el) [se PEE yo] *n.* • brush
cepillo de dientes (el) *n.* • toothbrush
¿Dónde está mi cepillo de dientes?
Where is my toothbrush?

cerca [SER ca] *adv.* • close, nearby
cerca de *prep.* • close to
Eduardo vive cerca.
Eduardo lives nearby.

Mi casa está cerca de la iglesia.
My house is close to the church.

cercano, a [ser CA no] *adj.* • near (neighboring), close
El cine más cercano está en la avenida Taquendama.
The closest movie theater is on Taquendama Avenue.

cerdo (el) [SER do] *n.* • pig
Araceli es la veterinaria en la granja de cerdos.
Araceli is the veterinarian at the pig farm.

cereal (el) [se re AL] *n.* • cereal
Creo que hay más de cien tipos de cereal en el mercado.
I think there are more than one hundred kinds of cereal at the market.

cereza (la) [se RE sa] *n.* • cherry
Michigan es un estado que produce cerezas.
Michigan is a state that produces cherries.

cerillo (el) [se REE yo] *n.* • match
Necesitamos un cerillo para encender las velas.
We need a match to light the candles.

cerrado, a [se RRA do] *adj.* • closed
En general los museos están cerrados los lunes.
In general, museums are closed on Mondays.

cerrar [se RRAR] *v.* • to close
cerrar con llave *n.* • to lock
Voy a cerrar la ventana.
I'm going to close the window.

Olvidamos cerrar la casa con llave.
We forgot to lock the house.

cerveza (la) [ser BE sa] *n.* • beer
Esa cerveza es alemana.
That beer is German.

cesta (la) [SES ta] *n.* • basket
Manuel lleva cestas al mercado.
Manuel takes baskets to the market.

ciclismo (el) [see CLEES mo] *n.* • cycling (sport)
El ciclismo es más popular en Europa que en los Estados Unidos.
Cycling is more popular in Europe than in the United States.

ciclomotor (el) [see clo mo TOR] *n.* • moped
Eduardo tiene ciclomotor.
Eduardo has a moped.

ciego, a [SYE go] *adj.* • blind
ciego, a (el, la) *n.* • blind person
Esa mujer es ciega.
That woman is blind.

Ese ciego es abogado.
That blind man is a lawyer.

cielo (el) [SYE lo] *n.* • sky, heaven
¡Qué bonito es el cielo!
The sky is so beautiful!

ciencia (la) [SYEN sya] *n.* • science
Biología es la ciencia que estudia la vida.
Biology is the science that studies life.

ciencia ficción (la) [SYEN sya feec SYON] *n.* • science fiction
¿Me puedes recomendar unos buenos autores de ciencia ficción?
Can you recommend some good science fiction authors?

científico, a [syen TEE fi ko] *adj.* • scientific
científico, a (el, la) *n.* • scientist
No sé la explicación científica del origen de la luna.
I do not know the scientific explanation of the origin of the moon.

Anita quiere ser científica.
Anita wants to be a scientist.

cierto, a [SYER to] *adj.* • true, sure, certain
¿Es cierto que el presidente cena con nosotros esta noche?
Is it true that the President is dining with us tonight?

cigarrillo (el) [see ga RREE yo] *n.* • cigarette
No me gusta salir con muchachos que huelen a cigarrillos.
I do not like to go out with boys who smell like cigarettes.

cine (el) [SEE ne] *n.* • movie theater
Nos espera en el cine.
She's waiting for us at the movie theater.

cinta (la) [SEEN ta] *n.* • ribbon; tape
Necesito una cinta azul.
I need a blue ribbon.

cinto (el) [SEEN to] *n.* • belt (narrow), sash
Tengo que devolver este vestido porque no tiene cinto.
I have to return this dress because it does not have a belt.

cintura (la) [seen TU ra] *n.* • waist
La natación es un buen ejercicio para la cintura.
Swimming is good exercise for the waist.

cinturón (el) [seen tu RON] *n.* • belt
cinturón de seguridad (el) *n.* • seatbelt
El cinturón marrón va muy bien con este pantalón, ¿no?
The brown belt goes well with these pants, don't you think?

circo (el) [SEER co] *n.* • circus
Los niños se divierten con los payasos del circo.
Children enjoy the circus clowns.

circular [seer cu LAR] *v.* • to circulate; to circle.
circular *adj.* • circular
circular (el) *n.* • circular, flier
El aire no circula por el salón.
The air is not circulating about the hall.

Este globo es circular.
This globe is circular.

La información está en el circular.
The information is in the flier.

círculo (el) [SEER cu lo] *n.* • circle
Tenemos que formar un círculo.
We have to form a circle.

ciruela (la) [seer WE la] *n.* • plum
¿Cuándo es la temporada de ciruelas?
When is the season for plums?

cita (la) [SEE ta] *n.* • date, appointment
Robertito no sabe todavía que tiene una cita con el dentista.
Robertito still does not know that he has an appointment with the dentist.

ciudad (la) [see u DAD] *n.* • city
Santa Fe es una ciudad con varias influencias culturales.
Santa Fe is a city with several cultural influences.

civil [see BEEL] *adj.* • civil, civilian
Mi primo sale del ejército y regresa a la vida civil.
My cousin is leaving the army and returning to civilian life.

claramente [cla ra MEN te] *adv.* • clearly
La maestra explica claramente los conceptos nuevos.
The teacher explains the new ideas clearly.

clarinete (el) [cla ree NE te] *n.* • clarinet
¿Hay un concierto para clarinete y orquesta?
Is there a concert for clarinet and orchestra?

claro, a [CLA ro] *adj.* • clear
¡claro que no! *intj.* • of course not!
¡claro que sí! *intj.* • of course!
Es una explicación clara del problema.
It is a clear explanation of the problem.

clase (la) [CLA se] *n.* • class
¿Cuántos estudiantes hay en la clase?
How many students are in the class?

clásico, a [CLA see co] *adj.* • classic, classical
Bill siempre se duerme en los conciertos de música clásica.
Bill always falls asleep in classical music concerts.

clavar [cla BAR] *v.* • to nail
Necesito un martillo para clavarlo bien.
I need a hammer to nail it well.

clavel (el) [cla BEL] *n.* • carnation
Rosa usa claveles en su boda.
Rosa wears carnations at her wedding.

clavo (el) [CLA bo] *n.* • nail (carpentry)
No tienen clavos de una pulgada en la ferretería.
They do not have one-inch nails at the hardware store.

clima (el) [CLEE ma] *n.* • weather, climate
Perú tiene varios climas.
Peru has several climates.

cobre (el) [CO bre] *n.* • copper
Compro pulseras de cobre.
I buy copper bracelets.

cocina (la) [co SEE na] *n.* • kitchen; cuisine
Mi cocina necesita más utensilios.
My kitchen needs more utensils.

cocinar [co see NAR] *v.* • to cook
Esta semana cocina mi papá.
This week my dad cooks.

cocinero, a (el, la) [co see NE ro] *n.* • cook
Mi papá es un cocinero muy bueno.
My dad is a very good cook.

coctel (el) [COC tel] *n.* • cocktail; cocktail party
La anfitriona prepara un coctel de camarones para el coctel mañana.
The hostess prepares shrimp cocktail for tomorrow's cocktail party.

cochino (el) [co CHEE no] *n.* • pig
Los cochinos me dan miedo.
Pigs scare me.

codo (el) [CO do] *n.* • elbow
Juan tiene el codo roto.
Juan has a broken elbow.

coherente [co e REN te] *adj.* • coherent
Nadie está coherente después de un accidente.
No one is coherent after an accident.

cohete (el) [co E te] *n.* • rocket
El cohete se estalla a la altura esperada.
The rocket explodes at the expected height.

col (la) [COL] *n.* • cabbage
¿Te gusta la ensalada de col?
Do you like cabbage salad?

cola (la) [CO la] *n.* • tail; line (of people)
Nuestro perro no tiene cola.
Our dog doesn't have a tail.

Hay una cola en la taquilla.
There is a line at the box office.

colección (la) [co lec SYON] *n.* • collection
La colección de impresionistas en este museo es excelente.
The Impressionist collection in this museum is excellent.

coleccionar [co lec SYO NAR] *v.* • to collect
La profesora Cervantes colecciona cerámica.
Professor Cervantes collects pottery.

coleccionista (el, la) [co lec syo NEES ta] *n.* • collector
Tal vez podemos vender esta antigüedad a un coleccionista.
Maybe we can sell this antique to a collector.

colegio (el) [co LE hyo] *n.* • school
El colegio de los niños está cerca de la casa.
The children's school is close to the house.

colgar [col GAR] *v.* • to hang

yo	cuelgo
tú	cuelgas
usted	cuelga
él, ella	cuelga
nosotros, as	colgamos
vosotros, as	colgáis
ustedes	cuelgan
ellos, ellas	cuelgan

Necesito hacer espacio para colgar mi ropa de invierno.
I need to make some room to hang my winter clothes.

coliflor (la) [co lee FLOR] *n.* • cauliflower
Liana me promete la receta de su ensalada de coliflor.
Liana promises me the recipe for her cauliflower salad

color (el) [co LOR] *n.* • color
Mi color favorito es verde.
My favorite color is green.

colorear [co lo re AR] *v.* • to color
Los niños quieren colorear en sus libros.
The children want to color in their books.

colorido, a [co lo REE do] *adj.* • colorful
Los textiles hechos en Guatemala son coloridos.
Textiles made in Guatemala are colorful.

columpio (el) [co LUM pyo] *n.* • swing
Nadie usa los columpios cuando hay nieve.
Nobody uses the swings when there is snow.

collar (el) [co YAR] *n.* • necklace
Bárbara prefiere los collares cortos.
Barbara prefers short necklaces.

comedia (la) [co ME dya] *n.* • comedy, play
Queremos ver una comedia en vez de ciencia ficción.
We want to see a comedy instead of science fiction.

comedor (el) [co me DOR] *n.* • dining room
¿Puedes traer más sillas al comedor?
Can you bring more chairs to the dining room?

comenzar [co men SAR] *v.* • to begin, to start

yo	comienzo
tú	comienzas
usted	comienza
él, ella	comienza
nosotros, as	comenzamos
vosotros, as	comenzáis
ustedes	comienzan
ellos, ellas	comienzan

La ceremonia de graduación comienza a las diez.
The graduation ceremony starts at ten.

comer [co MER] *v.* • to eat
Los Schmidt comen a las seis.
The Schmidts eat at six.

cometa (la) [co ME ta] *n.* • kite
Hay una cometa en el cielo.
There is a kite in the sky.

cómico, a [CO mee co] *adj.* • funny, amusing
cómico, a (el, la) *n.* • comedian
Esta película es muy cómica.
This movie is very funny.

El cómico es amigo de mi primo.
The comedian is a friend of my cousin.

comida (la) [co MEE da] *n.* • meal, dinner; food
No me gusta la comida demasiado picante.
I do not like food that is too spicy.

como [CO mo] *adv.* • as, like
tan....como *adv.* • as...as
Lo hacemos como usted.
We'll do this like you do.

Kansas no es tan poblado como California.
Kansas is not as populated as California.

cómo [CO mo] *adv.* • how
No sé cómo voy a pagar el coche.
I don't know how I'm going to pay for the car.

¿Cómo se puede ir a Yellowstone?
How can you get to Yellowstone?

cómodo, a [CO mo do] *adj.* • comfortable
Esta silla no es cómoda.
This chair is not comfortable.

compacto, a [com PAC to] *adj.* • compact
Un automóvil compacto usa menos gasolina que un automóvil deportivo.
A compact car uses less gas than a sports car.

compañero, a (el, la) [com pa NYE ro] *n.* • companion, partner; mate
compañero de clase • classmate
compañero de oficina • officemate
Uno de mis compañeros de clase es de Costa Rica.
One of my classmates is from Costa Rica.

compañía (la) [com pa NYEE a] *n.* • company
¿Para qué compañía trabaja Julián?
For what company does Julián work?

comparar [com pa RAR] *v.* • to compare
Necesito comparar precios antes de comprar esa chaqueta.
I need to compare prices before buying that jacket.

compartir [com par TEER] *v.* • to share
Los niños comparten los juegos.
The children share the games.

completamente [com ple ta MEN te] *adv.* • completely
Tengo que hacerlo completamente.
I have to do it completely.

completar [com ple TAR] *v.* • to finish, to complete
¿Completas el rompecabezas?
Are you finishing the jigsaw puzzle?

comportarse [com por TAR se] *v.* • to behave
Los niños se comportan muy bien en la fiesta.
The children behave very well at the party.

comprar [com PRAR] *v.* • to buy
Todavía no sé lo que voy a comprar para el Día de la Madre.
I still do not know what I am going to buy for Mother's Day.

comprender [com pren DER] *v.* • to understand
Todavía no comprendo muy bien.
I still do not understand very well.

compromiso (el) [com pro MEE so] *n.* • engagement, obligation
Quiero asistir a esa conferencia pero tengo otro compromiso.
I want to attend that lecture, but I have another engagement.

computadora (la) [com pu ta DO ra] *n.* • computer
Mi computadora tiene una pantalla de blanco y negro.
My computer has a black and white monitor.

comunidad (la) [co mu nee DAD] *n.* • community
La comunidad local de artistas tiene una exhibición este fin de semana.
The local community of artists has an exhibit this weekend.

con [CON] *prep.* • with
conmigo • with me
contigo • with you
Con el dinero que ahorro voy de vacaciones contigo.
With the money I am saving, I will go on a vacation with you.

concierto (el) [con SYER to] *n.* • concert
Joel no puede conseguir boletos para el concierto de rock.
Joel can't get tickets for the rock concert.

conclusión (la) [con clu SYON] *n.* • conclusion
La conclusión del jurado es que el acusado es inocente.
The conclusion of the jury is that the defendant is innocent.

concha (la) [CON cha] *n.* • shell
Hay muchas conchas en la playa.
There are lots of shells on the beach.

concurso (el) [con CUR so] *n.* • contest
El concurso de cocina es en el auditorio.
The cooking contest is in the auditorium.

conducir [con du SEER] *v.* • to drive, to conduct

yo	conduzco
tú	conduces
usted	conduce
él, ella	conduce
nosotros, as	conducimos
vosotros, as	conducís
ustedes	conducen
ellos, ellas	conducen

¿Quién nos conduce al cine?
Who is driving us to the movies?

conductor, a (el, la) [con duc TOR] *n.* • driver
Pepe es buen conductor.
Pepe is a good driver.

conejo (el) [co NE ho] *n.* • rabbit
Sarah tiene un conejo que se llama "Algodón".
Sarah has a rabbit named "Cotton."

confundido, a [con fun DEE do] *adj.* • confused
No entiendo este mapa; estoy confundido.
I do not understand this map; I am confused.

confundir [con fun DEER] *v.* • to confuse
confundirse • to be confused
La geometría me confunde.
Geometry confuses me.

Las direcciones son muy difíciles. ¡No te confundas!
The directions are very difficult. Don't get confused!

confusión (la) [con fu SYON] *n.* • confusion, chaos
Hay confusión al fin de un partido.
There is confusion at the end of a game.

conocer [co no SER] *v.* • to know (a person or a place)

yo	conozco
tú	conoces
usted	conoce
él, ella	conoce
nosotros, as	conocemos
vosotros, as	conocéis
ustedes	conocen
ellos, ellas	conocen

¿Conoces a mi sobrina?
Do you know my niece?

conseguir [con se GEER] *v.* • to get

yo	consigo
tú	consigues
usted	consigue
él, ella	consigue
nosotros, as	conseguimos
vosotros, as	conseguís
ustedes	consiguen
ellos, ellas	consiguen

¿Puedes conseguir los boletos?
Can you get the tickets?

conserje (el, la) [con SER he] *n.* • concierge, porter
El conserje te puede dar la información que quieres.
The concierge can give you the information you want.

conserva (la) [con SER ba] *n.* • jam, preserves
Tenemos suficientes duraznos para preparar las conservas.
We have enough peaches to prepare the preserves.

conquista (la) [con KEES ta] *n.* • conquest
La conquista de Tenochtitlán fue en el año 1521.
The conquest of Tenochtitlan was in 1521.

consonante (la) [con so NAN te] *n.* • consonant
"Ñ" no es una consonante del alfabeto inglés.
"Ñ" is not a consonant in the English alphabet.

construir [cons tru EER] *v.* • to build, to construct

yo	construyo
tú	construyes
usted	construye
él, ella	construye
nosotros, as	construimos
vosotros, as	construís
ustedes	construyen
ellos, ellas	construyen

Esa empresa construye hospitales.
That company builds hospitals.

contacto (el) [con TAC to] *n.* • contact
lentes de contacto (los) *n.* • contact lenses
El contacto entre estudiantes nacionales y extranjeros es beneficioso.
The contact between domestic and foreign students is beneficial.

contar [con TAR] *v.* • to count; to tell
contar con *v.* • to count on

yo	cuento
tú	cuentas
usted	cuenta
él, ella	cuenta
nosotros, as	contamos
vosotros, as	contáis
ustedes	cuentan
ellos, ellas	cuentan

Margarita cuenta el dinero.
Margarita is counting the money.

Cuento con tu ayuda.
I count on your help.

contento, a [con TEN to] *adj.* • happy, cheerful
Pedro está muy contento hoy.
Pedro is very happy today.

contestar [con tes TAR] *v.* • to answer
No puede contestar la pregunta.
He can't answer the question.

continuación (la) [con ti nua SYON] *n.* • follow-up, continuation
a continuación • next, following
Esta reunión es una continuación de la de anoche.
This meeting is a continuation of the one last night.

continuar [con tee NUAR] *v.* • to continue
Elisa continúa el trabajo de su padre.
Elisa is continuing her father's work.

contra [CON tra] *prep.* • against
llevar la contra *coll.* • to disagree with
La raqueta se apoya contra la pared.
The racket is leaning against the wall.

contraste (el) [con TRAS te] *n.* • contrast
Estudiamos el contraste entre los ricos y los pobres.
We are studying the contrast between the rich and the poor.

contrato (el) [con TRA to] *n.* • contract, lease
Firmamos un contrato para alquilar la casa.
We're signing a lease to rent the house.

control (el) [con TROL] *n.* • control
Todo está bajo control.
Everything is under control.

controlar [con tro LAR] *v.* • to control
El problema de José es que siempre quiere controlar todo.
José's problem is that he always wants to control everything.

convencer [con ben SER] *v.* • to convince

yo	convenzo
tú	convences
usted	convence
él, ella	convence
nosotros, as	convencemos
vosotros, as	convencéis
ustedes	convencen
ellos, ellas	convencen

No puedo convencer a mi mamá; no puedo ir.
I can't convince my mother; I can't go.

conversación (la) [con ber sa SYON] *n.* • conversation, talk
Mi madre tiene una conversación con la directora.
My mother is having a conversation with the principal.

conversar [con ber SAR] *v.* • to talk, to converse, to chat
Puedo conversar en español pero no en inglés.
I can talk in Spanish but not in English.

convertirse [con ber TEER se] *v.* • to become, to change

yo	me	convierto
tú	te	conviertes
usted	se	convierte
él, ella	se	convierte
nosotros, as	nos	convertimos
vosotros, as	os	convertís
ustedes	se	convierten
ellos, ellas	se	convierten

Las orugas se convierten en mariposas.
Caterpillars become butterflies.

copa (la) [CO pa] *n.* • glass (for liquor); cup
la Copa Mundial • the world soccer championship
Estas copas son de mi abuela.
These glasses are my grandmother's.

copia (la) [CO pya] *n.* • copy
¿Me das una copia de tu poema?
Will you give me a copy of your poem?

corazón (el) [co ra SON] *n.* • heart
Mi hermanita dibuja corazones en las cartas a nuestro abuelo.
My little sister draws hearts on the letters to our grandfather.

cordón (el) [cor DON] *n.* • string, twine
¿Quieres atar la caja con ese cordón?
Do you want to tie the box with that string?

correctamente [co rrec ta MEN te] *adv.* • correctly
Nathan siempre se comporta correctamente.
Nathan always behaves correctly.

correcto, a [co RREC to] *adj.* • correct, right
Alano tiene la respuesta correcta.
Alano has the correct answer.

corregir [co rre HEER] *v.* • to correct

yo	**corrijo**
tú	**corriges**
usted	**corrige**
él, ella	**corrige**
nosotros, as	**corregimos**
vosotros, as	**corregís**
ustedes	**corrigen**
ellos, ellas	**corrigen**

Me siento incómodo cuando me corriges en público.
I feel uncomfortable when you correct me in public.

correo (el) [co RRE o] *n.* • post office; mail
Hay mucho correo hoy.
There is a lot of mail today.

correr [co RRER] *v.* • to run
Humberto corre todos los días.
Humberto runs every day.

cortar [cor TAR] *v.* • to cut
Helen va a cortar el patrón de mi vestido.
Helen is going to cut my dress pattern.

cortés [cor TES] *adj.* • courteous, polite
El maestro de literatura es muy cortés con los estudiantes.
The literature teacher is very polite with the students.

cortina (la) [cor TEE na] *n.* • curtain
Todavía no tenemos cortinas en la cocina.
We still don't have curtains in the kitchen.

corto, a [COR to] *adj.* • short (length)
Es un libro de cuentos cortos.
It's a book of short stories.

cosa (la) [CO sa] *n.* • thing
¿qué cosa? *coll.* • what? what's that?
¿Qué es esa cosa debajo de tu cama?
What is that thing under your bed?

coser [co SER] *v.* • to sew
Muy pocos hombres saben coser.
Very few men know how to sew.

costa (la) [COS ta] *n.* • coast
Chile tiene una costa muy larga.
Chile has a very long coast.

costar [cos TAR] *v.* • to cost

yo	cuesto
tú	cuestas
usted	cuesta
él, ella	cuesta
nosotros, as	costamos
vosotros, as	costáis
ustedes	cuestan
ellos, ellas	cuestan

¿Cuánto cuesta esta bici?
How much does this bike cost?

costumbre (la) [cos TUM bre] *n.* • custom, tradition
La costumbre de romper piñatas es de origen mexicano.
The custom of breaking piñatas is of Mexican origin.

crecer [cre SER] *v.* • to grow

yo	crezco
tú	creces
usted	crece
él, ella	crece
nosotros, as	crecemos
vosotros, as	crecéis
ustedes	crecen
ellos, ellas	crecen

Los bebés crecen rápidamente.
Babies grow very fast.

creencia (la) [cre EN sya] *n.* • belief
No tenemos las mismas creencias.
We don't have the same beliefs.

creer [cre ER] *v.* • to believe
creer que • to think that
creo que sí • I think so
Creo en los ángeles, ¿y tú?
I believe in angels, do you?

Creo que debo ir a la reunión.
I think that I should go to the meeting.

crema (la) [CRE ma] *n.* • cream; lotion
De postre quiero fresas con crema.
For dessert I want strawberries with cream.

criado, a (el, la) [CRYA do] *n.* • servant, maid (f.)
La criada ayuda a mi mamá.
The maid helps my mother.

crimen (el) [CREE men] *n.* • crime
Hay mucho crimen en la ciudad.
There is a lot of crime in the city.

criminal (el, la) [cree mee NAL] *n.* • criminal
El criminal está en la cárcel.
The criminal is in jail.

cristal (el) [crees TAL] *n.* • crystal, glass
¿Quién vive en una casa de cristal?
Who lives in a glass house?

crítico, a (el, la) [CREE tee co] *n.* • critic
crítica (la) *n.* • criticism, critique
El crítico escribe una crítica para el periódico.
The critic writes a critique for the newspaper.

cruzar [cru SAR] *v.* • to cross
No puedo cruzar la calle sin mi hermano mayor.
I can't cross the street without my big brother.

cuaderno (el) [cwa DER no] *n.* • notebook
Necesitamos un cuaderno para la clase de historia.
We need a notebook for history class.

cuadra (la) [CWA dra] *n.* • block
El acuario está a tres cuadras de aquí.
The aquarium is three blocks from here.

cuadrado, a [cwa DRA do] *adj.* • square
cuadrado (el) *n.* • square
No puedo dibujar un cuadrado sin regla.
I can't draw a square without a ruler.

cuadro (el) [CWA dro] *n.* • picture, painting
Christine quiere comprar un cuadro para la sala.
Christine wants to buy a painting for the living room.

¿cuál? [CWAL] *pron.* • which?, which one?
cualquier *adj.* • any
¿Cuál de los dos libros prefieres?
Which of the two books do you prefer?

Cualquier estudiante puede entender esta lección.
Any student can understand this lesson.

cuando [CWAN do] *conj.* • when
¿cuándo? *adv.* • when?
Siempre ayudo a mi madre cuando llego a casa.
I always help my mother when I get home.

¿Cuándo estudias?
When do you study?

¿cuánto?, a [CWAN to] *adj.* • how much?
¿Cuánto cuesta el libro?
How much does the book cost?

¿cuántos?, as [CWAN tos] *adj.* • how many?
¿Cuántos libros tienes?
How many books do you have?

cuarto (el) [CWAR to] *n.* • room; quarter, fourth
El palacio de Buckingham tiene más de cien cuartos.
Buckingham Palace has more than a hundred rooms.

Un cuarto de la clase está en la cafetería.
A fourth of the class is in the cafeteria.

cubeta (la) [cu BE ta] *n.* • pail, bucket
Esa cubeta ya no sirve porque tiene un agujero en el fondo.
That bucket is not useful anymore because it has a hole in the bottom.

cubierta (la) [cu BYER ta] *n.* • book cover
cubierto, a *adj.* • covered
cubierto (el) *n.* • table setting
¿Cuántas cubiertas necesitas?
How many book covers do you need?

cubo (el) [CU bo] *n.* • cube
El cubo es una figura geométrica de tres dimensiones.
A cube is a geometric figure of three dimensions.

cubrir [cu BREER] *v.* • to cover
Cubrimos los muebles nuevos con sábanas.
We cover the new furniture with sheets.

cuchara (la) [cu CHA ra] *n.* • spoon
cucharada [cu cha RA d̲a] *n.* • spoonful
Me faltan dos cucharas.
I'm missing two spoons.

cuchillo (el) [cu CHEE yo] *n.* • knife
No necesitamos cuchillos; comemos comida japonesa con palillos chinos.
We don't need knives; we are eating Japanese food with chopsticks.

cuello (el) [CWE yo] *n.* • neck
Los cisnes tienen cuellos largos.
Swans have long necks.

cuenta (la) [CWEN ta] *n.* • bill; check
Primero pago las cuentas y luego te digo si tengo dinero para regalos.
First I will pay the bills, and then I'll tell you if I have money for gifts.

cuento (el) [CWEN to] *n.* • story, tale
cuento de hadas (el) *n.* • fairy tale
Te voy a decir un cuento.
I'm going to tell you a story.

cuerda (la) [CWER da] *n.* • rope, cord, string
Necesito una cuerda más larga.
I need a much longer string.

cuero (el) [CWE ro] *n.* • leather
Mis botas de cuero son mis favoritas.
My leather boots are my favorite ones.

cuerpo (el) [CWER po] *n.* • body
¡Me duele todo el cuerpo!
My whole body hurts!

cuestión (la) [cwes TYON] *n.* • matter
La cuestión que queremos resolver es cómo trabajar en este proyecto.
The matter we want to resolve is how to work on this project.

cuidado (el) [cwee DA do] *n.* • care
cuidadoso, a *adj.* • careful
¡cuidado! *intj.* • be careful! careful!
Trabaja con cuidado.
She works with care.

¡Cuidado! Esa olla está caliente.
Be careful! That pot is hot.

cuidar [cweeDAR] *v.* • to take care of, to look after
Hoy le toca a mi marido cuidar a los niños.
Today is my husband's turn to take care of the children.

culebra (la) [cu LE bra] *n.* • (small) snake
Aprendemos mucho sobre culebras en la clase de biología.
We're learning a lot about snakes in biology class.

culpable [cul PA ble] *adj.* • guilty
culpable (el, la) *n.* • guilty person
Yo creo que Teresa es culpable.
I think Teresa is guilty.

cultivar [cul te BAR] *v.* • to grow; to till, to cultivate
Este año no cultivamos zanahorias en el jardin.
This year we are not growing carrots in the garden.

cultura (la) [cul TU ra] *n.* • culture
cultural *adj.* • cultural
Estudiamos la cultura griega.
We're studying Greek culture.

cumpleaños (el) [cum ple A nyos] *n.* • birthday
Yo siempre celebro mi cumpleaños.
I always celebrate my birthday.

cuna (la) [CU na] *n.* • cradle, crib
Mi tía decora la cuna para el bebé.
My aunt is decorating the cradle for the baby.

cuñado (el) [cu NYA do] *n.* • brother-in-law
cuñada (la) *n.* • sister-in-law
Mi cuñada nos visita esta semana.
My sister-in-law is visiting us this week.

curioso, a [cu RYO so] *adj.* • curious
Mi gata siempre está en un aprieto por ser tan curiosa.
My cat is always in trouble for being so curious.

CH

champú (el) [cham PU] *n.* • shampoo
dar champú *v.* • to shampoo
Por favor, cómprame un champú para el pelo seco.
Please buy me a shampoo for dry hair.

chapulín (el) [cha pu LEEN] *n.* • grasshopper (Mexico)
Los chapulines viven en el jardín.
Grasshoppers live in the garden.

chaqueta (la) [cha KE ta] *n.* • jacket
No laves la chaqueta en la lavadora.
Do not wash the jacket in the washer.

charlar [char LAR] *v.* • to chat
Diana trabaja y estudia; no tiene tiempo para charlar.
Diana works and studies; she does not have time to chat.

cheque (el) [CHE ke] *n.* • check
chequera (la) *n.* • checkbook
¿Cuántos cheques quedan en la chequera?
How many checks are left in the checkbook?

chicle (el) [CHEE cle] *n.* • gum
Mi mamá nunca me permite masticar chicle.
My mother never lets me chew gum.

chico (el) [CHEE co] *n.* • boy
chica (la) *n.* • girl
Esa chica es muy inteligente.
That girl is very intelligent.

chile (el) [CHEE le] *n.* • chili pepper
¿Qué tipo de chile tiene esta salsa?
What kind of chili pepper does this sauce have?

chimenea (la) [chee me NE a] *n.* • fireplace; chimney
Lilia trae la madera para la chimenea.
Lilia brings the wood for the fireplace.

chiste (el) [CHEES te] *n.* • joke
Este cómico tiene buenos chistes.
This comedian has good jokes.

chocolate (el) [cho co LA te] *n.* • chocolate
A Carmen le gusta comer chocolate.
Carmen likes to eat chocolate.

chofer (el) [cho FER] *n.* • driver
Peter es el chofer designado después de la fiesta.
Peter is the designated driver after the party.

chubasco (el) [chu BAS co] *n.* • short, heavy storm; downpour
Es un chubasco, nada más.
It's a downpour, nothing more.

chuleta (la) [chu LE ta] *n.* • chop, cutlet
A Sandra le gusta preparar chuletas de puerco.
Sandra likes to fix pork chops.

D

damas (las) [DA mas] *n.* • checkers
Me gusta jugar a las damas.
I like to play checkers.

daño (el) [DA nyo] *n.* • damage
No hay mucho daño al carro.
There isn't much damage to the car.

dar [DAR] *v.* • to give

yo	doy
tú	das
usted	da
él, ella	da
nosotros, as	damos
vosotros, as	dais
ustedes	dan
ellos, ellas	dan

Mi papá me da dinero.
My father gives me money.

dato (el) [DA to] *n.* • fact, a piece of information
datos (los) *n.* • data
Los datos del experimento son procesados y analizados.
The data from the experiment are processed and analyzed.

de [DE] *prep.* • of, from, about
de acuerdo • OK
de nada • you are welcome
de repente *adv.* • suddenly
estar de acuerdo *v.* • to agree

1. To indicate source of origin
Soy de Colombia.
I am from Colombia.

2. To indicate possession
Los amigos de Patricia vienen a su casa de vez en cuando.
Patricia's friends come over to her house every now and then.

debajo [de BA ho] *adv.* • underneath, below
debajo de *prep.* • under
La caja está debajo del sillón.
The box is under the chair.

débil [DE beel] *adj.* • weak
Vicki está débil por su enfermedad.
Vicki is weak because of her illness.

decepción (la) [de cep SYON] *n.* • disappointment
¡Qué decepción!
What a disappointment!

decir [de SEER] *v.* • to say, to tell

yo	digo
tú	dices
usted	dice
él, ella	dice
nosotros, as	decimos
vosotros, as	decís
ustedes	dicen
ellos, ellas	dicen

Siempre digo la verdad.
I always tell the truth.

decisión (la) [de see SYON] *n.* • decision
La decisión es unánime.
The decision is unanimous.

decoración (la) [de co ra SYON] *n.* • decoration, ornamentation
¡Qué decoraciones tan bonitas!
What pretty decorations!

decorar [de co RAR] *v.* • to decorate
Lucía decora su casa en un estilo contemporáneo.
Lucía is decorating her house in a contemporary style.

dedo (el) [DE do] *n.* • finger
dedo del pie (el) *n.* • toe
Tenemos diez dedos.
We have ten fingers.

defecto (el) [de FEC to] *n.* • fault, defect
Esta licuadora tiene unos defectos.
This blender has some defects.

dejar [de HAR] *v.* • to leave (behind), to abandon, to allow
dejar de *v.* • to stop, to cease
Mamá no nos deja ver esa película.
Mother won't let us see that movie.

Miguel quiere dejar de fumar.
Miguel wants to stop smoking.

del [DEL] *cont.* de + el (see **de**) • of the, from the
Necesito ver el índice del libro.
I need to see the index of the book.

delantal (el) [de lan TAL] *n.* • apron
Usa tu delantal en la cocina por favor.
Please wear your apron in the kitchen.

delante [de LAN te] *adv.* • in front, ahead
delante de *prep.* • in front of
José está delante de Juan.
José is in front of Juan.

delfín (el) [del FEEN] *n.* • dolphin
Los delfines son muy inteligentes.
Dolphins are very intelligent.

delgado, a [del GA d̲o] *adj.* • thin, slim
Marisa es tan delgada.
Marisa is so thin.

delicado, a [de lee CA d̲o] *adj.* • delicate, fine
La porcelana es delicada.
Porcelain is delicate.

delicioso, a [de lee SYO so] *adj.* • delicious
El postre es delicioso.
The dessert is delicious.

demasiado, a [de ma SYA d̲o] *adj.* • too much; too many
demasiado *adv.* • too; too much
Hay demasiadas moscas aquí.
There are too many flies here.

Pedro come demasiado.
Pedro eats too much.

democrático, a [de mo CRA tee co] *adj.* • democratic
Tenemos un sistema democrático.
We have a democratic system.

dentista (el, la) [den TEES ta] *n.* • dentist
Mi hermano tiene miedo al dentista.
My brother is afraid of the dentist.

deporte (el) [de POR te] *n.* • sport
Luisa practica varios deportes.
Luisa plays several sports.

deportista (el, la) [de por TEES ta] *n.* • athlete, sportsman, sportswoman
Pepe quiere ser deportista profesional.
Pepe wants to be a professional athlete.

derecho, a [de RE cho] *adj.* • right
derecha (la) • *n.* right side
Me duele el brazo derecho.
My right arm hurts.

La escuela está a la derecha.
The school is on the right.

derecho (el) [de RE cho] *n.* • right, privilege
derecho *adv.* • straight ahead
No tienes derecho de entrar en mi cuarto.
You don't have the right to enter my room.

derramar [de rra MAR] *v.* • to spill
El bebé siempre derrama su leche.
The baby always spills his milk.

desaparecer [de sa pa re SER] *v.* • to disappear

yo	desaparezco
tú	desapareces
usted	desaparece
él, ella	desaparece
nosotros, as	desaparecemos
vosotros, as	desaparecéis
ustedes	desaparecen
ellos, ellas	desaparecen

Juan desaparece cuando hay muchos quehaceres.
Juan disappears when there are a lot of chores.

desayuno (el) [de sa YU no] *n.* • breakfast
El desayuno incluye cereal con leche.
Breakfast includes cereal with milk.

descansar [des can SAR] *v.* • to rest
Jorge descansa después de la fiesta.
Jorge rests after the party.

descender [de sen DER] *v.* • to go down, to descend

yo	desciendo
tú	desciendes
usted	desciende
él, ella	desciende
nosotros, as	descendemos
vosotros, as	descendéis
ustedes	descienden
ellos, ellas	descienden

La reina desciende la escalera
The queen descends the stairs.

describir [des cree BEER] *v.* • to describe
La maestra de historia describe la vida en la Edad Media.
The history teacher describes life in the Middle Ages.

desde [DES de] *prep.* • from, since
Puedo ver mejor desde aquí.
I can see better from here.

desear [de se AR] *v.* • to want, to wish, to desire
Dorothy desea regresar a casa.
Dorothy wants to go back home.

deseo (el) [de SE o] *n.* • wish, desire
Mi deseo es viajar a Europa.
My wish is to travel to Europe.

desfile (el) [des FEE le] *n.* • parade
El Desfile de las Rosas es en Pasadena.
The Rose Bowl Parade is in Pasadena.

desierto (el) [de SYER to] *n.* • desert
El Sahara está en Africa
The Sahara Desert is in Africa.

desobediente [de so be DYEN te] *adj.* •
disobedient, naughty
A Papá Noel no le gustan los niños desobedientes.
Santa Claus does not like disobedient children.

despacio [des PA syo] *adv.* • slow; slowly
Habla más despacio por favor.
Please speak more slowly.

despedida (la) [des pe DEE da] *n.* • farewell
despedida de soltera (la) *n.* • bridal shower
Preparamos una despedida de soltera para María.
We're preparing a bridal shower for María.

despegar [des pe GAR] *v.* • to take off; to unglue
El avión a Lima despega a las 8 p.m.
The plane to Lima takes off at 8 p.m.

despertador (el) [des per ta DOR] *n.* • alarm clock
Pongo el despertador a las seis y veinte.
I set the alarm clock for 6:20.

despertar [des per TAR] *v.* • to wake (someone)
despertarse *v.* • to wake up

yo	me	despierto
tú	te	despiertas
usted	se	despierta
él, ella	se	despierta
nosotros, as	nos	despertamos
vosotros, as	os	despertáis
ustedes	se	despiertan
ellos, ellas	se	despiertan

Me despierto más tarde en el invierno.
I wake up later in the winter.

después [des PWES] *adv.* • later, afterward
después de *adv.* • after
Te veo después.
I'll see you later.

Vamos de compras después de las clases.
We're going shopping after school.

detective (el) [de tec TEE be] *n.* • detective
Sherlock Holmes es el detective más famoso de todos.
Sherlock Holmes is the most famous detective of all.

detener [de te NER] *v.* • to stop, to arrest
El policía detiene a los jóvenes.
The policeman stops the young men.

detestar [de tes TAR] *v.* • to hate, to detest
Maricela detesta las espinacas.
Maricela hates spinach.

detrás [de TRAS] *adv.* • in back, behind
detrás de *prep.* • in back of, behind
La escoba está detrás de esa puerta.
The broom is behind that door.

Los árboles están delante de la casa y el jardín está detrás.
The trees are in front of the house, and the garden is in back.

deuda (la) [DEU da] *n.* • debt
No tengo ninguna deuda.
I don't have a single debt.

devolver [de bol BER] *v.* • to return, to give back

yo	devuelvo
tú	devuelves
usted	devuelve
él, ella	devuelve
nosotros, as	devolvemos
vosotros, as	devolvéis
ustedes	devuelven
ellos, ellas	devuelven

Devuelvo los libros a la biblioteca.
I return the books to the library.

día (el) [DEE a] *n.* • day
día de fiesta • holiday
día libre • free day, day off
Hay siete días en una semana.
There are seven days in a week.

diablo (el) [DYAB lo] *n.* • demon, devil
¿Crees en el diablo?
Do you believe in the Devil?

diario, a [DYA ryo] *adj.* • daily
diario (el) *n.* • newspaper, journal
Richard hace sus ejercicios diarios.
Richard does his daily exercises.

dibujante (el, la) [dee bu HAN te] *n.* • illustrator
Juan es un dibujante excelente.
Juan is an excellent illustrator.

dibujar [dee bu HAR] *v.* • to draw
Me gusta dibujar en mi tiempo libre.
I like to draw in my free time.

dibujo (el) [dee BU ho] *n.* • drawing
El museo tiene una exhibición de los dibujos de Leonardo.
The museum has an exhibit of Leonardo's drawings.

diccionario (el) [deec syo NA ryo] *n.* • dictionary
La biblioteca tiene un diccionario español-inglés.
The library has a Spanish-English dictionary.

diciembre [dee SYEM bre] *n.* • December
Diciembre es un mes lleno de festividades.
December is a month full of festivities.

diente (el) [DYEN te] *n.* • tooth
El bebé ya tiene tres dientes.
The baby already has three teeth.

dieta (la) [DYE ta] *n.* • diet
La familia Díaz sigue una dieta estrictamente vegetariana.
The Díaz family follows a strictly vegetarian diet.

diferencia (la) [dee fe REN sya] *n.* • difference
No hay mucha diferencia entre estos productos.
There isn't much difference between these products.

diferente [dee fe REN te] *adj.* • different
No quiero éste; quiero algo diferente.
I don't want this one; I want something different.

difícil [dee FEE seel] *adj.* • difficult
Esta lección es muy difícil.
This lesson is very difficult.

dinero (el) [dee NE ro] *n.* • money
dinero en efectivo • cash
José le pide dinero a su padre.
José is asking his father for money.

dinosaurio (el) [dee no SAU ryo] *n.* • dinosaur
El museo tiene un esqueleto de dinosaurio.
The museum has a dinosaur skeleton.

dirección (la) [dee rec SYON] *n.* • address, direction
La dirección que buscamos está al norte de la ciudad.
The address we are looking for is on the north side of town.

director, a (el, la) [dee rec TOR] *n.* • director, principal
Felipe quiere ser director de cine.
Felipe wants to be a movie director.

dirigir [dee ree HEER] *v.* • to direct, to lead, to manage

yo	dirijo
tú	diriges
usted	dirige
él, ella	dirige
nosotro, as	dirigimos
vosotros, as	dirigís
ustedes	dirigen
ellos, as	dirigen

Mi tío dirige una empresa en California.
My uncle manages a company in California.

disco (el) [DEES co] *n.* • record
Este disco es muy popular ahora.
This record is very popular now.

discriminación (la) [dees cree mee na SYON] *n.* • discrimination; bigotry
La discriminación es un problema todavía.
Discrimination is still a problem.

disculpar [dees cul PAR] *v.* • to excuse, to forgive
discúlpeme *coll.* • excuse me, pardon me
No sé si me va a disculpar.
I don't know if she'll forgive me.

¡Discúlpeme! ¡Lo siento!
Excuse me! I'm sorry!

disfrutar [dees fru TAR] *v.* • to enjoy
Los niños disfrutan con las visitas de su tía Carmen.
The children enjoy the visits of their aunt Carmen.

disgustado, a [dees gus TA do] *adj.* • upset, annoyed
Mi papá está disgustado con la política del nuevo gobernador.
My father is upset with the policies of the new governor.

disgusto (el) [dees GUS to] *n.* • annoyance, displeasure
Ese ruido es un disgusto.
That noise is an annoyance.

distante [dees TAN te] *adj.* • distant, far away
El mercado no está muy distante.
The market isn't very far away.

distinto, a [dees TEEN to] *adj.* • different
El estilo de este pintor es distinto.
This painter's style is different.

diversión (la) [dee ber SYON] *n.* • entertainment, amusement
Ir al cine es una diversión popular en los Estados Unidos.
Going to the movies is popular entertainment in the United States.

divertido, a [dee ber TEE do] *adj.* • amusing, funny
Ese libro es muy divertido.
That book is very amusing.

divertirse [dee ber TEER se] *v.* • to have fun

yo	me	divierto
tú	te	diviertes
usted	se	divierte
él, ella	se	divierte
nosotros, as	nos	divertimos
vosotros, as	os	divertís
ustedes	se	divierten
ellos, ellas	se	divierten

Ellos siempre se divierten durante sus vacaciones.
They always have fun on their vacation.

doblar [do BLAR] *v.* • to fold; to turn
¿Me ayudas a doblar las invitaciones?
Will you help me fold the invitations?

docena (la) [do SE na] *n.* • dozen
Las rosas cuestan tres dólares la docena.
Roses cost three dollars a dozen.

doctor, a (el, la) [doc TOR] *n.* • doctor, Ph.D.
Jaime es doctor en matemáticas.
Jaime is a doctor of mathematics.

documental (el) [do cu men TAL] *n.* • documentary
Ese director escribe un documental muy interesante.
That director is writing a very interesting documentary.

dólar (el) [DO lar] *n.* • dollar
Te doy cinco dólares por ese reloj.
I'll give you five dollars for that watch.

doler [do LER] *v.* • to ache, to feel pain
Le duele la mano a Susita.
Susita's hand hurts.

dolor (el) [do LOR] *n.* • pain, ache; sorrow
dolor de cabeza *n.* • headache
dolor de estómago *n.* • stomach ache
Necesito una siesta; tengo un dolor de cabeza.
I need a nap; I have a headache.

dominó (el) [do mee NO] *n.* • dominoes
No tengo un juego de dominó.
I don't have a set of dominoes.

donde [DON de] *adv.* • where
¿dónde? *adv.* • where?
Éste es el hotel donde nos alojamos.
This is the hotel where we are staying.

¿Dónde está Alberto?
Where is Alberto?

dormido, a [dor MEE d̲o] *adj.* • asleep
El jefe está dormido en su oficina.
The boss is asleep in his office.

dormir [dor MEER] *v.* • to sleep
dormirse *v.* • to fall asleep

yo	me	duermo
tú	te	duermes
usted	se	duerme
él, ella	se	duerme
nosotros, as	nos	dormimos
vosotros, as	os	dormís
ustedes	se	duermen
ellos, ellas	se	duermen

Los atletas necesitan dormir bien.
Athletes need to sleep well.

dormitorio (el) [dor mee TO ryo] *n.* • bedroom; dormitory
Mi dormitorio está arriba.
My bedroom is upstairs.

drama (el) [DRA ma] *n.* • drama, play
Ella tiene un papel en el drama.
She has a role in the play.

dramático, a [dra MA tee co] *adj.* • dramatic
Carmen es una ópera dramática.
Carmen *is a dramatic opera.*

ducha (la) [DU cha] *n.* • shower
No me gustan las duchas frías.
I don't like cold showers.

ducharse [du CHAR se] *v.* • to take a shower

yo	me	ducho
tú	te	duchas
usted	se	ducha
él, ella	se	ducha
nosotros, as	nos	duchamos
vosotros, as	os	ducháis
ustedes	se	duchan
ellos, ellas	se	duchan

Voy a ducharme antes de salir.
I'm going to shower before I leave.

dueño, a (el, la) [DWE nyo] *n.* • owner
No conozco al dueño de esta tienda.
I don't know the owner of this store.

dulce [DUL se] *adj.* • sweet
dulce (el) *n.* • candy
Bernice es una niña muy dulce.
Bernice is a very sweet girl.

¿Quieres unos dulces?
Do you want some candy?

durante [du RAN te] *prep.* • during, while
Voy a comer durante la película.
I'm going to eat during the movie.

durazno (el) [du RAS no] *n.* • peach
Me gustan los duraznos con crema.
I like peaches with cream.

duro, a [DU ro] *adj.* • hard; firm; stern
Esta cama es dura.
This bed is firm.

E

eclipse (el) [e CLEEP se] *n.* • eclipse
Hay un eclipse el viernes.
There is an eclipse on Friday.

económico, a [e co NO mee co] *adj.* • economic
La forma más económica de viajar en Europa es por tren.
The most economic way to travel in Europe is by train.

ecuación (la) [e cwa SYON] *n.* • equation
En álgebra no estudiamos las ecuaciones diferenciales.
In algebra we do not study differential equations.

edad (la) [e DAD] *n.* • age
La edad mínima para votar es dieciocho años.
The minimum age to vote is eighteen.

edificio (el) [e dee FEE syo] *n.* • building
La Torre de Sears es el edificio más alto del mundo.
The Sears Tower is the tallest building in the world.

educación (la) [e du ca SYON] *n.* • education
educación física *n.* • physical education
La educación es una prioridad nacional.
Education is a national priority.

ejemplo (el) [e HEM plo] *n.* • example
por ejemplo • for example
Los ejemplos en el libro son muy útiles.
The examples in the book are very useful.

ejército (el) [e HER see to] *n.* • army
Los Estados Unidos tiene un ejército grande.
The U.S. has a big army.

ejote (el) [e HO te] *n.* • string bean (Mexico)
La cena de hoy es pollo asado y ensalada de ejotes.
Today's dinner is roast chicken and string bean salad.

el [EL] *art.* • the (m. sing.)
El coche está en el garaje.
The car is in the garage.

él [EL] *pron.* • he
¿Quién es él?
Who is he?

el que [EL KE] *rel. pron.* • the one that, the one who
¿Quién es el que va a traer las galletas a la reunión?
Who is the one who is going to bring the cookies to the meeting?

electricidad (la) [e lec tree see DAD] *n.* • electricity
Estudiamos las propiedades de la electricidad en la clase de física.
We study the properties of electricity in physics.

electricista (el, la) [e lec tree SEES ta] *n.* • electrician
El electricista repara la lámpara.
The electrician repairs the lamp.

electrónico, a [e lec TRO nee co] *adj.* • electronic
Estos juguetes electrónicos necesitan baterías.
These electronic toys need batteries.

elefante (el) [e le FAN te] *n.* • elephant
Hay muchos elefantes en África.
There are many elephants in Africa.

elegante [e le GAN te] *adj.* • elegant
Vamos a preparar una comida elegante.
We are going to prepare an elegant meal.

ella [E ya] *pron.* • she
Ella está en la biblioteca.
She is in the library.

ellos, as [E yos] *pron.* • they (pl.)
ellos, as mismos, as • (they) themselves, by themselves
todos, as ellos, as • all of them
Ellos celebran porque pueden terminar el proyecto ellos mismos.
They are celebrating because they are able to finish the project by themselves.

emergencia (la) [e mer HEN sya] *n.* • emergency
Debes decirles que es una emergencia.
You should tell them that it is an emergency.

emisora (la) [e mee SO ra] *n.* • broadcasting station
El canal 13 es la emisora de la universidad.
Channel 13 is the broadcasting station for the university.

emoción (la) [e mo SYON] *n.* • emotion, feeling
¡Qué emoción! • How exciting!
El amor es una emoción compleja.
Love is a complex emotion.

emocionante [e mo syo NAN te] *adj.* • exciting
Las historias de Marco Polo son muy emocionantes.
Stories about Marco Polo are very exciting.

emocionar [e mo syo NAR] *v.* • to move, to thrill
Las buenas noticias nos emocionan.
The good news thrills us.

empezar [em pe SAR] *v.* • to start, to begin

yo	empiezo
tú	empiezas
usted	empieza
él, ella	empieza
nosotros, as	empezamos
vosotros, as	empezáis
ustedes	empiezan
ellos, ellas	empiezan

El semestre empieza en enero.
The semester starts in January.

empleado, a [em ple A do] *adj.* • employed
empleado, a (el, la) *n.* • employee
La compañía busca veinte empleados nuevos.
The company is looking for twenty new employees.

empleo (el) [em PLE o] *n.* • job, work
Tengo empleo en la biblioteca.
I have a job at the library.

empujar [em pu HAR] *v.* • to push
Empuja el botón por favor.
Push the button, please.

en [EN] *prep.* • in, at, on, by
en forma *coll.* • in shape
en punto *coll.* • on the dot
en seguida *adv.* • immediately, right away
Los mapas están en el escritorio en la oficina de Loretta.
The maps are on the desk in Loretta's office.

Hago ejercicios para estar en forma.
I exercise to be in shape.

encantado, a [en can TA d̲o] *adj.* • delighted, enchanted
encantado, a de conocerle • glad to meet you
Mi hermano está encantado con su nuevo equipo de buceo.
My brother is delighted with his new diving equipment.

encantar [en can TAR] *v.* • to charm, to delight
Esa niñita me encanta.
That little girl delights me.

enciclopedia (la) [en see clo PE d̲ya] *n.* • encyclopedia
La biblioteca tiene dos enciclopedias.
The library has two encyclopedias.

encima [en SEE ma] *adv.* • on top
encima de *prep.* • on top of, upon, above
El papel que quieres está encima.
The paper that you want is on top.

Mi bolsa está encima de la mesa.
My purse is on top of the table.

encontrar [en con TRAR] *v.* • to find
encontrarse *v.* • to meet

yo	me	encuentro
tú	te	encuentras
usted	se	encuentra
él, ella	se	encuentra
nosotros, as	nos	encontramos
vosotros, as	os	encontráis
ustedes	se	encuentran
ellos, ellas	se	encuentran

Luisa necesita encontrar un apartamento más grande.
Luisa needs to find a bigger apartment.

encuesta (la) [en CWES ta] *n.* • survey, poll
¿Vas a participar en la encuesta?
Are you going to take part in the survey?

enchufe (el) [en CHU fe] *n.* • (electric) plug
Los enchufes no deben ser accesibles al bebé.
The plugs must not be accessible to the baby.

enemigo, a (el, la) [e ne MEE go] *n.* • enemy
Todos los superhéroes tienen enemigos.
All superheroes have enemies.

enero [e NE ro] *n.* • January
Mi cumpleaños es en enero.
My birthday is in January.

enfermería (la) [en fer me REE a] *n.* • infirmary
Los estudiantes enfermos están en la enfermería.
The sick students are in the infirmary.

enfermero, a (el, la) [en fer ME ro] *n.* • nurse
Beth es enfermera certificada.
Beth is a registered nurse.

enfermo, a [en FER mo] *adj.* • ill, sick
Andy está enfermo después de comer cincuenta tacos.
Andy is ill after eating fifty tacos.

enfrente [en FREN te] *adv.* • in front of, opposite
enfrente de *prep.* • in front of
El monumento está enfrente del teatro.
The monument is in front of the theater.

enlatado, a [en la TA d̲o] *adj.* • canned
Durante el invierno tengo que usar tomates enlatados.
During the winter I have to use canned tomatoes.

enojado, a [e no HA d̲o] *adj.* • angry, upset
Mi madre está enojada conmigo.
My mother is angry with me.

enorme [e NOR me] *adj.* • huge, enormous
Ese elefante es enorme.
That elephant is enormous.

enrollar [en ro YAR] *v.* • to roll up (a sheet)
Tienes que enrollar los mapas.
You have to roll up the maps.

ensalada (la) [en sa LA d̲a] *n.* • salad
¿Prefieres sopa o ensalada?
Do you prefer soup or salad?

enseñar [en se NYAR] *v.* • to teach
Linda enseña en un colegio.
Linda teaches in a high school.

entender [en ten DER] *v.* to understand

yo	entiendo
tú	entiendes
usted	entiende
él, ella	entiende
nosotros, as	entendemos
vosotros, as	entendéis
ustedes	entienden
ellos, ellas	entienden

No entiendo la lección.
I don't understand the lesson.

entero, a [en TE ro] *adj.* • whole, complete, entire
El proyecto entero está listo.
The entire project is ready.

entonces [en TON ses] *adv.* • then, at that time; in that case
... y entonces Caperucita decidió seguir el camino más corto...
... and then Little Red Riding Hood decided to follow the shortest way...

entrada (la) [en TRA da] *n.* • entrance
Te espero en la entrada.
I'll wait for you at the entrance.

entrar [en TRAR] *v.* • to enter
No podemos entrar sin llave.
We can't enter without a key.

entre [EN tre] *prep.* • between
Entre Juana y María no hay secretos.
There are no secrets between Juana and María.

entregar [en tre GAR] *v.* • to give, to deliver; to hand in
Tenemos que entregar la tarea hoy.
We have to hand in the assignment today.

entrevista (la) [en tre BEES ta] *n.* • interview
El periódico publica una serie de entrevistas con Pérez de Cuellar.
The paper is publishing a series of interviews with Pérez de Cuellar.

enviado, a (el, la) [en BYA do] *n.* • representative, delegate, envoy
La señora García es la enviada del gobernador.
Mrs. García is the governor's representative.

enviar [en BYAR] *v.* • to send
Por favor envía estas cartas por correo aéreo.
Please send these letters by air mail.

equipaje (el) [e kee PA he] *n.* • luggage, baggage
¿Dónde está tu equipaje?
Where is your luggage?

equipo (el) [e KEE po] *n.* • team; equipment
Este año tenemos muy buen equipo de baloncesto.
This year we have a very good basketball team.

error (el) [e RROR] *n.* • mistake
Hay muchos errores en el manuscrito.
There are many errors in the manuscript.

escalera (la) [es ca LE ra] *n.* • ladder; staircase
Mi vecina me presta su escalera cuando necesito limpiar las ventanas.
My neighbor lends me her ladder when I need to wash the windows.

escalón (el) [es ca LON] *n.* • step
Cuidado en el escalón.
Be careful on the step.

escoba (la) [es CO ba] *n.* • broom
Necesito una escoba para barrer el piso.
I need a broom to sweep the floor.

escoger [es co HER] *v.* • to choose, to pick
Es difícil escoger entre tantos colores.
It's hard to choose from among so many colors.

escolar [es co LAR] *adj.* • school (related)
El programa escolar incluye un curso de arte.
The school curriculum includes an art class.

esconder [es con DER] *v.* • to hide, to conceal
Manuel siempre esconde mis zapatos.
Manuel always hides my shoes.

escribir [es cree BEER] *v.* • to write
Mi hermano me escribe cartas sobre sus viajes.
My brother writes me letters about his travels.

escritor, a (el, la) [es cree TOR] *n.* • writer
Ernest Hemingway es un escritor norteamericano.
Ernest Hemingway is a North American writer.

escritorio (el) [es cree TO ryo] *n.* • desk
Este escritorio es sólido.
This desk is solid.

escuchar [es cu CHAR] *v.* • to listen to
Prefiero escuchar la música rock.
I prefer to listen to rock music.

escuela (la) [es CWE la] *n.* • school
La escuela está en la esquina.
The school is on the corner.

escultura (la) [es cul TU ra] *n.* • sculpture
La escultura frente a la escuela representa un estudiante.
The sculpture facing the school represents a student.

ese, a [E se] *adj.* • that
Ese perro es muy inteligente.
That dog is very intelligent.

ése, a [E se] *pron.* • that one
Este libro es tuyo, ése es mío.
This book is yours, that one is mine.

esnob (el, la) [es NOB] *n.* • snob
Algunos amigos de Patricia son esnobs.
Some of Patricia's friends are snobs.

espacio (el) [es PA syo] *n.* • space, room
Mi oficina tiene suficiente espacio para todas mis cosas.
My office has enough room for all my things.

espaguetis (los) [es pa GE tees] *n.* • spaghetti
Preparo espaguetis con albóndigas.
I'm preparing spaghetti with meatballs.

espalda (la) [es PAL da] *n.* • back
La tensión me produce dolor de espalda.
Stress gives me back pain.

espantoso, a [es pan TO so] *adj.* • horrible, frightening
El monstruo en esa película es espantoso.
The monster in that movie is horrible.

español, a [es pa NYOL] *adj.* • Spanish
español (el) *n.* • Spanish (language)
español, a (el, la) *n.* • Spaniard

Los estudiantes españoles llegan mañana.
The Spanish students arrive tomorrow.

¿Hablas español?
Do you speak Spanish?

espárrago (el) [es PA rra go] *n.* • asparagus
No sé cocinar espárragos.
I do not know how to cook asparagus.

especial [es pe SYAL] *adj.* • special
Tengo una sorpresa especial para ti.
I have a special surprise for you.

especialmente [es pe syal MEN te] *adv.* • especially
Esta tarea es especialmente difícil.
This assignment is especially difficult.

espectador, a (el, la) [es pec ta DOR] *n.* • spectator
No soy atleta, soy espectador.
I'm not an athlete, I'm a spectator.

espejo (el) [es PE ho] *n.* • mirror
Romper un espejo no significa mala suerte.
To break a mirror does not mean bad luck.

esperar [es pe RAR] *v.* • to wait for; to hope
Te esperamos en el restaurante.
We'll wait for you in the restaurant.

espinaca (la) [es pee NA ca] *n.* • spinach
Popeye come espinacas para ser fuerte.
Popeye eats spinach to be strong.

esposa (la) [es PO sa] *n.* • wife
La esposa de Roberto es una bailarina de ballet.
Roberto's wife is a ballet dancer.

esposo (el) [es PO so] *n.* • husband
El esposo de Lucille es contador.
Lucille's husband is an accountant.

esquí (el) [es KEE] *n.* • ski; skiing
El esquí es un deporte de invierno.
Skiing is a winter sport.

esquiar [es KYAR] *v.* • to ski
Prefiero esquiar a campo travieso.
I prefer to cross-country ski.

esquina (la) [es KEE na] *n.* • corner
Nuestra escuela está en la esquina.
Our school is on the corner.

estación (la) [es ta SYON] *n.* • station; season
La estación de tren es ahora un restaurante.
The train station is now a restaurant.

Hay cuatro estaciones en el año.
There are four seasons in the year.

estacionamiento (el) [es ta syo na MYEN to] *n.* • parking lot
El estacionamiento está cerca del correo.
The parking lot is near the post office.

estacionar [es ta syo NAR] *v.* • to park
Nunca recuerdo dónde estacionamos el automóvil.
I never remember where we park the car.

estadio (el) [es TA dyo] *n.* • stadium
Este magnífico estadio tiene una capacidad de cien mil personas.
This magnificent stadium has a capacity of one hundred thousand people.

estado (el) [es TA do] *n.* • state
¿Quién es el gobernador del estado?
Who is the governor of the state?

Estados Unidos (los) [es TA dos u NEE dos] *n.* • United States
Los Estados Unidos están en Norteamérica.
The United States is in North America.

estampilla (la) [es tam PEE ya] *n.* • stamp
Tengo que comprar estampillas en el correo.
I have to buy stamps at the post office.

estanque (el) [es TAN ke] *n.* • pond
Hay un estanque en la granja.
There is a pond on the farm.

estante (el) [es TAN te] *n.* • bookshelf
El carpintero viene hoy para instalar los estantes.
The carpenter comes today to install the bookshelves.

estar [es TAR] *v.* • to be (see *also ser*)
estar contento, a • to be happy
estar enojado, a • to be upset, to be angry
estar furioso, a • to be furious
estar triste • to be sad

yo	estoy
tú	estás
usted	está
él, ella	está
nosotros, as	estamos
vosotros, as	estáis
ustedes	están
ellos, ellas	están

¿Dónde está Pablo?
Where is Pablo?

este (el) [ES te] *n.* • east
Boston está en el este.
Boston is in the east.

este, a [ES te] *adj.* • this
Este libro es para ti.
This book is for you.

éste, a [ES te] *pron.* • this one
Ese libro es mío, éste es de Roberto.
That book is mine, this one is Roberto's.

estimado, a [es tee MA d̲o] *adj.* • dear
Estimado cliente,
En su carta anterior......
Dear customer,
In your previous letter......

estómago (el) [es TO ma go] *n.* • stomach
El estómago de la vaca está dividido en cuatro secciones.
The cow's stomach is divided into four sections.

estornudar [es tor nu DAR] *v.* • to sneeze
Cuando ella estornuda, siempre usa su pañuelo.
When she sneezes, she always uses her handkerchief.

estrecho, a [es TRE cho] *adj.* • narrow
estrecho (el) *n.* • strait
La camioneta no pasa, este camino es estrecho.
The pick-up truck will not pass; this road is narrow.

estrella (la) [es TRE ya] *n.* • star
Mira, hay una estrella fugaz.
Look, there's a shooting star.

estudiante (el, la) [es tu DYAN te] *n.* • student
Algunos estudiantes no tienen becas.
Some students do not have scholarships.

estudiar [es tu DYAR] *v.* • to study
Estudiamos cinco asignaturas este semestre.
We study five subjects this term.

estufa (la) [es TU fa] *n.* • stove
Necesitamos comprar una nueva estufa.
We need to buy a new stove.

estupendo, a [es tu PEN do] *adj.* • fabulous, awesome
Me parece estupendo que aprendas español.
I think it is fabulous that you are learning Spanish.

estúpido, a [es TU pee do] *adj.* • stupid
Es un error estúpido.
It is a stupid mistake.

examen (el) [eks A men] *n.* • test, exam
El examen de matemáticas es viernes.
The math exam is Friday.

excelente [eks e LEN te] *adj.* • excellent
El sonido de este disco es excelente.
The sound of this record is excellent.

éxito (el) [EKS ee to] *n.* • success
El libro es un éxito.
The book is a success.

exótico, a [eks O tee co] *adj.* • exotic
Esa maestra lleva ropa muy exótica.
That teacher wears very exotic clothes.

experimento (el) [eks pe ree MEN to] *n.* • experiment
Manuel prepara su experimento de química.
Manuel is preparing his chemistry experiment.

experto, a (el, la) [eks PER to] *n.* • expert
Alfredo es el experto aquí.
Alfredo is the expert here.

explicar [eks plee CAR] *v.* • to explain
¿Puedes explicar el problema?
Can you explain the problem?

expresar [eks pre SAR] *v.* • to express
Todos pueden expresar su opinión.
Everyone can express his opinion.

expresión (la) [eks pre SYON] *n.* • expression
"Por favor" es una expresión importante.
"Please" is an important expression.

extintor (el) [eks teen TOR] *n.* • extinguisher
Hay tres extintores en cada piso del edificio.
There are three extinguishers on each floor of the building.

extranjero, a [eks tran HE ro] *adj.* • foreign
extranjero, a (el, la) *n.* • foreigner
Quiero vivir en un país extranjero por dos años.
I want to live in a foreign country for two years.

Esos tres hombres son extranjeros.
Those three men are foreigners.

extrañar [eks tra NYAR] *v.* • to miss, to long for
Extraño el clima tropical.
I miss the tropical weather.

extraño, a [eks TRA nyo] *adj.* • strange
Es una situación extraña.
It's a strange situation.

extraordinario, a [eks tra or dee NA ryo] *adj.* • extraordinary
La natación es un ejercicio extraordinario.
Swimming is an extraordinary exercise.

F

fábrica (la) [FAB ree ca] *n.* • factory
Las fábricas están fuera de la ciudad.
The factories are outside of the city.

fábula (la) [FA bu la] *n.* • fable, tale
Tenemos que escribir una fábula original para la clase de composición.
We have to write an original fable for composition class.

fabuloso, a [fa bu LO so] *adj.* • fabulous, wonderful
Es un desfile fabuloso.
It is a fabulous parade.

fácil [FA seel] *adj.* • easy
La tarea es fácil.
The assignment is easy.

fácilmente [FA seel men te] *adv.* • easily
Podemos hacerlo fácilmente.
We can do it easily.

falda (la) [FAL da] *n.* • skirt
La falda corta está de moda otra vez.
Short skirts are in fashion again.

falso, a [FAL so] *adj.* • false, fake
Joseph siempre declara un peso falso en su licencia de manejar.
Joseph always gives a false weight on his driver's license.

faltar [fal TAR] *v.* • to lack; to miss (to not attend)
hacerle falta a uno (alguna cosa) *coll.* • to need (something)
Me faltan cinco dólares.
I'm missing five dollars.

Elisa falta a la clase hoy.
Elisa is missing class today.

Me hace falta más tiempo.
I need more time.

fallar [fa YAR] *v.* • to fail, disappoint; to break, to give way
Mis hijos no me fallen.
My children don't disappoint me.

familia (la) [fa MEE lya] *n.* • family
A mi familia le gusta viajar.
My family likes to travel.

familiar [fa mee LYAR] *adj.* • family, familiar
familiar (el, la) *n.* • relative, family member
Tenemos una celebración familiar.
We're having a family celebration.

José es familiar de mi cuñada.
José is my sister-in-law's relative.

famoso, a [fa MO so] *adj.* • famous
Pablo Picasso es un pintor famoso.
Pablo Picasso is a famous painter.

fantasma (el) [fan TAS ma] *n.* • ghost
¿Tienes miedo a los fantasmas?
Are you afraid of ghosts?

fantástico, a [fan TAS tee co] *adj.* • fantastic
¡Qué idea tan fantástica!
What a fantastic idea!

farmacéutico, a (el, la) [far ma SE u tee co] *n.* • pharmacist
El padre de Anita es farmacéutico.
Anita's father is a pharmacist.

farmacia (la) [far MA sya] *n.* • drugstore, pharmacy
Por favor ve a la farmacia y compra unas aspirinas.
Please go to the drugstore and buy some aspirin.

faro (el) [FA ro] *n.* • headlight; lighthouse
El carro necesita faros nuevos.
The car needs new headlights.

farol (el) [fa ROL] *n.* • streetlight
Los faroles no funcionan esta noche.
The streetlights aren't working tonight.

favor (el) [fa BOR] *n.* • favor
por favor • please
Hazme el favor de traducir esta carta.
Do me the favor of translating this letter.

favorito, a [fa bo REE to] *adj.* • favorite
El verano es mi estación favorita.
Summer is my favorite season.

febrero [fe BRE ro] *n.* • February
Febrero es el mes más corto del año.
February is the shortest month of the year.

fecha (la) [FE cha] *n.* • date (in a calendar or schedule)
¿Cuál es la fecha hoy?
What is today's date?

felicitación (la) [fe lee see ta SYON] *n.* • congratulations
La tarjeta sólo dice "Felicitaciones en tu cumpleaños".
The card only says "Congratulations on your birthday."

feliz [fe LEES] *adj.* • happy
¡Feliz cumpleaños!
Happy Birthday!

feo, a [FE o] *adj.* • ugly
Yo creo que es una escultura muy fea.
I think it is a very ugly sculpture.

feria (la) [FE rya] *n.* • fair
La feria anual es en agosto.
The annual fair is in August.

feroz [fe ROS] *adj.* • fierce
Los tiburones son animales feroces.
Sharks are fierce animals.

ferrocarril (el) [fe rro ca RREEL] *n.* • railroad
Las líneas de ferrocarril son excelentes en Europa.
The railroads are excellent in Europe.

festejar [fes te HAR] *v.* • to celebrate
Festejamos el cumpleaños de los niños con una merienda campestre.
We celebrate the children's birthday with a picnic.

festival (el) [fes tee BAL] *n.* • festival
¿Quieres ir al festival de cine?
Do you want to go to the film festival?

ficción (la) [feek SYON] *n.* • fiction
¿Te gusta leer la ciencia ficción?
Do you like to read science fiction?

fiebre (la) [FYE bre] *n.* • fever
Ricardito ya no tiene fiebre.
Ricardito does not have a fever anymore.

fiesta (la) [FYES ta] *n.* • party
La fiesta empieza a las ocho.
The party starts at eight.

fila (la) [FEE la] *n.* • line (of people); row
Los boletos son para la fila número ocho.
The tickets are for row number eight.

fin (el) [FEEN] *n.* • end, ending
fin de semana (el) *n.* • weekend
Vamos a estudiar astronomía este fin de semana.
We are going to study astronomy this weekend.

final [fee NAL] *adj.* • final, last
final (el) *n.* • ending, end
Estamos al final de este proyecto.
We are at the end of this project.

fino, a [FEE no] *adj.* • fine (good quality)
Esta lana es muy fina.
This wool is of very fine quality.

físico, a (el, la) [FEE see co] *n.* • physicist
Los físicos estudian el átomo.
Physicists study the atom.

flaco, a [FLA co] *adj.* • skinny
Juan es muy flaco.
Juan is very skinny.

flan (el) [FLAN] *n.* • custard
Flan es un postre favorito en España.
Custard is a favorite dessert in Spain.

flor (la) [FLOR] *n.* • flower
Hay muchas flores en el jardín.
There are a lot of flowers in the garden.

flotar [flo TAR] *v.* • to float
Para nadar, necesitas saber flotar.
To swim you need to know how to float.

fondo (el) [FON do] *n.* • bottom
La revista está al fondo del montón.
The magazine is at the bottom of the pile.

forma (la) [FOR ma] *n.* • form, shape
en forma de • in the shape of, in the form of
Con tres meses de ejercicio vamos a estar en forma.
With three months of exercise we will be in shape.

formar [for MAR] *v.* • to form
Queremos formar un grupo para conversar en español.
We want to form a group to converse in Spanish.

fortaleza (la) [for ta LE sa] *n.* • fortress
Hay una fortaleza española en San Juan, Puerto Rico.
There is a Spanish fortress in San Juan, Puerto Rico.

fósforo (el) [FOS fo ro] *n.* • match
¿Tienes fósforos?
Do you have matches?

foto (la) [FO to] *n.* • photo, snapshot
fotografía (la) [fo to gra FEE a] *n.* • photograph; photography
¿Tienes una foto de tu hijo?
Do you have a photo of your son?

francés, a [fran SES] *adj.* • French
francés (el) *n.* • French (language)
francés, a (el, la) *n.* • Frenchman, French woman
¿Hablas francés?
Do you speak French?

La cocina francesa es muy complicada.
French cuisine is very complicated.

frase (la) [FRA se] *n.* • sentence; phrase
Juan escribe la frase en la pizarra.
Juan is writing the sentence on the board.

frecuente [fre KWEN te] *adj.* • frequent
Las visitas de mis abuelos no son muy frecuentes.
My grandparents' visits are not very frequent.

frecuentemente [fre kwen te MEN te] *adv.* • frequently
Silvia va a fiestas frecuentemente.
Silvia goes to parties frequently.

fregadero (el) [fre ga DE ro] *n.* • kitchen sink
Lavo los platos en el fregadero.
I wash dishes in the kitchen sink.

freno (el) [FRE no] *n.* • brake
Los frenos no funcionan muy bien.
The brakes aren't working very well.

frente (la) [FREN te] *n.* • forehead
Hay una mosca en la frente de Pablo.
There is a fly on Pablo's forehead.

fresa (la) [FRE sa] *n.* • strawberry
Este año cultivamos fresas en nuestro jardín.
This year we are growing strawberries in our garden.

fresco, a [FRES co] *adj.* • fresh
El restaurante de la calle Central siempre tiene pescado fresco.
The restaurant on Central Street always carries fresh fish.

frijol (el) [free HOL] *n.* • bean
Mi sopa favorita es la sopa de frijoles.
My favorite soup is bean soup.

frío, a [FREE o] *adj.* • cold
El vino blanco se sirve frío.
White wine is served cold.

frito, a [FREE to] *adj.* • fried
Rafael no come comida frita por razones de salud.
Rafael does not eat fried food for health reasons.

frontera (la) [fron TE ra] *n.* • border
No necesitamos pasaportes para cruzar la frontera.
We don't need passports to cross the border.

frustración (la) [frus tra SYON] *n.* • frustration
Virginia Wolf habla de la frustración de no poder ser libre.
Virginia Wolf talks about the frustration of not being able to be free.

frustrado, a [frus TRA do] *adj.* • frustrated; failed
Ella está frustrada con este proyecto.
She is frustrated with this project.

fruta (la) [FRU ta] *n.* • fruit
Comemos ensalada de fruta hoy.
We're eating fruit salad today.

fuego (el) [FWE go] *n.* • fire
No debes jugar con fuego.
You shouldn't play with fire.

fuente (la) [FWEN te] *n.* • fountain
Hay una fuente en la plaza.
There is a fountain in the plaza.

fuera de [FWE ra] *prep.* • out of
Jorge está fuera de la oficina.
Jorge is out of the office.

fuerte [FWER te] *adj.* • strong; loud
fuerte (el) *n.* • fort
Hércules es el héroe más fuerte de la mitología griega.
Hercules is the strongest hero in Greek mythology.

fumar [fu MAR] *v.* • to smoke (a cigarette, cigar or pipe)
Se prohibe fumar aquí.
Smoking is prohibited here.

funcionar [fun see o NAR] *v.* • to work, to function
Kay nos enseña cómo funciona la nueva computadora.
Kay teaches us how the new computer works.

fútbol (el) [FUT bol] *n.* • soccer
fútbol americano (el) *n.* • football
El fútbol es un deporte popular en Latinoamérica.
Soccer is a popular sport in Latin America.

futuro (el) [fu TU ro] *n.* • future
No podemos predecir el futuro.
We can't predict the future.

G

gafas (las) [GA fas] *n.* • glasses
gafas de sol (las) *n.* • sunglasses
¿Dónde están mis gafas?
Where are my glasses?

galleta (la) [ga YE ta] *n.* • cookie
galleta salada *n.* • cracker
Las galletas saladas son para la sopa de frijoles.
The crackers are for the bean soup.

gallina (la) [ga YEE na] *n.* • hen, chicken
Las gallinas son animales ruidosos.
Hens are noisy animals.

gallo (el) [GA yo] *n.* • rooster
El gallo se despierta temprano.
The rooster wakes up early.

gana (la) [GA na] *n.* • desire, longing
tener ganas de • to want to, to feel like
¿Tienes ganas de comer enchiladas?
Do you feel like eating enchiladas?

ganar [ga NAR] *v.* • to win, to earn
Los atletas olímpicos quieren ganar medallas.
The Olympic athletes want to win medals.

ganso (el) [GAN so] *n.* • goose
Los gansos migran al sur en el invierno.
Geese migrate south in winter.

garaje (el) [ga RA he] *n.* • garage
El garaje tiene espacio para dos automóviles.
The garage has space for two cars.

garganta (la) [gar GAN ta] *n.* • throat
La cantante cuida la garganta.
The singer takes care of her throat.

gas (el) [GAS] *n.* • gas (vapor)
Esta reacción química produce un gas azul.
This chemical reaction produces a blue gas.

gasolina (la) [ga so LEE na] *n.* • gas (fuel)
Mi automóvil necesita gasolina pero no tengo dinero.
My car needs gas but I don't have any money.

gasolinera (la) [ga so lee NE ra] *n.* • gas station
La gasolinera está en la esquina.
The gas station is on the corner.

gastar [gas TAR] *v.* • to spend
Susana gasta mucho dinero en la ropa.
Susana spends a lot of money on clothes.

gasto (el) [GAS to] *n.* • expense
¿Tiene una lista de gastos?
Do you have a list of expenses?

gatito, a (el, la) [ga TEE to] *n.* • kitten
Los gatitos son juguetones.
The kittens are playful.

gato, a (el, la) [GA to] *n.* • cat
Elisa tiene tres gatos.
Elisa has three cats.

gelatina (la) • [he la TEE na] *n.* • gelatine
La gelatina es nuestro postre favorito.
Gelatine is our favorite dessert.

gemelos, as (los, las) [he ME los] *n.* • twins
Los gemelos son idénticos.
The twins are identical.

general [he ne RAL] *adj.* • general, usual
Por regla general Michael no come carne.
As a general rule Michael does not eat meat.

generalmente [he ne ral MEN te] *adv.* • generally
Las hojas de los árboles generalmente se caen en octubre.
The leaves on the trees generally fall in October.

generoso, a [he ne RO so] *adj.* • generous
El padrino de Michelle es muy generoso.
Michelle's godfather is very generous.

gente (la) [HEN te] *n.* • people
Hay mucha gente en la feria.
There are a lot of people at the fair.

geografía (la) [he o gra FEE a] *n.* • geography
En la clase de geografía estudiamos unos lugares interesantes.
In geography class we study some interesting places.

gerente (el) [he REN te] *n.* • manager
Tomás es el gerente de esa tienda.
Tomás is the manager of that store.

gesto (el) [HES to] *n.* • gesture
Los estudiantes practican diferentes gestos en su clase de teatro.
The students practice different gestures in their theater class.

gigante (el) [hee GAN te] *n.* • giant
No hay gigantes en el mundo.
There are no giants in the world.

gimnasia (la) [heem NA sya] *n.* • gymnastics
El equipo de gimnasia va a ganar el campeonato.
The gymnastics team is going to win the championship.

gimnasio (el) [heem NA syo] *n.* • gymnasium
La fiesta de graduación es en el gimnasio de la escuela.
The graduation party is in the school gymnasium.

girasol (el) [hee ra SOL] *n.* • sunflower
El girasol es una flor amarilla.
The sunflower is a yellow flower.

globo (el) [GLO bo] *n.* • balloon
¿Me ayudas a inflar los globos?
Will you help me blow up the balloons?

gobierno (el) [go bee ER no] *n.* • government
El gobierno de los Estados Unidos reside en Washington.
The government of the United States is located in Washington.

golf (el) [GOLF] *n.* • golf
No tengo palos de golf.
I don't have golf clubs.

golfo (el) [GOL fo] *n.* • gulf
Leemos sobre el Golfo Pérsico.
We're reading about the Persian Gulf.

goma (la) [GO ma] *n.* • rubber
Pepito juega con la pelota de goma.
Pepito plays with the rubber ball.

grabadora (la) [gra ba DO ra] *n.* • tape recorder
Traemos la grabadora a la fiesta.
We're bringing the tape recorder to the party.

grabar [gra BAR] *v.* • to record
Voy a grabar la clase para Ricardo.
I'm going to record the class for Ricardo.

gracias (las) [GRA syas] *n.* • thanks
dar las gracias *n.* • to thank
Gracias por tu ayuda.
Thanks for your help.

gracioso, a [gra SYO so] *adj.* • cute, funny; graceful
El bebé es muy gracioso.
The baby is very cute.

grado (el) [GRA do] *n.* • degree, grade
El termómetro marca cien grados.
The thermometer reads one hundred degrees.

gran [GRAN] *adj.* • great, grand
Plácido Domingo es un gran cantante.
Plácido Domingo is a great singer.

granadilla (la) [gra na DEE ya] *n.* • passion fruit
En Costa Rica se comen granadillas.
In Costa Rica they eat passion fruit.

grande [GRAN de] *adj.* • big, large
Necesito un reloj grande para la sala.
I need a big clock for the living room.

granja (la) [GRAN ha] *n.* • farm
La granja está en el campo.
The farm is in the country.

granjero, a (el, la) [gran HE ro] *n.* • farmer
El granjero se despierta temprano.
The farmer wakes up early.

gripe (la) [GREE pe] *n.* • flu
No voy al trabajo porque tengo gripe.
I'm not going to work because I have the flu.

gris [GREES] *adj.* • gray
Juan compra un traje gris.
Juan is buying a gray suit.

gritar [gri TAR] *v.* • to shout, to scream
Los niños gritan al ver el monstruo.
The children scream on seeing the monster.

grueso, a [gru E so] *adj.* • heavy, thick
Necesito un abrigo más grueso.
I need a heavier coat.

grupo (el) [GRU po] *n.* • group
El grupo de biología va de excursión.
The biology group is going on a field trip.

guajolote (el) [gwa ho LO te] *n.* • turkey
El guajolote es más grande que la gallina.
The turkey is bigger than the hen.

guante (el) [GWAN te] *n.* • glove
Susan usa guantes para manejar.
Susan wears gloves to drive.

guapa [GWA pa] *adj.* • beautiful (woman)
Luisa es guapa.
Luisa is beautiful.

guapo [GWA po] *adj.* • handsome
José Diaz es el muchacho más guapo de la escuela.
José Diaz is the most handsome boy in the school.

guardar [gwar DAR] *v.* • to keep, to store, to guard
El profesor guarda los exámenes.
The professor keeps the exams.

guayaba (la) [gwa YA ba] *n.* • guava
La conserva de guayaba es de Puerto Rico.
Guava jam is from Puerto Rico.

guerra (la) [GE rra] *n.* • war
Estudiamos la Segunda Guerra Mundial
We are studying the Second World War.

guía (el, la) [GEE a] *n.* • guide
El guía nos dice la historia del edificio.
The guide tells us the history of the building.

guiar [GEE ar] *v.* • to guide
Este señor nos guía al restaurante.
This gentleman will guide us to the restaurant.

guisante (el) [gee SAN te] *n.* • pea
¿Te gusta la sopa de guisantes?
Do you like pea soup?

guitarra (la) [gee TA rra] *n.* • guitar
Danny toca la guitarra en la fiesta.
Danny plays the guitar at the party.

gusano (el) [gu SA no] *n.* • worm
El pescador usa gusanos como cebo.
The fisherman uses worms as bait.

gustar [gus TAR] *v.* • to like, to appeal to
Nos gusta la comida guatemalteca.
We like Guatemalan food.

Me gustan los tacos.
I like tacos.

H

haber [a BER] *aux. v.* to have (as auxiliary to a past participle)

yo	he
tú	has
usted	ha
él, ella	ha
nosotros, as	habemos
vosotros, as	habéis
ustedes	han
ellos, ellas	han

Yo he aprendido español.
I have learned Spanish.

habitación (la) [a bee ta SYON] *n.* • room
Este hotel tiene ochocientas habitaciones.
This hotel has eight hundred rooms.

habitante (el, la) [a bee TAN te] *n.* • inhabitant
¿Cuántos habitantes tiene este pueblo?
How many inhabitants does this town have?

hablar [a BLAR] *v.* • to speak
Juana habla tres idiomas.
Juana speaks three languages.

hacer [a SER] *v.* • to do; to make
hacerse • to become; to turn into
hacer la cama • to make the bed
hacer las maletas • to pack (lugagge)
hacerse el tonto, la tonta *coll.* • to play the fool, to act dumb
hace + time + **que** • for + time
hace buen tiempo • it is nice weather
hace calor • it is warm, it is hot
hace fresco • it is cool
hace frío • it is cold
hace mal tiempo • it is bad weather
hace sol • it is sunny
hace viento • it is windy

yo	hago
tú	haces
usted	hace
él, ella	hace
nosotros, as	hacemos
vosotros, as	hacéis
ustedes	hacen
ellos, ellas	hacen

Hace dos meses que no te veo.
I haven't seen you for two months.

Julia hace su tarea.
Julia does her homework.

Miguel se hizo millonario cuando ganó la lotería.
Miguel became a millionaire when he won the lottery.

hacia [A sya] *prep.* • to, toward
Los gitanos van hacia la ciudad.
The gypsies go toward the city.

hacienda (la) [a SYEN da] *n.* • (large) farm
Esta hacienda tiene ganado y caballos de carreras.
This farm has cattle and race horses.

hada (el) (f.) [A da] *n.* • fairy
Cenicienta tiene una hada madrina.
Cinderella has a fairy godmother.

hallar [a YAR] *v.* • to find, to come across
No hallo mi collar de perlas.
I can't find my pearl necklace.

hambre (el) (f.) [AM bre] *n.* • hunger
tener hambre *v.* • to be hungry
El hambre es un problema mundial.
Hunger is a world problem.

harina (la) [a REE na] *n.* • flour
Necesito harina para hacer el pastel.
I need flour to make the cake.

harina de avena (la) [a REE na DE a BE na] *n.* • oatmeal
Comemos harina de avena para el desayuno.
We eat oatmeal for breakfast.

hasta [AS ta] *prep.* • until
hasta luego • see you later
hasta mañana • see you tomorrow
hasta pronto • see you soon
hasta la vista • see you soon, until we meet again
Tengo que estudiar hasta las cinco.
I have to study until 5 o'clock.

hay [I] *v.* • there is; there are
hay que • to have to, must
Hay tres libros que debo leer.
There are three books I should read.

Hay que limpiar la casa.
We have to clean the house.

heladería (la) [e la de REE a] *n.* • ice cream store
Esta heladería tiene cincuenta sabores de helados.
This ice cream store has fifty ice cream flavors.

helado (el) [e LA do] *n.* • ice cream
Tenemos helado de postre.
We have ice cream for dessert.

helicóptero (el) [e lee COP te ro] *n.* • helicopter
El presidente llega en helicóptero.
The president arrives by helicopter.

heno (el) [E nol] *n.* • hay
El heno es para el nacimiento.
The hay is for the Christmas crib.

hermano (el) [er MA no] *n.* • brother
hermana (la) *n.* • sister
Lilia tiene tres hermanos pero no tiene hermanas.
Lilia has three brothers, but she does not have sisters.

hermanastro (el) [er ma NAS tro] *n.* • stepbrother
hermanastra (la) *n.* • stepsister
Ahora mis hermanastros y yo nos llevamos bien.
Now my stepbrothers and I get along well.

hermoso, a [er MO so] *adj.* • beautiful
El puesto del sol es hermoso.
The sunset is beautiful.

héroe (el) [E ro e] *n.* • hero
heroína (la) [e ro EE na] *n.* • heroine
Al final el héroe y la heroína son felices.
At the end the hero and the heroine are happy.

herrero (el) [e RRE ro] *n.* • blacksmith
El herrero trabaja con metales.
The blacksmith works with metals.

hervido, a [er BEE do] *adj.* • boiled
¿Quieres huevos hervidos para desayunar?
Do you want boiled eggs for breakfast?

hielo (el) [YE lo] *n.* • ice
Mi bebida necesita más hielo.
My drink needs more ice.

hierba (la) [YER ba] *n.* • grass
Después de la lluvia la hierba está verde.
After the rain the grass is green.

hierro (el) [YE rro] *n.* • iron
La reja antigua está hecha de hierro.
The old grill is made of iron.

hijo (el) [EE ho] *n.* • son
hija (la) *n.* • daughter
Los hijos de la señora Viveros son muy juguetones.
Mrs. Viveros' sons are very playful.

hijastro (el) [ee HAS tro] *n.* • stepson
hijastra (la) *n.* • stepdaughter
Tengo una hijastra de mi segundo matrimonio.
I have a stepdaughter from my second marriage.

hipopótamo (el) [ee po PO ta mo] *n.* • hippopotamus
Los hipopótamos viven en África y en zoológicos.
Hippopotamuses live in Africa and in zoos.

historia (la) [ees TO rya] *n.* • history; story
Estudio la historia de la conquista española.
I study the history of the Spanish Conquest.

histórico, a [ees TO ree co] *adj.* • historical
Hércules no es un personaje histórico.
Hercules is not an historical character.

hoja (la) [O ha] *n.* • leaf; sheet of paper
Ese árbol todavía no tiene hojas.
That tree still doesn't have leaves.

¿Me prestas una hoja de papel?
Will you lend me a sheet of paper?

hola [O la] *intj.* • hello
¡Hola! Me llamo Malvina.
Hello! My name is Malvina.

hombre (el) [OM bre] *n.* • man
hombre de nieve • snowman
Ese hombre es mi tío.
That man is my uncle.

hombro (el) [OM bro] *n.* • shoulder
Los futbolistas protegen sus hombros.
The football players protect their shoulders.

hondo, a [ON do] *adj.* • deep
El lago Superior es muy hondo.
Lake Superior is very deep.

hongo (el) [ON go] *n.* • mushroom, fungus
Hay muchos tipos de hongos en el bosque.
There are many kinds of mushrooms in the forest.

honor (el) [o NOR] *n.* • honor
de honor, honorable *adj.* • honorable
Don Quijote es un hombre de honor.
Don Quixote is an honorable man.

hora (la) [O ra] *n.* • hour; time
La hora de comer es a las seis.
Dinner time is at six.

horario (el) [o RA ryo] *n.* • schedule, timetable
El horario de clases está en la biblioteca.
The class schedule is in the library.

hormiga (la) [or MEE ga] *n.* • ant
¡Hay tantas hormigas!
There are so many ants!

horno (el) [OR no] *n.* • oven
horno de microondas *n.* • microwave oven
El pastel está en el horno.
The cake is in the oven.

horrible [o REE ble] *adj.* • horrible
Dante describe el infierno como un sitio horrible.
Dante describes hell as a horrible place.

horror (el) [o RROR] *n.* • horror
Durante la víspera de Todos los Santos hay películas de horror en la televisión.
During Halloween there are horror movies on TV.

hospital (el) [os pee TAL] *n.* • hospital
Kathy está en el hospital.
Kathy is in the hospital.

hotel (el) [o TEL] *n.* • hotel
Necesitamos reservaciones para el hotel.
We need reservations for the hotel.

hoy [OY] *adv.* • today
hoy día • nowadays
Hoy es domingo y no trabajo.
Today is Sunday, and I do not work.

Hoy día todo el mundo tiene coche.
Nowadays everyone has a car.

hueso (el) [WE so] *n.* • bone
El perro muerde su hueso.
The dog bites its bone.

huevo (el) [WE bo] *n.* • egg
Preparo huevos rancheros para el desayuno.
I prepare eggs ranchero style for breakfast.

húmedo, a [U me do] *adj.* • wet, damp; humid
Necesito secar esta toalla húmeda.
I need to dry this damp towel.

humo (el) [U mo] *n.* • smoke
La sección de fumadores está llena de humo.
The smoking section is full of smoke.

humor (el) [u MOR] *n.* • mood
Pepe está de mal humor.
Pepe is in a bad mood.

huracán (el) [u ra CAN] *n.* • hurricane
Un huracán destruye edificios.
A hurricane destroys buildings.

I

ida (la) [EE da] *n.* • departure; trip
ida(s) y venida(s) *coll.* • coming(s) and going(s)
ida y vuelta • round trip
Mañana es la ida de Rosario.
Tomorrow is Rosario's departure.

idea (la) [ee DE a] *n.* • idea
¡No tengo la menor idea!
I don't have the slightest idea!

idealismo (el) [ee de al EES mo] *n.* • idealism
No es idealismo querer una sociedad justa.
It is not idealism to desire a just society.

idealista (el, la) [ee de al EES ta] *n.* • idealist
Elena es idealista.
Elena is an idealist.

identificación (la) [ee den tee fee ca SYON] *n.* • identification
La licencia de conducir es la identificación más común.
A driver's license is the most common identification.

idioma (el) [ee DYO ma] *n.* • language
En Puerto Rico hablan el idioma español.
In Puerto Rico they speak the Spanish language.

iglesia (la) [ee GLE sya] *n.* • church
La boda es en la Iglesia San Antonio.
The wedding is at Saint Anthony's Church.

igual [ee GWAL] *adj.* • equal, the same
Tenemos que dividir el dinero en dos cantidades iguales.
We have to divide the money into two equal amounts.

impaciente [eem pa cee EN te] *adj.* • impatient
La maestra es impaciente con nosotros.
The teacher is impatient with us.

impermeable [eem per me A ble] *adj.* • waterproof
impermeable (el) *n.* • raincoat
Voy a traer el impermeable; creo que va a llover.
I'm going to bring my raincoat; I think it's going to rain.

importante [eem por TAN te] *adj.* • important
El presidente de la compañía está en una reunión importante.
The president of the company is at an important meeting.

imposible [eem po SEE ble] *adj.* • impossible
Lo que pides es imposible.
What you ask is impossible.

incendio (el) [een SEN dyo] *n.* • fire
Este incendio es desastroso.
This fire is disastrous.

incómodo, a [een CO mo do] *adj.* • uncomfortable
El viaje fue largo e incómodo.
The trip was long and uncomfortable.

incorrecto, a [een co RREC to] *adj.* • incorrect; not proper
La respuesta es incorrecta.
The answer is incorrect.

Es incorrecto interrumpir cuando otra persona habla.
It is not proper to interrupt when another person speaks.

increíble [een cre EE ble] *adj.* • incredible, unbelievable
Los avances de la tecnología moderna son increíbles.
The advances of modern technology are incredible.

independencia (la) [een de pen DEN sya] *n.* • independence
Algunos países africanos todavía no tienen su independencia.
Some African countries still do not have their independence.

indicar [een dee CAR] *v.* • to indicate, to direct, to instruct, to point out
La maestra indica los países en el mapa.
The teacher points out the countries on the map.

individual [een dee bee du AL] *adj.* • individual
Es una decisión individual.
It's an individual decision.

infeliz [een fe LEES] *adj.* • unhappy
¿Por qué estás tan infeliz?
Why are you so unhappy?

influenza (la) [een flu EN sa] *n.* • flu
Miguel tiene la influenza.
Miguel has the flu.

información (la) [een for ma SYON] *n.* • information
La información que quieres está en la biblioteca.
The information that you want is in the library.

ingeniero, a (el, la) [een he NYE ro] *n.* • engineer
Mi primo es ingeniero en el ejército.
My cousin is an engineer in the army.

inglés, a [een GLES] *adj.* • English
inglés (el) *n.* • English (language)
inglés, a (el, la) *n.* Englishman, English woman
Thomas es inglés.
Thomas is English.

La bandera inglesa es conocida en todo el mundo.
The English flag is known all over the world.

ingrediente (el) [een gre d̲ee EN te] *n.* • ingredient
Los ingredientes para las tortitas son fáciles de conseguir.
The ingredients for the crepes are easy to get.

injusto, a [een HUS to] *adj.* • unfair, unjust
Ese sistema es injusto a los estudiantes.
That system is unfair to the students.

inmediatamente [een me d̲ee a ta MEN te] *adv.* • immediately
Necesito el dinero inmediatamente.
I need the money immediately.

inocente [ee no SEN te] *adj.* • innocent
El ladrón dice que es inocente.
The thief says he is innocent.

insecto (el) [een SEC to] *n.* • insect
No me gustan los insectos.
I don't like insects.

inseparable [een se pa RA ble] *adj.* • inseparable
Luisa y Verónica son amigas inseparables.
Luisa and Verónica are inseparable friends.

insistir [een sees TEER] *v.* • to insist
insistir en *v.* • to insist on
No quiero ir, pero mamá insiste.
I don't want to go, but Mom insists.

Lola insiste en salir temprano.
Lola insists on leaving early.

inspeccionar [een spec syo NAR] *v.* • to inspect, to check
Los jueces inspeccionan los proyectos.
The judges inspect the projects.

instrucción (la) [eens truc SYON] *n.* • instruction, direction
Las instrucciones son muy complejas.
The directions are very complex.

instructor, a (el, la) [eens truc TOR] *n.* • instructor
El instructor es el autor de varios libros.
The instructor is the author of several books.

instrumento (el) [eens tru MEN to] *n.* • instrument
¿Sabes cuántos instrumentos tiene una orquesta?
Do you know how many instruments are in an orchestra?

insultar [een sul TAR] *v.* • to insult
No me gustan las bromas que insultan a otros.
I don't like jokes that insult others.

inteligencia (la) [een te lee HEN sya] *n.* • intelligence
Los científicos dicen que hay varios tipos de inteligencia.
Scientists say that there are several types of intelligence.

inteligente [een te lee HEN te] *adj.* • intelligent, sharp
Susana es la chica más inteligente de la clase.
Susana is the most intelligent girl in the class.

interés (el) [een te RES] *n.* • interest
La ciencia no tiene interés para Lupe.
Lupe has no interest in science.

interesante [een te re SAN te] *adj.* • interesting
La mitología india es diferente e interesante.
Indian mythology is different and interesting.

interior (el) [een te RYOR] *n.* • interior
Hay murciélagos en el interior de esta cueva.
There are bats in the interior of this cave.

internacional [een ter na syo NAL] *adj.* • international
Los Juegos Olímpicos son competencias internacionales.
The Olympic Games are international competitions.

interrupción (la) [een te rrup SYON] *n.* • interruption
No puedo terminar mi tarea con tantas interrupciones.
I cannot finish my homework with so many interruptions.

investigación (la) [een bes tee ga SYON] *n.* • investigation, research
Mi hermana escribe un trabajo de investigación.
My sister is writing a research paper.

investigar [een bes tee GAR] *v.* • to research, to investigate
Columbo investiga los crímenes.
Columbo investigates crimes.

invierno (el) [een BYER no] *n.* • winter
Cuando es invierno en los Estados Unidos, es verano en Chile.
When it is winter in the United States, it is summer in Chile.

invitar [een bee TAR] *v.* • to invite, to ask out
Rosalía nos invita a su fiesta de cumpleaños.
Rosalía invites us to her birthday party.

ir [EER] *v.* • to go
irse *v.* • to leave

yo	me	voy
tú	te	vas
usted	se	va
él, ella	se	va
nosotros, as	nos	vamos
vosotros, as	os	váis
ustedes	se	van
ellos, ellas	se	van

¿Adónde vas?
Where are you going?

isla (la) [EES la] *n.* • island
El estado de Hawai tiene muchas islas.
The state of Hawaii has many islands.

izquierdo, a [ees kee ER do] *adj.* • left
Escribe con la mano izquierda porque es zurdo.
He writes with his left hand because he is left-handed.

J

jabón (el) [ha BON] *n.* • soap
Sandra se baña con jabón perfumado.
Sandra bathes with perfumed soap.

jalar [ha LAR] *v.* • to pull
Hay que jalar la puerta.
You have to pull the door.

jalea (la) [ha LE a] *n.* • jelly
Mi mamá cocina jalea de durazno.
My mother cooks peach jelly.

jamás [ha MAS] *adv.* • never
Jamás voy al cine.
I never go to the movies.

jamón (el) [ha MON] *n.* • ham
Hay huevos con jamón para el desayuno.
There are ham and eggs for breakfast.

jardín (el) [har DEEN] *n.* • garden
El perro destruye las flores en el jardín.
The dog destroys the flowers in the garden.

jaula (la) [HOW la] *n.* • cage
Los animales de este zoológico no están en jaulas.
The animals in this zoo are not in cages.

jefe (el) [HE fe] *n.* • boss
El jefe habla con los empleados.
The boss talks with the employees.

jinete (el) [hee NE te] *n.* • horseman, rider
El rodeo de este fin de semana presenta treinta jinetes.
This weekend's rodeo presents thirty riders.

jirafa (la) [hee RA fa] *n.* • giraffe
La jirafa come las hojas altas de los árboles.
The giraffe eats the top leaves of the trees.

joven [HO ben] *adj.* • young
joven (el, la) *n.* • young man, young woman
jóvenes (los) *n.* • young people
Los jóvenes escuchan "La hora joven" en la radio.
The young people listen to the "Youth Hour" on the radio.

joya (la) [HO ya] *n.* • jewel
La reina tiene muchas joyas.
The queen has many jewels.

joyería (la) [ho ye REE a] *n.* • jewelry store
Compro mis pendientes en la joyería del centro.
I buy my earrings in the jewelry store downtown.

joyero, a (el, la) [ho YE ro] *n.* • jeweler
La reina tiene un joyero personal.
The queen has a personal jeweler.

juego (el) [HWE go] *n.* • game
No me gusta este juego.
I don't like this game.

jugador, a (el, la) [hu ga DOR] *n.* • player
Un equipo de baloncesto tiene cinco jugadores.
A basketball team has five players.

jugar [hu GAR] *v.* • to play (a game)

yo	juego
tú	juegas
usted	juega
él, ella	juega
nosotros, as	jugamos
vosotros, as	jugáis
ustedes	juegan
ellos, ellas	juegan

Steven juega al baloncesto.
Steven plays basketball.

jugo (el) [HU go] *n.* • juice
Hoy hay jugo de naranja y de manzana.
Today there is orange and apple juice.

jugoso, a [hu GO so] *adj.* • juicy
Estas peras son jugosas.
These pears are juicy.

juguete (el) [hu GE te] *n.* • toy
Los niños juegan con sus juguetes.
The children play with their toys.

juicio (el) [HWEE syo] *n.* • trial
El juicio no es público.
The trial is not public.

julio [HU lyo] *n.* • July
Mi prima se casa en julio.
My cousin is getting married in July.

junio [HU nyo] *n.* • June
Hace calor en junio.
It's warm in June.

junto, a [HUN to] *adj.* • together; united
junto a *prep.* • next to
Ana y Raúl siempre llegan juntos.
Ana and Raúl always arrive together.

El señor que está junto a Juan es de México.
The man who is next to Juan is from Mexico.

jurar [hu RAR] *v.* • to swear
Juramos proteger a nuestra patria.
We swear to protect our country.

justo, a [HUS to] *adj.* • fair, just
Creo que las reglas son justas.
I believe the rules are fair.

juventud (la) [hu ben TUD] *n.* • youth
Mi abuelo habla mucho de su juventud.
My grandfather talks a lot about his youth.

K

kilo (el) [KI lo] *n.* • kilo
Ese saco pesa tres kilos.
That sack weighs three kilos.

kilogramo (el) [ki lo GRA mo] *n.* • kilogram
Un kilogramo tiene mil gramos.
A kilogram has one thousand grams.

kilómetro (el) [ki LO me tro] *n.* • kilometer
Son treinta kilómetros de mi casa a mi oficina.
It is thirty kilometers from my house to my office.

L

la [LA] *art.* • the (f. sing.)
La profesora Gómez enseña las clases de español.
Professor Gómez teaches the Spanish classes.

labio (el) [LA byo] *n.* • lip
La bruja tiene labios verdes.
The witch has green lips.

laboratorio (el) [la bo ra TO ryo] *n.* • laboratory
El laboratorio de fotografía está cerrado durante el verano.
The photography lab is closed during the summer.

lado (el) [LA do] *n.* • side
al lado de *prep.* • next to
Un triángulo tiene tres lados.
A triangle has three sides.

ladrón, a (el, la) [la DRON] *n.* • thief, burglar
El ladrón está en la cárcel.
The burglar is in jail.

lagarto (el) [la GAR to] *n.* • lizard
Los lagartos viven en zonas tropicales.
Lizards live in tropical areas.

lago (el) [LA go] *n.* • lake
Ellos tienen una casa en las orillas del lago.
They have a house on the lakeshore.

lágrima (la) [LA gree ma] *n.* • tear
Me siento triste al ver tus lágrimas.
I feel sad when I see your tears.

lámpara (la) [LAM pa ra] *n.* • lamp
La lámpara necesita una bombilla.
The lamp needs a light bulb.

lancha (la) [LAN cha] *n.* • motorboat
Compramos una lancha nueva.
We're buying a new motorboat.

largo, a [LAR go] *adj.* • long
Un metro es más largo que una yarda.
A meter is longer than a yard.

las [LAS] *art.* • the (f. pl.)
Las muchachas estudian para el examen.
The girls study for the exam.

lástima (la) [LAS tee ma] *n.* • pity
¡Qué lástima! • What a pity!
¡Qué lástima! María no puede venir este domingo.
What a pity! María cannot come this Sunday.

lata (la) [LA ta] *n.* • bore, annoyance; can
¡Qué lata! • What an annoyance!
Reciclamos las latas de aluminio.
We recycle aluminum cans.

¡Qué lata! Tenemos que llenar los formularios por triplicado.
What an annoyance! We have to fill out the forms in triplicate.

latino, a [la TEE no] *adj.* • Latin
latino, a (el, la) *n.* • Latin (person)
El español es una lengua de origen latino.
Spanish is a language of Latin origin.

latoso, a [la TO so] *adj.* • annoying, pesty
Nadie quiere trabajar con Judy, es muy latosa.
Nobody wants to work with Judy; she is very annoying.

lavadora (la) [la ba DO ra] *n.* • washer
La lavadora cuesta doscientos dólares.
The washer costs two hundred dollars.

lavandería (la) [la ban de REE a] *n.* • laundry, laundry room
La lavandería está en el sótano del edificio.
The laundry room is in the building's basement.

lavaplatos (el) [la ba PLA tos] *n.* • dishwasher
El lavaplatos y el refrigerador están en la cocina.
The dishwasher and the refrigerator are in the kitchen.

lavar [la BAR] *v.* • to wash
lavarse *v.* • to wash oneself
Mi hermano lava su ropa en el dormitorio.
My brother washes his clothes in the dorm.

lección (la) [lec SYON] *n.* • lesson
Empezamos la lección nueva mañana.
We begin the new lesson tomorrow.

leche (la) [LE che] *n.* • milk
Me gusta la leche con chocolate.
I like milk with chocolate.

lechuga (la) [le CHU ga] *n.* • lettuce
Por favor dame la lechuga para la ensalada.
Please give me the lettuce for the salad.

leer [le ER] *v.* • to read
A Elena le encanta leer.
Elena loves to read.

legumbre (la) [le GUM bre] *n.* • vegetable
Una dieta sana contiene legumbres.
A healthy diet contains vegetables.

lejos [LE hos] *adv.* • far; far away
Los Ángeles está lejos de Nueva York.
Los Angeles is far from New York.

lengua (la) [LEN gwa] *n.* • tongue; language
Las papilas del gusto están en la lengua.
Our taste buds are on the tongue.

lentamente [len ta MEN te] *adv.* • slowly
La vieja camina lentamente.
The old woman walks slowly.

lente (el) [LEN te] *n.* • lens
lentes (los) *n.* • glasses
¿Dónde están mis lentes?
Where are my glasses?

lento, a [LEN to] *adj.* • slow
El progreso es lento.
Progress is slow.

leña (la) [LE nya] *n.* • firewood
Raúl corta leña en el bosque.
Raúl is cutting firewood in the forest.

león, a (el, la) [le ON] *n.* • lion, lioness
león marino (el) *n.* • sea lion
El león es el rey de la selva.
The lion is the king of the jungle.

leopardo (el) [le o PAR do] *n.* • leopard
El leopardo es un felino salvaje.
The leopard is a wild feline.

letra (la) [LE tra] *n.* • letter (of the alphabet)
¿Cuántas letras hay en el alfabeto?
How many letters are in the alphabet?

letrero (el) [le TRE ro] *n.* • sign
El letrero dice que aquí se habla español.
The sign says that Spanish is spoken here.

levantar [le ban TAR] *v.* • to raise
levantarse *v.* • to get up
Elisa siempre levanta la mano en la clase.
Elisa always raises her hand in class.

Me levanto a las seis de la mañana todos los días.
I get up at six a.m. every day.

libertad (la) [lee ber TAD] *n.* • freedom, liberty
La libertad es un derecho humano.
Freedom is a human right.

libertador, a (el, la) [lee ber ta DOR] *n.* • liberator
Los libertadores de la patria son héroes nacionales.
The country's liberators are national heroes.

libra (la) [LEE bra] *n.* • pound
Una libra tiene 454 gramos.
A pound contains 454 grams.

libre [LEE bre] *adj.* • free
No tengo mucho tiempo libre.
I don't have much free time.

librería (la) [lee bre REE a] *n.* • bookstore
¿Dónde está la librería?
Where is the bookstore?

libro (el) [LEE bro] *n.* • book
Necesito un libro de la biblioteca.
I need a book from the library.

licuadora (la) [lee cwa DO ra] *n.* • blender
Mi licuadora tiene tres velocidades.
My blender has three speeds.

líder (el) [LEE der] *n.* • leader
¿Conoces al líder?
Do you know the leader?

liebre (la) [LYE bre] *n.* • hare
Las liebres no son conejos.
Hares are not rabbits.

limón (el) [lee MON] *n.* • lemon
Necesitamos jugo de limón para esta receta.
We need lemon juice for this recipe.

limpiar [leem PYAR] *v.* • to clean
Tenemos que limpiar las ventanas.
We have to clean the windows.

limpio, a [LEEM pyo] *adj.* • clean
La casa de Cristina siempre está limpia.
Cristina's house is always clean.

línea (la) [LEE ne a] *n.* • line
La línea telefónica no funciona.
The phone line does not work.

liso, a [LEE so] *adj.* • smooth; flat
Un espejo es una superficie lisa.
A mirror is a smooth surface.

listo, a [LEES to] *adj.* • smart, clever (with *ser*); ready (with *estar*)
Juan es muy listo.
Juan is very clever.

¿Estás listo?
Are you ready?

literatura (la) [lee te ra TU ra] *n.* • literature
Este año no tengo clase de literatura.
This year I do not have a literature class.

lobo (el) [LO bo] *n.* • wolf
Un lobo vive cerca de mi casa.
A wolf lives near my house.

local [lo CAL] *adj.* • local
Es un programa local.
It's a local program.

loción (la) [lo SYON] *n.* • lotion
loción de afeitar *n.* • aftershave
Le regalo una loción de afeitar a mi papá para su cumpleaños.
I give aftershave lotion to my dad for his birthday.

loco, a [LO co] *adj.* • crazy (with *estar*); mad, insane (with *ser*)
¿Estás loco?
Are you crazy?

El protagonista de la novela se vuelve loco.
The novel's protagonist goes insane.

locura (la) [lo CU ra] *n.* • madness, craziness
Es una locura vender el carro por diez dólares.
It is madness to sell the car for ten dollars.

locutor, a (el, la) [lo cu TOR] *n.* • announcer
El locutor menciona el accidente.
The announcer mentions the accident.

lodo (el) [LO do] *n.* • mud
Tus botas están cubiertas de lodo.
Your boots are covered with mud.

loro (el) [LO ro] *n.* • parrot
El loro repite las palabras.
The parrot repeats the words.

los [LOS] *art.* • the (m. pl.)
Los libros son de España.
The books are from Spain.

luego [LWE go] *adv.* • then, later
Primero limpiamos la casa, luego vamos a la playa.
First we'll clean the house, then we'll go to the beach.

lugar (el) [lu GAR] *n.* • place
Es un lugar interesante, pero no me gusta.
It is an interesting place, but I don't like it.

luna (la) [LU na] *n.* • moon
¿Cuándo es la luna llena?
When is the full moon?

lunes (el) [LU nes] *n.* • Monday
No tengo fiestas los lunes.
I don't have parties on Mondays.

luz (la) [LUS] *n.* • light
Las luces de la ciudad son bonitas.
The lights of the city are pretty.

LL

llamar [ya MAR] *v.* • to call
llamarse *v.* • to call oneself, to be named
me llamo • my name is
Por favor llama a mi hermana.
Please call my sister.

La chica se llama Juanita.
The girl's name is Juanita.

llano, a [YA no] *adj.* • flat, even
llano (el) *n.* • plain
Hay mucha tierra llana en Illinois.
There is a lot of flat land in Illinois.

Iowa es una región de llanos.
Iowa is a region of plains.

llanta (la) [YAN ta] *n.* • tire (of a car)
¿Sabes cambiar la llanta?
Do you know how to change the tire?

llave (la) [YA be] *n.* • key
llavero (el) *n.* • key chain
El dependiente no tiene llave para la caja fuerte.
The clerk does not have a key for the safe.

llegada (la) [ye GA d̲a] *n.* • arrival
La llegada del vuelo 95 es a las 6 de la tarde.
The arrival of flight 95 is at 6:00 p.m.

llegar [ye GAR] *v.* • to arrive
Mis papás llegan mañana.
My parents arrive tomorrow.

lleno, a [YE no] *adj.* • full; crowded
El vaso está lleno.
The glass is full.

llevar [ye BAR] *v.* • to carry; take
¿Puedes llevar mis libros?
Can you carry my books?

llorar [yo RAR] *v.* • to cry
¡Ese bebé llora mucho!
That baby cries a lot!

llover [yo BER] *v.* • to rain
Llueve durante el verano.
It rains during the summer.

M

madera (la) [ma DE ra] *n.* • wood
La mesa es de madera.
The table is made of wood.

madrastra (la) [ma DRAS tra] *n.* • stepmother
La madrastra de Cenicienta no es buena persona.
Cinderella's stepmother is not a good person.

madre (la) [MA dre] *n.* • mother
El día de la madre en Latinoamérica es el diez de mayo.
Mother's Day in Latin America is on May tenth.

madrina (la) [ma DREE na] *n.* • godmother
Mi madrina es mi tía.
My godmother is my aunt.

maduro, a [ma DU ro] *adj.* • mature, ripe
Los duraznos no están maduros.
The peaches are not ripe.

maestro, a (el, la) [ma ES tro] *n.* • teacher
El maestro de español es de Barcelona.
The Spanish teacher is from Barcelona.

mágico, a [MA hee co] *adj.* • magic, magical
El museo de arte es un sitio mágico.
The art museum is a magical place.

magnífico, a [mag NEE fee co] *adj.* • magnificent, awesome
El Cañón de Colorado es magnífico.
The Grand Canyon is awesome.

mago (el) [MA go] *n.* • magician,wizard
Doug Henning y David Copperfield son magos.
Doug Henning and David Copperfield are magicians.

maíz (el) [ma EES] *n.* • corn
Las tortillas son de maíz.
Tortillas are made of corn.

mal [MAL] *adv.* • bad, badly
mal educado *adj.* • bad mannered
El niño se porta mal con la niñera.
The child behaves badly with the babysitter.

El muchacho es mal educado.
The boy is bad mannered.

maleta (la) [ma LE ta] *n.* • suitcase
Mi maleta está en el aeropuerto.
My suitcase is at the airport.

malo, a [MA lo] *adj.* • bad; sick
Esa película es mala.
That movie is bad.

mamá (la) [ma MA] *n.* • mother
Mi mamá es enfermera.
My mother is a nurse.

mancha (la) [MAN cha] *n.* • stain, spot
Esa camisa tiene una mancha.
That shirt has a spot.

mandar [man DAR] *v.* • to command, to order; to send
El maestro de educación física nos manda correr tres kilómetros.
The physical education teacher orders us to run three kilometers.

manejar [ma ne HAR] *v.* • to drive
Mi madre me enseña a manejar.
My mother is teaching me to drive.

manera (la) [ma NE ra] *n.* • way, style
Lo hacemos de la misma manera.
We do it the same way.

mango (el) [MAN go] *n.* • mango (tropical fruit)
Los mangos son deliciosos.
Mangoes are delicious.

manguera (la) [man GE ra] *n.* • garden hose
La manguera está en el garaje.
The hose is in the garage.

mano (la) [MA no] *n.* • hand
la mano derecha • right hand
la mano izquierda • left hand
dar la mano *v.* • to shake hands
Es muy difícil dibujar manos.
It is very difficult to draw hands.

manso, a [MAN so] *adj.* • tame, gentle (animal)
Lassie es un perro muy manso.
Lassie is a very gentle dog.

manta (la) [MAN ta] *n.* • blanket
La manta de lana está en la tintorería.
The wool blanket is at the dry cleaners.

mantel (el) [man TEL] *n.* • tablecloth
El mantel de encaje es de mi abuela.
The lace tablecloth is from my grandmother.

mantener [man te NER] *v.* • to maintain, to support

yo	mantengo
tú	mantienes
usted	mantiene
él, ella	mantiene
nosotros, as	mantenemos
vosotros, as	mantenéis
ustedes	mantienen
ellos, ellas	mantienen

La esposa mantiene al esposo mientras él estudia.
The wife supports her husband while he studies.

mantequilla (la) [man te KEE ya] *n.* • butter
¿Quieres pan con mantequilla?
Do you want bread with butter?

manual (el) [ma NUAL] *n.* • manual, instruction book
No sabemos operar esta máquina; el manual está perdido.
We do not know how to operate this machine; the manual is lost.

manzana (la) [man SA na] *n.* • apple
El pastel de manzana es un postre típico de los Estados Unidos.
Apple pie is a traditional dessert of the United States.

mañana (la) [ma NYA na] *n.* • morning
mañana *adv.* • tomorrow
Vamos a España mañana por la mañana.
We're going to Spain tomorrow morning.

mapa (el) [MA pa] *n.* • map
Alberto dibuja un mapa de Europa.
Alberto is drawing a map of Europe.

mapache (el) [ma PA che] *n.* • raccoon
El mapache es un animal nocturno.
The raccoon is a nocturnal animal.

maquillaje (el) [ma kee YA he] *n.* • make-up
¿Tu mamá te permite usar maquillaje?
Does your mother let you use make-up?

máquina (la) [MA kee na] *n.* • machine
máquina de escribir *n.* • typewriter
¿Sabes usar una máquina de coser?
Do you know how to use a sewing machine?

mar (el) [MAR] *n.* • sea
El Mar de Cortés también se llama el Golfo de California.
The Sea of Cortés is also called the Gulf of California.

maravilla (la) [ma ra BEE ya] *n.* • marvel, wonder
Es una maravilla escuchar la voz de esa señora.
It's a wonder to listen to that woman's voice.

maravilloso, a [ma ra bee YO so] *adj.* • marvelous
Roma es una ciudad maravillosa.
Rome is a marvelous city.

margarina (la) [mar ga REE na] *n.* • margarine
Prefiero la mantequilla a la margarina.
I prefer butter to margarine.

margarita (la) [ma ga REE ta] *n.* • daisy
Las margaritas son flores de primavera.
Daisies are spring flowers.

marido (el) [ma REE do] *n.* • husband
El marido de Lucrecia es Antonio.
Lucrecia's husband is Antonio.

mariposa (la) [ma ree PO sa] *n.* • butterfly
Las mariposas pasan el invierno en México.
Butterflies spend the winter in Mexico.

mariquita (la) [ma ree KEE ta] *n.* • ladybug
Las mariquitas son insectos útiles.
Ladybugs are useful insects.

mármol (el) [MAR mol] *n.* • marble (stone)
Hay muchas esculturas de mármol en el museo.
There are many marble sculptures in the museum.

marrón [ma RRON] *adj.* • brown
Creo que el suéter marrón te queda bien.
I think the brown sweater suits you well.

martes (el) [MAR tes] *n.* • Tuesday
El concierto de violín es el martes.
The violin concert is on Tuesday.

martillo (el) [mar TEE yo] *n.* • hammer
Necesitamos un martillo para reparar esta silla.
We need a hammer to fix this chair.

marzo [MAR so] *n.* • March
La primavera empieza en marzo.
Spring starts in March.

más [MAS] *adv.* • more
más *prep.* • plus
Ella quiere más pastel.
She wants more cake.

Dos más uno son tres.
Two plus one is three.

máscara (la) [MAS ca ra] *n.* • mask
Tenemos que llevar máscaras al baile.
We have to wear masks to the dance.

matar [ma TAR] *v.* • to kill
El torero mata al toro.
The bullfighter kills the bull.

mate (el) [MA te] *n.* • maté, a South American herb and herbal tea
El mate es una bebida tradicional en Argentina.
Maté is a traditional drink in Argentina.

matemáticas (las) [ma te MA tee cas] *n.* • mathematics
Las matemáticas es mi asignatura favorita.
Mathematics is my favorite subject.

máximo, a [MAKS ee mo] *adj.* • maximum
La máxima calificación en el exámen es cien.
The maximum grade in the exam is one hundred.

mayo [MA yo] *n.* • May
El año escolar termina en mayo.
The school year ends in May.

mayores (los) [ma YO res] *n.* • adults, elders
Mis padres me enseñan a respetar a los mayores.
My parents teach me to respect adults.

mecánico, a (el, la) [me CA nee co] *n.* • mechanic
El mecánico de la compañía repara el refrigerador.
The company mechanic repairs the refrigerator.

mecanógrafo, a (el, la) [me ca NO gra fo] *n.* • typist
El mecanógrafo termina el documento hoy.
The typist is finishing the document today.

medalla (la) [me DA ya] *n.* • medal
Anita espera ganar una medalla hoy.
Anita hopes to win a medal today.

media (la) [ME dya] *n.* • stocking
Susita lleva medias negras.
Susita is wearing black stockings.

mediano, a [me DYA no] *adj.* • medium (size)
Carlos es un hombre de estatura mediana.
Carlos is a man of medium height.

medianoche (la) [me dya NO che] *n.* • midnight
El tren llega a medianoche.
The train arrives at midnight.

medicina (la) [me dee SEE na] *n.* • medicine
La medicina está en la mesita de noche.
The medicine is on the nightstand.

médico, a (el, la) [ME dee co] *n.* • physician
Los médicos en esta clínica son muy eficientes.
The physicians in this clinic are very efficient.

medio, a [ME dyo] *adj.* • half; middle
ir a medias *v.* • to go fifty-fifty
término medio (el) *n.* • average
Te veo en media hora.
I'll see you in a half hour.

El ensayo trata de la clase media.
The essay deals with the middle class.

mediodía (el) [me dyo DEE a] *n.* • noon
Jaime sale a mediodía.
Jaime is leaving at noon.

mejilla (la) [me HEE ya] *n.* • cheek
¿Te gusta bailar mejilla a mejilla?
Do you like to dance cheek to cheek?

mejor [me HOR] *adj., adv.* • better; best
lo mejor • the best
mejor...que • better...than
Mi abuelo está mejor hoy.
My grandfather is better today.

Este libro es mejor que el otro.
This book is better than the other one.

melocotón (el) [me lo co TON] *n.* • peach
Estos melocotones no están maduros todavía.
These peaches aren't ripe yet.

melón (el) [me LON] *n.* • cantaloupe, melon
¿Prefieres melón o toronja?
Do you prefer melon or grapefruit?

menos [ME nos] *adv.* • less
Este año hay menos nieve que el año pasado.
This year there is less snow than last year.

mensaje (el) [men SA he] *n.* • message
No entiendo el mensaje en el tablero de anuncios.
I don't understand the message on the bulletin board.

mentir [men TEER] *v.* • to lie

yo	miento
tú	mientes
usted	miente
él, ella	miente
nosotros, as	mentimos
vosotros, as	mentís
ustedes	mienten
ellos, ellas	mienten

No debes mentir.
You shouldn't lie.

mentira (la) [men TEE ra] *n.* • lie
¿Dices mentiras?
Do you tell lies?

menú (el) [me NU] *n.* • menu
Hay muchos platos típicos en el menú.
There are lots of typical dishes on the menu.

menudo, a [me NU do] *adj.* • small, unimportant
a menudo *adv.* • often
Comemos tortillas a menudo en mi casa.
We often eat tortillas at home.

mercado (el) [mer CA do] *n.* • market
Vamos al mercado los sábados.
We go to the market on Saturdays.

merienda (la) [me ree EN da] *n.* • afternoon snack, bite to eat
¿Adónde vamos para la merienda?
Where shall we go for a bite to eat?

mermelada (la) [mer me LA da] *n.* • jam, marmalade
Mi mamá hace mermeladas deliciosas.
My mother makes delicious jams.

mes (el) [MES] *n.* • month
Abril es mi mes favorito.
April is my favorite month.

mesero (el) [me SE ro] *n.* • waiter
mesera (la) *n.* • waitress
Los meseros en este restaurante son muy amables.
The waiters in this restaurant are very nice.

meta (la) [ME ta] *n.* • goal
La meta de Elena es ser astronauta.
Elena's goal is to be an astronaut.

método (el) [ME to do] *n.* • method
El profesor usa un método nuevo.
The professor is using a new method.

métrico, a [ME tree co] *adj.* • metric
El sistema métrico es un sistema universal
The metric system is a universal system.

metro (el) [ME tro] *n.* • meter; subway
La estación del metro está a unas cuadras de aquí.
The subway station is a few blocks from here.

mexicano, a [me hee CA no] *adj.* • Mexican
mexicano, a (el, la) *n.* • Mexican (person)
El chocolate es de origen mexicano.
Chocolate is of Mexican origin.

Los mexicanos hablan español.
Mexicans speak Spanish.

mezclar [mes CLAR] *v.* • to mix
Tenemos que mezclar los colores.
We have to mix the colors.

mi [ME] *adj.* • my
Mi tío es abogado.
My uncle is a lawyer.

miedo (el) [MYE do] *n.* • fear
tener miedo *v.* • to fear, to be afraid
Tengo miedo de manejar en Los Ángeles.
I'm afraid to drive in Los Angeles.

miembro (el) [MYEM bro] *n.* • member
Los miembros del club votan por un nuevo presidente mañana.
The club members vote for a new president tomorrow.

miércoles (el) [MYER co les] *n.* • Wednesday
Mañana es miércoles.
Tomorrow is Wednesday.

milla (la) [MEE ya] *n.* • mile
Una milla es más larga que un kilómetro.
A mile is longer than a kilometer.

millón (el) [mee YON] *n.* • million
La lotería tiene tres millones de dólares esta semana.
The lotto has three million dollars this week.

mimado, a [mee MA d̲o] *adj.* • spoiled, pampered
Ella es una persona inteligente pero muy mimada.
She is a smart person but very spoiled.

mineral (el) [mee ne RAL] *n.* • mineral
Hay refrescos y agua mineral en el refrigerador.
There is pop and mineral water in the refrigerator.

minuto (el) [mee NU to] *n.* • minute
Una hora tiene sesenta minutos.
An hour has sixty minutes.

mío, a [MEE o] *adj.* • mine
Estos cuadernos son míos.
These notebooks are mine.

mirar [mee RAR] *v.* • to look at, to watch
Me gusta mirar las estrellas.
I like to look at the stars.

mismo, a [MEES mo] *adj.* • same
Leemos el mismo libro.
We are reading the same book.

misterio (el) [mees te RYO so] *n.* • mystery
Agatha Christie escribe novelas de misterio.
Agatha Christie writes mystery novels.

misterioso, a [mees te RYO so] *adj.* • mysterious
Estoy leyendo "La casa misteriosa" y me gusta mucho.
I'm reading "The Mysterious House" and I like it a lot.

mitad (la) [mee TA<u>D</u>] *n.* • half
La mitad de diez es cinco.
Half of ten is five.

mochila (la) [mo CHEE la] *n.* • backpack
Mi tarea está en mi mochila.
My homework is in my backpack.

moderno, a [mo DER no] *adj.* • modern
Éste es un barrio moderno y tiene todas las comodidades.
This is a modern neighborhood, and it has all the conveniences.

modesto, a [mo DES to] *adj.* • modest
Eduardo no es una persona modesta; es muy vanidoso.
Eduardo is not a modest person; he is very vain.

modista (el, la) [mo DEES ta] *n.* • seamstress, dressmaker
La modista de mi mamá hace el vestido para mí.
My mother's seamstress is making the dress for me.

mojado, a [mo HA do] *adj.* • wet
La ropa está mojada; por favor ponla en la secadora.
The clothes are wet; please put them in the dryer.

molestar [mo les TAR] *v.* • to bother, to annoy
Los mosquitos me molestan durante el verano.
Mosquitoes bother me during the summer.

momento (el) [mo MEN to] *n.* • moment
en un momento • right away, in a moment
¿Me puedes esperar un momento?
Can you wait for me a moment?

moneda (la) [mo NE da] *n.* • coin; currency
El dólar americano es una moneda internacional.
The U.S. dollar is an international currency.

monetario, a [mo ne TA ryo] *adj.* • monetary, of money
El valor monetario de este cuadro no importa; tiene valor sentimental.
The monetary value of this painting does not matter; it has sentimental value.

mono (el) [MO no] *n.* • monkey
El zoológico tiene varias especies de monos.
The zoo has several species of monkeys.

monstruo (el) [MONS truo] *n.* • monster
El monstruo en la película es horrible.
The monster in the movie is horrible.

montaña (la) [mon TA nya] *n.* • mountain
Orizaba es la montaña más alta de México.
Orizaba is the highest mountain in Mexico.

montar [mon TAR] *v.* • to mount, to ride
Me gusta montar a caballo.
I like to ride horseback.

monumento (el) [mo nu MEN to] *n.* • monument
En la plaza hay un monumento a Simón Bolívar.
There is a monument to Simon Bolivar in the plaza.

morado, a [mo RA do] *adj.* • purple
¿Dónde está mi lápiz morado?
Where is my purple pencil?

morder [mor DER] *v.* • to bite
Pedro muerde su labio cuando está nervioso.
Pedro bites his lip when he is nervous.

morirse [mo REER] *v.* • to die

yo	me	muero
tú	te	mueres
usted	se	muere
él, ella	se	muere
nosotros, as	nos	morimos
vosotros, as	os	morís
ustedes	se	mueren
ellos, ellas	se	mueren

Mis plantas se mueren por la contaminación.
My plants are dying because of the pollution.

mosca (la) [MOS ca] *n.* • fly
Las moscas son molestas.
Flies are bothersome.

mosquito (el) [mos KEE to] *n.* • mosquito
Hay demasiados mosquitos en el verano.
There are too many mosquitoes during summer.

mostrar [mos TRAR] *v.* • to show

yo	muestro
tú	muestras
usted	muestra
él, ella	muestra
nosotros, as	mostramos
vosotros, as	mostráis
ustedes	muestran
ellos, ellas	muestran

La dependiente nos muestra diferentes estilos.
The clerk shows us different styles.

mover [mo BER] *v.* • to move (things, not for people moving from one address to another)
moverse *v.* to move (oneself)

yo	me	muevo
tú	te	mueves
usted	se	mueve
él, ella	se	mueve
nosotros, as	nos	movemos
vosotros, as	os	movéis
ustedes	se	mueven
ellos, ellas	se	mueven

El esposo mueve los muebles de la sala.
The husband is moving the living room furniture.

El perro no se mueve de la puerta.
The dog isn't moving from the door.

mozo (el) [MO so] *n.* • waiter, young man
moza (la) *n.* • young woman
El mozo trae la comida y las bebidas.
The waiter brings the food and drinks.

muchacho (el) [mu CHA cho] *n.* • boy
muchacha (la) *n.* • girl
Los muchachos de la escuela preparan una fiesta para el maestro.
The boys and girls at school prepare a party for the teacher.

mucho, a [MU cho] *adj.* • much, a lot
mucho *adv.* • a lot, very much
Tengo mucho trabajo.
I have a lot of work.

Te quiero mucho.
I love you very much.

mueble (el) [MWE ble] *n.* • piece of furniture
muebles (los) *n.* • furniture
Los muebles en mi casa son viejos.
The furniture in my house is old.

mueblería (la) [mwe ble REE a] *n.* • furniture store
Compramos el sillón en la mueblería Colonial
We're buying the armchair at the Colonial furniture store.

mujer (la) [mu HER] *n.* • woman
¿Quién es esa mujer?
Who is that woman?

mundial [mun DYAL] *adj.* • worldwide, of the world
Este autor tiene fama mundial.
This author has worldwide fame.

mundo (el) [MUN do] *n.* • world
todo el mundo *pron.* • everybody, everyone
Quiero viajar alrededor del mundo.
I want to travel around the world.

muñeca (la) [mu NYE ca] *n.* • doll; wrist
Patricia tiene una muñeca nueva.
Patricia has a new doll.

Usamos el reloj en la muñeca izquierda.
We wear watches on the left wrist.

muralla (la) [mu RA ya] *n.* • wall; barrier
La ciudad española de Ávila está rodeada por una muralla.
The Spanish city of Avila is surrounded by a wall.

museo (el) [mu SE o] *n.* • museum
El museo tiene una exhibición especial de los dibujos de Goya.
The museum has a special exhibit of Goya's drawings.

música (la) [MU see ca] *n.* • music
La música es un lenguaje universal.
Music is a universal language.

músico, a [Mu see co] *adj.* • musical
músico, a (el, la) *n.* • musician
Andrés Segovia es un músico y compositor español.
Andrés Segovia is a Spanish musician and composer.

muy [MUY] *adv.* • very
Estamos muy contentos.
We are very happy.

N

nacer [na SER] *v.* • to be born

yo	nazco
tú	naces
usted	nace
él, ella	nace
nosotros, as	nacemos
vosotros, as	nacéis
ustedes	nacen
ellos, ellas	nacen

¿Cuántos bebés nacen en este hospital?
How many babies are born in this hospital?

nacido, a [na SEE do] *adj.* • born
recién nacido, a (el, la) *n.* • newborn
Las personas nacidas el 29 de febrero nacen en un año bisiesto.
People born on February 29 are born in a leap year.

nación (la) [na SYON] *n.* • nation, country
España es una nación europea.
Spain is a European nation.

nacional [na syo NAL] *adj.* • national
El béisbol es un deporte nacional.
Baseball is a national sport.

nacionalidad (la) [na syo na lee DAD] *n.* • nationality
¿De qué nacionalidad es el profesor?
What nationality is the professor?

nada [NA da] *pron.* • nothing
No hay nada en el refrigerador.
There is nothing in the refrigerator.

nadar [na DAR] *v.* • to swim
Nadamos todos los sábados por la mañana.
We swim every Saturday morning.

nadie [NA dye] *pron.* • no one, nobody
No había nadie en el consultorio del médico.
There was nobody in the doctor's office.

naranja (la) [na RAN ha] *n.* • orange
Hay jugo de naranja o de tomate para el desayuno.
There is orange or tomato juice for breakfast.

nariz (la) [na REES] *n.* • nose
El humo me irrita la nariz y los ojos.
Smoke irritates my nose and my eyes.

natación (la) [na ta SYON] *n.* • swimming
La natación es un deporte popular.
Swimming is a popular sport.

naturaleza (la) [na tu ra LE sa] *n.* • nature; outdoors
naturaleza muerta *n.* • still life
¿Te gusta la naturaleza?
Do you like the outdoors?

navaja (la) [na BA ha] *n.* • pocket knife
navaja de afeitar *n.* • razor
¿Tienes una navaja?
Do you have a pocket knife?

Navidad (la) [na bee DAD] *n.* • Christmas
Vamos a pasar la Navidad en Madrid.
We're going to spend Christmas in Madrid.

necesario, a [ne se SA ryo] *adj.* • necessary; needed
Trae todas las cosas necesarias.
He's bringing all the necessary things.

necesitar [ne se see TAR] *v.* • to need
Necesitas estudiar más.
You need to study more.

negativo, a [ne ga TEE bo] *adj.* • negative
Una persona que no escucha da una impresión negativa.
A person who doesn't listen gives a negative impression.

negocio (el) [ne GO syo] *n.* • business
Hay tres nuevos negocios en el centro de la ciudad.
There are three new businesses downtown.

negro, a [NE gro] *adj.* • black
¿Dónde está el gato negro?
Where is the black cat?

nene, a (el, la) [NE ne] *n.* • baby
El nene tiene tres meses.
The baby is three months old.

nervioso, a [ner BYO so] *adj.* • nervous
Todos estamos nerviosos con el exámen de química.
We are all nervous about the chemistry exam.

nevar [ne BAR] *v.* • to snow
nieva • it is snowing, it snows
No nieva en Panamá.
It does not snow in Panama.

nevera (la) [ne BE ra] *n.* • refrigerator
No hay nada en mi nevera.
There is nothing in my refrigerator.

nido (el) [NEE do] *n.* • nest
Las ardillas construyen nidos grandes.
Squirrels build big nests.

niebla (la) [NYE bla] *n.* • fog
Londres es una ciudad famosa por su niebla.
London is a city famous for its fog.

nieto, a (el, la) [NYE to] *n.* • grandson, granddaughter; grandchild
Doña María tiene cuatro nietos.
Doña María has four grandchildren.

nieve (la) [NYE be] *n.* • snow
Me gustan los paisajes con nieve.
I like landscapes with snow.

ninguno, a [neen GU no] *adj.* • (not) any, no, none
pron. • none
Ninguna amiga mía puede asistir al concierto.
No friend of mine is able to attend the concert.

Tengo muchas amigas pero ninguna puede asistir al concierto.
I have many friends, but none is able to attend the concert.

niño, a (el, la) [NEE nyo] *n.* • child; boy; girl
Los niños juegan en el jardín.
The children are playing in the garden.

no [NO] *adv.* • no, not
Elena no canta bien.
Elena doesn't sing well.

noche (la) [NO che] *n.* • night
Se pueden ver las estrellas por la noche.
You can see the stars at night.

nombrar [nom BRAR] *v.* • to name
¿Puedes nombrar tres ríos españoles?
Can you name three Spanish rivers?

nombre (el) [NOM bre] *n.* • name
No me acuerdo de su nombre.
I can't remember his name.

norte (el) [NOR te] *n.* • north
Los gansos migran al norte en el verano.
Geese migrate north in the summer.

nosotros, as [no SO tros] *pron.* • we
Nosotros decidimos lo que vamos a hacer con el dinero.
We will decide what we are going to do with the money.

nota (la) [NO ta] *n.* • grade, mark; note
Eduardo tiene muy buenas notas.
Eduardo has very good grades.

noticias (las) [no TEE syas] *n.* • news
Las noticias son a las siete.
The news is at seven.

novela (la) [no BE la] *n.* • novel
telenovela (la) *n.* • soap opera
Tenemos que leer tres novelas del siglo XIX para la clase de literatura.
We have to read three nineteenth-century novels for literature class.

noviembre [no BYEM bre] *n.* • November
Nieva mucho en noviembre.
It snows a lot in November.

novio, a (el, la) [NO byo] *n.* • boyfriend; groom; girlfriend; bride
La novia de Miguel es la hermana de mi novio.
Miguel's girlfriend is my boyfriend's sister.

nube (la) [NU be] *n.* • cloud
Estudiamos la clasificación de las nubes en la clase de ciencias.
We study the classification of clouds in science class.

nudo (el) [NU do] *n.* • knot
¿Qué tipo de nudo es éste?
What kind of knot is this?

nuestro, a [NWES tro] *adj.* • our
Nuestra casa está en la calle División.
Our house is on Division Street.

nuevo, a [NWE bo] adj. • new
Roberto compra un automóvil nuevo.
Roberto is buying a new car.

número (el) [NU me ro] *n.* • number
El número ganador de la lotería se anuncia en los periódicos.
The winning number of the lottery is announced in the newspapers.

nunca [NUN ca] *adv.* • never
Nunca digo mentiras.
I never tell lies.

nutritivo, a [nu tree TEE bo] *adj.* • nutritious
Las naranjas son nutritivas y sabrosas.
Oranges are nutritious and delicious.

O

obedecer [o be de SER] *v.* • to obey

yo	obedezco
tú	obedeces
usted	obedece
él, ella	obedece
nosotros, as	obedecemos
vosotros, as	obedecéis
ustedes	obedecen
ellos, ellas	obedecen

Los soldados obedecen las órdenes de sus superiores.
Soldiers obey the orders of their superiors.

objetar [ob he TAR] *v.* • to object
Ella objeta ese comentario.
She objects to that comment.

objeto (el) [ob HE to] *n.* • object
El museo Metropolitano tiene una colección de objetos prehispánicos.
The Metropolitan Museum has a collection of pre-Hispanic objects.

obra (la) [O bra] *n.* • play (theater); work (of art, literature)
Creo que el Teatro Savoy presenta una obra diferente cada semana.
I think that the Savoy Theater presents a different play every week.

obrero, a (el, la) [o BRE ro] *n.* • worker (blue collar)
La fábrica necesita obreros calificados.
The factory needs qualified workers.

obtener [ob te NER] *v.* • to obtain

yo	obtengo
tú	obtienes
usted	obtiene
él, ella	obtiene
nosotros, as	obtenemos
vosotros, as	obtenéis
ustedes	obtienen
ellos, ellas	obtienen

Para obtener la licencia de manejar debes tener dieciséis años.
To obtain a driver's license you must be sixteen years old.

océano (el) [o SE a no] *n.* • ocean
El Océano Pacífico es muy grande.
The Pacific Ocean is very big.

octubre [oc TU bre] *n.* • October
Mi cumpleaños es en octubre.
My birthday is in October.

ocupación (la) [o cu pa SYON] *n.* • profession; military occupation
Tiene una ocupación muy interesante.
He has a very interesting occupation.

ocupado, a [o cu PA do] *adj.* • busy
El jefe siempre está ocupado.
The boss is always busy.

ocurrir [o cu RREER] *v.* • to occur, to happen
Tengo frío; siempre ocurre cuando voy al cine.
I'm cold; this always happens when I go to the movies.

odiar [o DYAR] *v.* • to hate
Odio tener que levantarme temprano.
I hate to have to get up early.

oeste (el) [o ES te] *n.* • west
Seattle está al oeste de Chicago.
Seattle is west of Chicago.

oficial [o fee SYAL] *adj.* • official
La lista oficial tiene los nombres completos de los estudiantes.
The official list has the students' full names.

oficina (la) [o fee SEE na] *n.* • office
La oficina del director está en el tercer piso.
The principal's office is on the third floor.

ofrecer [o fre SER] *v.* • to offer

yo	ofrezco
tú	ofreces
usted	ofrece
él, ella	ofrece
nosotros, as	ofrecemos
vosotros, as	ofrecéis
ustedes	ofrecen
ellos, ellas	ofrecen

El professor ofrece traer la solucíon de la tarea.
The professor is offering to bring the answer to the homework.

oído (el) [o EE do] *n.* • (inner) ear
Necesito protegerme los oídos cuando nado.
I need to protect my ears when I swim.

oír [o EER] *v.* • to hear

yo	oigo
tú	oyes
usted	oye
él, ella	oye
nosotros, as	oímos
vosotros, as	oís
ustedes	oyen
ellos, ellas	oyen

¿Me puedes oír?
Can you hear me?

ojo (el) [O ho] *n.* • eye
echar un ojo *coll.* • to check
El cloro de la piscina me irrita los ojos.
The chlorine in the swimming pool irritates my eyes.

ola (la) [O la] *n.* • wave
Los niños juegan en las olas.
The children play in the waves.

oler [o LER] *v.* • to smell

yo	huelo
tú	hueles
usted	huele
él, ella	huele
nosotros, as	olemos
vosotros, as	oléis
ustedes	huelen
ellos, ellas	huelen

Me gusta oler las flores de la primavera.
I like to smell the spring flowers.

olvidar [ol bee DAR] *v.* • to forget
Siempre olvido dónde pongo mis llaves.
I always forget where I put my keys.

olla (la) [O ya] *n.* • pot
olla de presión *n.* • pressure cooker
Los frijoles están en la olla.
The beans are in the pot.

ómnibus (el) [OM nee bus] *n.* • bus
La línea de ómnibuses tiene la terminal al norte de la ciudad.
The bus line has its terminal north of town.

opinar [o pee NAR] *v.* • to think, to have an opinion
¿Qué opinas tú?
What do you think?

opinión (la) [o pee NYON] *n.* • opinion
No es buena idea en mi opinión.
It isn't a good idea in my opinion.

oportunidad (la) [o por tu nee DAD] *n.* • opportunity
Quiero tener la oportunidad de viajar antes de casarme.
I want to have the opportunity to travel before I get married.

oración (la) [o ra SYON] *n.* • sentence; prayer
Tenemos que traducir cien oraciones para la tarea de mañana.
We have to translate one hundred sentences for tomorrow's homework.

orden (la) [OR den] *n.* • command, order
Estas órdenes vienen directamente de la oficina del alcalde.
These orders come directly from the mayor's office.

oreja (la) [o RE ha] *n.* • ear
¿Tienes las orejas abiertas?
Do you have pierced ears?

orilla (la) [o REE ya] *n.* • edge, shore
Mira esos veleros en la orilla, ¡qué bonitos!
Look at those sailboats on the shore; they're so beautiful!

organización (la) [or ga nee sa SYON] *n.* • organization
Estudiamos la organización social de los incas.
We're studying the social organization of the Incas.

orgullo (el) [or GU yo] *n.* • pride
El jardín es el orgullo de mi papá.
The garden is my father's pride.

orgulloso, a [or gu YO so] *adj.* • proud
El papá está orgulloso de sus hijos.
The father is proud of his children.

oro (el) [O ro] *n.* • gold
El Museo del Oro está en Bogotá.
The Gold Museum is in Bogotá.

orquesta (la) [or KES ta] *n.* • orchestra
La temporada de la orquesta sinfónica empieza en septiembre.
The season for the symphony orchestra starts in September.

oscuro, a [os CU ro] *adj.* • dark
El teatro está oscuro cuando llegamos.
The theater is dark when we arrive.

oso (el) [O so] *n.* • bear
Mario quiere conseguir boletos para el partido de los Osos de Chicago.
Mario wants to get tickets for the Chicago Bears' game.

otoño (el) [o TO nyo] *n.* • autumn, fall
La feria de la cosecha es en otoño.
The harvest fair is in autumn.

otro, a [O tro] *adj.* • other, another
¿Quieres otro pedazo de pastel?
Do you want another piece of cake?

oveja (la) [o BE ha] *n.* • sheep
La lana viene de las ovejas.
Wool comes from sheep.

P

paciencia (la) [pa see EN sya] *n.* • patience
La maestra tiene mucha paciencia.
The teacher has a lot of patience.

paciente [pa SYEN te] *adj.* • patient
paciente (el, la) *n.* • patient
Mi mamá es tan paciente con mi hermanito.
My mother is so patient with my little brother.

padre (el) [PA dre] *n.* • father
El padre de María vive en Sudamérica.
María's father lives in South America.

padres (los) [PA dres] *n.* • parents
Mis padres me visitan dos veces al año.
My parents visit me twice a year.

padrino (el) [pa DREE no] *n.* • godfather
Mi padrino vive en la misma ciudad que mis padres.
My godfather lives in the same city as my parents.

pagar [pa GAR] *v.* • to pay
No puedo pagar la cuenta.
I can't pay the bill.

página (la) [PA hee na] *n.* • page
¿Cuántas páginas tiene el libro?
How many pages does the book have?

país (el) [pa EES] *n.* • country
Estoy orgulloso de mi país.
I am proud of my country.

pájaro (el) [PA ha ro] *n.* • bird
No me gusta ver pájaros en jaulas.
I do not like to see birds in cages.

pala (la) [PA la] *n.* • shovel
Debemos comprar unas palas este invierno.
We should buy some shovels this winter.

palabra (la) [pa LA bra] *n.* • word
Cuando no entiendo una palabra, consulto el diccionario.
When I do not understand a word, I consult the dictionary.

palacio (el) [pa LA syo] *n.* • palace
La ciudad de México es conocida como la ciudad de los palacios.
Mexico City is known as the city of palaces.

palmera (la) [pal ME ra] *n.* • palm tree
Me gustaría estar en una hamaca bajo las palmeras.
I would like to be in a hammock under the palm trees.

palo (el) [PA lo] *n.* • stick; small board
Tenemos que cambiar varios palos en la cerca.
We have to replace several boards in the fence.

pan (el) [PAN] *n.* • bread
No puedo comer pan dulce porque estoy a dieta.
I cannot eat sweet bread because I am on a diet.

panadería (la) [pa na de REE a] *n.* • bakery
La panadería abre a las 6:30 de la mañana.
The bakery opens at 6:30 a.m.

panadero, a (el, la) [pa na DE ro] *n.* • baker
El panadero hace el pan a las cuatro de la mañana.
The baker makes bread at 4 a.m.

pantalones (los) [pan ta Lo nes] *n.* • pants
Tengo que recoger los pantalones de la tintorería.
I have to pick up the pants from the dry cleaners.

paño (el) [PA nyo] *n.* • cloth, rag
Necesito un paño viejo para limpiar la sala.
I need an old cloth to clean the living room.

pañuelo (el) [pa NYWE lo] *n.* • handkerchief
Tengo una colección de pañuelos antiguos que me dejó mi mamá.
I have a collection of old handkerchiefs that my mother left me.

papa (la) [PA pa] *n.* • potato
La papa es originalmente de Sudamérica.
Potatoes are originally from South America.

papá (el) [pa PA] *n.* • father, dad
Mi papá trabaja para una compañía de automóviles.
My father works for an automobile company.

papel (el) [pa PEL] *n.* • paper; role (in a play)
No tengo papel.
I don't have any paper.

paquete (el) [pa KE te] *n.* • package
El paquete con tu regalo llega la semana entrante.
The package with your gift will arrive next week.

par (el) [PAR] *n.* • pair, couple
Tengo un par de boletos para el teatro, ¿quieres venir?
I have a couple of tickets for the theater; do you want to come?

para [PA ra] *prep.* • for, to, in order to, by
1. To express a deadline
La tarea es para mañana.
The homework is for tomorrow.

2. To indicate destination, purpose or goal
Este autobús va para Santa Fe.
This bus goes to Santa Fe.

Ángela estudia para (ser) física.
Ángela is studying to become a physicist.

3. To specify intention
Los niños preparan una sorpresa para mamá.
The children prepare a surprise for mom.

parabrisas (el) [pa ra BREE sas] *n.* • windshield
El automóvil tiene un parabrisas roto.
The car has a broken windshield.

paracaídas (el) [pa ra ka EE das] *n.* • parachute
No me interesa saltar en paracaídas.
I am not interested in jumping with a parachute.

parado, a [pa RA do] *adj.* • standing; stopped
parada de autobús (la) *n.* • bus stop
Cristina todavía está parada en la esquina.
Cristina is still standing on the corner.

La parada de autobús está a tres cuadras.
The bus stop is three blocks away.

paraguas (el) [pa RA gwas] *n.* • umbrella
Marisela usa paraguas porque llueve.
Marisela uses an umbrella because it is raining.

parar [pa RAR] *v.* • to stop
El policía para el automóvil por exceso de velocidad.
The police officer stops the car for speeding.

parcial [par SYAL] *adj.* • partial
¿Aceptan pagos parciales?
Will they accept partial payments?

parecer [pa re SER] *v.* • to seem
Me parece que no le gusta a Miguel.
It seems to me that Miguel does not like it.

pared (la) [pa RED] *n.* • wall
Tenemos que pintar las paredes.
We have to paint the walls.

pariente, a (el, la) [pa RYEN te] *n.* • relative
La mayoría de mis parientes viven en Nuevo México.
Most of my relatives live in New Mexico.

párrafo (el) [PA rra fo] *n.* • paragraph
La maestra de gramática nos enseña a escribir un párrafo.
The grammar teacher teaches us how to write a paragragh.

parte (la) [PAR te] *n.* • part
¿Qué parte del pollo prefieres?
What part of the chicken do you prefer?

partido (el) [par TEE do] *n.* • game; political party
El partido de voleibol es el viernes.
The volleyball game is on Friday.

Es miembro del partido Socialista.
He's a member of the Socialist Party.

pasado, a [pa SA do] *adj.* • past; last
Mi abuela piensa en los días pasados.
My grandmother is thinking about days long past.

No recuerdo la celebración el año pasado.
I don't remember the celebration last year.

pasajero, a (el, la) [pa sa HE ro] *n.* • passenger
Los pasajeros suben al avión.
The passengers board the plane.

pasar [pa SAR] *v.* • to pass, spend (time)
Pasamos nuestras vacaciones en Bariloche.
We spend our holidays in Bariloche.

pasatiempo (el) [pa sa TYEM po] *n.* • hobby, pastime
Mi pasatiempo favorito es leer libros.
My favorite pastime is reading books.

pasear [pa se AR] *v.* • to stroll; to take a short pleasure trip
Roberto pasea con su novia por el parque.
Roberto takes a stroll with his girlfriend through the park.

paseo (el) [pa SE o] *n.* • walk; ride; short trip
El fin de semana vamos de paseo a las montañas.
On the weekend we're taking a trip to the mountains.

pasillo (el) [pa SEE yo] *n.* • hall, hallway
Este pasillo conduce a la salida del edificio.
This hallway goes to the exit of the building.

pastel (el) [pas TEL] *n.* • cake
María hornea un pastel para la fiesta de Charles.
María bakes a cake for Charles' party.

pata (la) [PA ta] *n.* • paw, foot of an animal
Los gatos tienen cuatro patas.
Cats have four paws.

patín (el) [pa TEEN] *n.* • skate
patín de hielo *n.* • ice skate
Necesito patines nuevos; los que tengo están rotos.
I need new skates; the ones I have are broken.

patinaje (el) [pa tee NA he] *n.* • skating
patinaje sobre hielo *n.* • ice skating
patinaje sobre ruedas *n.* • roller skating
Las competencias de patinaje sobre hielo son muy interesantes.
The ice-skating competitions are very interesting.

patinar [pa tee NAR] *v.* • to skate
La señora López enseña a sus hijos a patinar.
Mrs. López teaches her children to skate.

pato, a (el, la) [PA to] *n.* • duck
Los patos migran al sur durante el invierno.
Ducks migrate south during the winter.

pavo (el) [PA bo] *n.* • turkey
El pavo es la cena tradicional en el día de acción de gracias.
Turkey is the traditional dinner on Thanksgiving Day.

payaso (el) [pa YA so] *n.* • clown
Los payasos son siempre parte del circo.
The clowns are always part of the circus.

pecho (el) [PE cho] *n.* • chest
Tiene una herida en el pecho.
He has a wound in his chest.

pedazo (el) [pe DA so] *n.* • piece
¿Quieres un pedazo de pan?
Do you want a piece of bread?

pedir [pe DEER] *v.* • to ask for, to request
pedir prestado *v.* • to borrow

yo	pido
tú	pides
usted	pide
él, ella	pide
nosotros, as	pedimos
vosotros, as	pedís
ustedes	piden
ellos, ellas	piden

Mi padre pide la cuenta.
My father asks for the bill.

peinar(se) [pay NAR] *v.* • to comb (oneself)
Rocío peina el cabello de su hermana.
Rocío is combing her sister's hair.

peine (el) [PAY ne] *n.* • comb
No me gusta prestar mi peine.
I do not like to lend my comb.

película (la) [pe LEE cu la] *n.* • movie
El festival de cine tiene varias películas en español.
The film festival has several movies in Spanish.

peligro (el) [pe LEE gro] *n.* • danger
El letrero en el edificio dice "PELIGRO, ALTO VOLTAJE."
The sign on the building says "DANGER, HIGH VOLTAGE."

peligroso, a [pe lee GRO so] *adj.* • dangerous
Las carreras de automóviles es un deporte peligroso.
Car racing is a dangerous sport.

pelo (el) [PE lo] *n.* • hair
Lupe tiene el pelo corto.
Lupe has short hair.

pelota (la) [pe LO ta] *n.* • ball
Diferentes deportes usan diferentes tipos de pelotas.
Different sports use different kinds of balls.

peluca (la) [pe LU ca] *n.* • wig
Tengo una peluca verde para la fiesta de disfraces.
I have a green wig for the costume party.

pena (la) [PE na] *n.* • grief, sorrow, pain
La situación me da pena.
The situation causes me pain.

pendientes (los) [pen DYEN tes] *n.* • earrings
Los pendientes con piedras de colores son muy populares.
Earrings with colored stones are very popular.

península (la) [pe NEEN su la] *n.* • peninsula
España está en la península Ibérica.
Spain is on the Iberian Peninsula.

pensar [pen SAR] *v.* • to think; to believe

yo	pienso
tú	piensas
usted	piensa
él, ella	piensa
nosotros, as	pensamos
vosotros, as	pensáis
ustedes	piensan
ellos, ellas	piensan

Ella piensa que él es muy listo.
She thinks he is very smart.

pensión (la) [pen SYON] *n.* • rooming house
En Europa, los estudiantes viven en pensiones.
In Europe students live in rooming houses.

peña (la) [PE nya] *n.* • cliff, rock
Los escaladores de roca suben a la peña.
The rock climbers climb the cliff.

peor [pe OR] *adj., adv.* • worse; worst
lo peor • the worst
peor que • worse than
peor...que • worse...than
Lo peor que me puede pasar ahora es perder mi beca.
The worst that can happen to me now is to lose my scholarship.

Mi tía está peor hou.
My aunt is worse today.

pepino (el) [pe PEE no] *n.* • cucumber
No me gustan pepinos en la ensalada.
I don't like cucumbers in my salad.

pequeño, a [pe KE nyo] *adj.* • small, little
Mi apartamento es pequeño.
My apartment is small.

pera (la) [PE ra] *n.* • pear
Me gustan las peras y las manzanas.
I like pears and apples.

perder [per DER] *v.* • to lose
perderse • to get lost, to be lost

yo	me	pierdo
tú	te	pierdes
usted	se	pierde
él, ella	se	pierde
nosotros, as	nos	perdemos
vosotros, as	os	perdéis
ustedes	se	pierden
ellos, ellas	se	pierden

Nuestro equipo no puede perder este partido.
Our team cannot lose this game.

Cuando voy a Chicago, siempre me pierdo.
When I go to Chicago, I always get lost.

perdonar [per do NAR] *v.* • to forgive
perdóname • pardon me, excuse me
La maestra no quiere perdonarnos por faltar a tres clases.
The teacher does not want to forgive us for missing three classes.

perezoso, a [pe re SO so] *adj.* • lazy
¡Qué perezosa eres!
You're so lazy!

perfectamente [per fec ta MEN te] *adv.* • perfectly
Diana habla francés perfectamente.
Diana speaks French perfectly.

perfecto, a [per FEC to] *adj.* • perfect
Nadie es perfecto.
Nobody is perfect.

perfume (el) [per FU me] *n.* • perfume
Siempre uso perfume francés.
I always wear French perfume.

perico (el) [pe REE co] *n.* • parrot
¿Es cierto que los pericos pueden hablar?
Is it true that parrots can talk?

periódico (el) [pe RYO d̲ee co] *n.* • newspaper
El periódico llega por la mañana.
The newspaper arrives in the morning.

periodista (el, la) [pe ryo D̲EES ta] *n.* • journalist
Varios periodistas asisten a la reunión.
Several journalists are attending the meeting.

perla (la) [PER la] *n.* • pearl
María usa collares de perlas.
María wears pearl necklaces.

permiso (el) [per MEE so] *n.* • permit, permission
Necesitamos un permiso escrito de nuestros padres para ir a la excursión.
We need written permission from our parents to go on the field trip.

permitir [per mee TEER] *v.* • to allow, to permit
El maestro no nos permite comer en clase.
The teacher does not allow us to eat in class.

pero [PE ro] *conj.* • but
El viaje es interesante pero tengo trabajo que hacer.
The trip is interesting, but I have work to do.

perro (el) [PE rro] *n.* • dog
Duncan prefiere perros a gatos.
Duncan prefers dogs to cats.

persona (la) [per SO na] *n.* • person
Pedro es una persona amable.
Pedro is a nice person.

pesado, a [pe SA do] *adj.* • heavy
Necesitamos varias personas para cargar este mueble; es muy pesado.
We need several people to carry this piece of furniture; it is very heavy.

pesca (la) [PES ca] *n.* • fishing
A mi abuelo le gusta la pesca.
My grandfather likes fishing.

pescado (el) [pes CA do] *n.* • fish (that has been cooked)
El pescado es muy sano.
Fish is very healthy.

pescador, a (el, la) [pes ca DOR] *n.* • fisherman, fisherwoman
Los pescadores salen al mar temprano por la mañana.
Fishermen go to sea early in the morning.

pescar [pes CAR] *v.* • to fish
Don Carlos enseña a pescar a su hija.
Don Carlos teaches his daughter to fish.

peso (el) [PE so] *n.* • weight; unit of money in several Latin American countries
Tenemos que descubrir el peso neto del paquete.
We have to discover the net weight of the package.

Vamos de vacaciones a México; necesitamos cambiar el dinero a pesos.
We are going to Mexico on vacation; we need to change the money to pesos.

pestaña (la) [pes TA nya] *n.* • eyelash
Me gustaría tener pestañas más largas.
I would like to have longer eyelashes.

petróleo (el) [pe TRO le o] *n.* • oil
El petróleo es un recurso no renovable.
Oil is a non-renewable resource.

pez (el) [PES] *n.* • fish (alive)
Tengo tres tipos de peces en mi acuario.
I have three kinds of fish in my aquarium.

piano (el) [PYA no] *n.* • piano
Mi hija está aprendiendo a tocar el piano.
My daughter is learning to play the piano.

picar [pee CAR] *v.* • to cut in small pieces, to chop; to sting; to bite
Por favor pica los tomates para la ensalada.
Please chop the tomatoes for the salad.

¡Cuidado! Esas moscas pican.
Careful! Those flies bite.

pícaro, a [PEE ca ro] *adj.* • roguish, mischievous
Mis hermanitas son un par de niñas pícaras.
My sisters are a couple of mischievous little girls.

pico (el) [PEE co] *n.* • beak
El canario tiene un pico pequeño.
The canary has a small beak.

pie (el) [PYE] *n.* • foot
¡Me duelen los pies!
My feet hurt!

piedra (la) [PYE dra] *n.* • stone
Los ópalos son piedras semi-preciosas.
Opals are semi-precious stones.

piel (la) [PYEL] *n.* • skin
Debes proteger tu piel del sol.
You should protect your skin from the sun.

pierna (la) [PYER na] *n.* • leg
Me duele la pierna después de correr.
My leg hurts after I run.

pijama (el) [pee HA ma] *n.* • pajamas
Necesito un pijama nuevo para mi viaje.
I need new pajamas for my trip.

piloto (el, la) [pee LO to] *n.* • pilot
James necesita volar diez horas más para obtener su licencia de piloto.
James needs to fly ten more hours to obtain his pilot's license.

pimienta (la) [pee MYEN ta] *n.* • pepper (condiment)
La sopa necesita más sal y pimienta.
The soup needs more salt and pepper.

pintar [peen TAR] *v.* • to paint
En la clase de arte pintamos retratos.
In art class we are painting portraits.

pintura (la) [peen TU ra] *n.* • painting
Mi primo tiene una colección de pinturas antiguas.
My cousin has a collection of old paintings.

piña (la) [PEE nya] *n.* • pineapple
Para la cena de Navidad cocinamos jamón con piña.
For Christmas dinner we cook ham with pineapple.

pirámide (la) [pee RA mee de] *n.* • pyramid
Las pirámides de Teotihuacán son muy interesantes.
The Teotihuacán pyramids are very interesting.

piscina (la) [pee SEE na] *n.* • swimming pool
La piscina pública se abre durante el verano.
The public swimming pool is open during the summer.

piso (el) [PEE so] *n.* • floor; apartment (in Spain)
La casa tiene un bonito piso de madera.
The house has a beautiful wooden floor.

pistola (la) [pees TO la] *n.* • gun
Jaime tiene una pistola de agua.
Jaime has a water gun.

pizarra (la) [pee SA rra] *n.* • blackboard
Necesito un borrador para la pizarra.
I need an eraser for the blackboard.

placer (el) [pla SER] *n.* • pleasure
Es un placer servirle.
It is a pleasure to serve you.

plan (el) [PLAN] *n.* • plan
La compañía tiene planes de comprar un nuevo sistema de comunicación.
The company has plans to buy a new communication system.

plancha (la) [PLAN cha] *n.* • iron
Mi mamá quiere una plancha de vapor para su cumpleaños.
My mother wants a steam iron for her birthday.

planchar [plan CHAR] *v.* • to iron
Ciertas fibras sintéticas no se necesitan planchar.
Certain synthetic fibers do not need to be ironed.

planeta (el) [pla NE ta] *n.* • planet
El sistema solar tiene nueve planetas.
The solar system has nine planets.

plano, a [PLA no] *adj.* • flat
Los estados del Medio Oeste son planos.
The Midwestern states are flat.

planta (la) [PLAN ta] *n.* • plant
planta baja • ground floor
Tengo varias plantas en mi casa que necesitan macetas más grandes.
I have several plants at home that need larger pots.

plantar [plan TAR] *v.* • to plant
Voy a plantar rosales.
I'm going to plant rose bushes.

plástico, a [PLAS tee co] *adj.* • plastic
Los juguetes plásticos están rotos.
The plastic toys are broken.

plata (la) [PLA ta] *n.* • silver
México es uno de los principales productores de plata.
Mexico is one of the main producers of silver.

plátano (el) [PLA ta no] *n.* • banana; plantain
El mono en el zoológico come tres kilos de plátanos diariamente.
The monkey at the zoo eats three kilograms of bananas daily.

plato (el) [PLA to] *n.* • plate
Carla escoge los platos que quiere usar.
Carla chooses the plates she wants to use.

playa (la) [PLA ya] *n.* • beach
Este verano vamos a la playa de vacaciones.
This summer we're going to the beach on vacation.

plaza (la) [PLA sa] *n.* • square, plaza
Hay una plaza en todas las ciudades españolas.
There is a square in every Spanish city.

pluma (la) [PLU ma] *n.* • pen; feather
Necesito una pluma roja para subrayar mis notas.
I need a red pen to underline my notes.

población (la) [po bla SYON] *n.* • population
La población de mi pueblo es 2,500.
The population of my town is 2,500.

pobre [PO bre] *adj.* • poor
pobre (el, la) *n.* • poor person
¡pobrecito, a! • poor thing!
Mi abuelo era pobre durante los años treinta.
My grandfather was poor during the thirties.

Ese pobre no tiene casa.
That poor man does not have a home.

poco, a [PO co] *adj.* • little; few
poco *adv.* • little, not much
poca importancia • no importance
Tengo pocos amigos.
I have few friends.

Eduardo habla poco cuando está nervioso.
Eduardo says little when he is nervous.

poder [po DER] *v.* • to be able to, can

yo	puedo
tú	puedes
usted	puede
él, ella	puede
nosotros, as	podemos
vosotros, as	podéis
ustedes	pueden
ellos, ellas	pueden

¿Puedes leer alemán?
Can you read German?

poema (el) [po E ma] *n.* • poem
Nuestra tarea es escribir un poema.
Our homework is to write a poem.

policía (la) [po lee SEE a] *n.* • police (force)
policía (el, la) *n.* • police officer
Debemos llamar a la policía.
We should call the police.

El policía es muy amable.
The police officer is very friendly.

polvo (el) [POL bo] *n.* • dust
El polvo me hace estornudar.
Dust makes me sneeze.

pollito (el) [po YEE to] *n.* • chick
Los pollitos siguen a su mamá gallina.
The chicks follow their mother hen.

pollo (el) [PO yo] *n.* • chicken
Mi plato favorito es arroz con pollo.
My favorite dish is chicken with rice.

poner [po NER] *v.* • to put
ponerse *v.* • to put on

yo	me	pongo
tú	te	pones
usted	se	pone
él, ella	se	pone
nosotros, as	nos	ponemos
vosotros, as	os	ponéis
ustedes	se	ponen
ellos, ellas	se	ponen

Los niños se ponen los abrigos porque hace frío.
The children put their coats on because it is cold.

por [POR] *prep.* • for, by, through

1. To express through, along, by
Me gusta pasear por el parque.
I like to walk through the park.

2. To express duration of time
Voy de vacaciones por tres meses.
I'm going on vacation for three months.

3. To indicate an exchange
Él cambia la camisa por un suéter.
He is exchanging the shirt for a sweater.

4. To express means of transportation
Viajan por tren.
They travel by train.

5. To indicate the objective of an errand (to go for...)
Voy por el periódico.
I am going to get the newspaper.

6. To express appreciation
Gracias por el regalo.
Thanks for the gift.

porque [POR ke] *conj.* • because
¿por qué? [por KE] *interr.* • why?
No voy porque estoy cansado.
I'm not going because I am tired.

¿Por qué estás tan cansado?
Why are you so tired?

portafolio (el) [por ta FO lyo] *n.* • briefcase
La abogada usa portafolio para llevar sus papeles.
The lawyer uses a briefcase to carry her papers.

portarse [por TAR se] *v.* • to behave
portarse mal *v.* • to misbehave
Los niños reciben regalos si se portan bien.
The children receive gifts if they behave well.

posada (la) [po SA da] *n.* • inn
Nos alojamos en la Posada San Ángel.
We're staying at San Angel Inn.

posibilidad (la) [po see bee lee DAD] *n.* • possibility
Existe la posibilidad de vida inteligente en otros planetas.
There is the possibility of intelligent life on other planets.

postre (el) [POS tre] *n.* • dessert
Prefiero comer fruta de postre.
I prefer to eat fruit for dessert.

pozo (el) [PO SO] *n.* • well
Echamos monedas al pozo de los deseos.
We throw coins in the wishing well.

precio (el) [pre SYO] *n.* • price
Los precios en esa tienda son buenos.
The prices in that store are good.

precioso, a [pre SYO so] *adj.* • precious
El zafiro es una piedra preciosa.
Sapphires are precious stones.

preferir [pre fe REER] *v.* • to prefer

yo	prefiero
tú	prefieres
usted	prefiere
él, ella	prefiere
nosotros, as	preferimos
vosotros, as	preferís
ustedes	prefieren
ellos, ellas	prefieren

Los estudiantes prefieren no tener exámenes.
Students prefer not to have exams.

pregunta (la) [pre GUN ta] *n.* • question
Las preguntas del examen no son fáciles.
The questions on the exam are not easy.

preguntar [pre gun TAR] *v.* • to ask
Me pregunta si conozco a esa chica.
He is asking me if I know that girl.

premio (el) [PRE myo] *n.* • prize
El premio es dos mil dólares.
The prize is two thousand dollars.

prendedor (el) [pren de DOR] *n.* • brooch, pin
Este prendedor es un regalo de mi abuela.
This brooch is a gift from my grandmother.

preparado, a [pre pa RA do] *adj.* • prepared
Todo está preparado para la fiesta.
Everything is prepared for the party.

preparar [pre pa RAR] *v.* • to prepare
La galería prepara una exhibición de arte cada año.
The gallery prepares an art exhibition every year.

presentar [pre sen TAR] *v.* • to present
El millonario presenta su retrato a la biblioteca.
The millionaire presents his portrait to the library.

presente [pre SEN te] *adj.* • present
Todo el mundo está presente en el examen final de historia.
Everybody is present at the final history exam.

presidente, a (el, la) [pre see DEN te] *n.* • president
El presidente de los Estados Unidos vive en Washington, D.C.
The President of the United States lives in Washington, D.C.

prestar [pres TAR] *v.* • to lend, to borrow
prestar atención *v.* • to pay attention
Tom me presta su automóvil para ir a la fiesta.
Tom lends me his car to go to the party.

primavera (la) [pree ma BE ra] *n.* • spring
La primavera empieza en marzo.
Spring starts in March.

primero, a [pree ME ro] *adj.* • first
primero, a (el, la) *n.* • the first one
El primero en llegar a la meta gana el maratón.
The first one to get to the finish line wins the marathon.

Rosa está en la primera fila.
Rosa is in the first row.

primo, a (el, la) [PREE mo] *n.* • cousin
Mis primos viven en Bogotá.
My cousins live in Bogota.

princesa (la) [preen SE sa] *n.* • princess
La princesa del cuento es muy buena.
The princess in the story is very good.

príncipe (el) [PREEN see pe] *n.* • prince
El príncipe es el hijo del rey.
The prince is the son of the king.

prismáticos (los) [prees MA tee cos] *n.* • binoculars
Estos prismáticos son para el teatro.
These binoculars are for the theater.

probar [pro BAR] *v.* • to try, to test; to prove

yo	pruebo
tú	pruebas
usted	prueba
él, ella	prueba
nosotros, as	probamos
vosotros, as	probáis
ustedes	prueban
ellos, ellas	prueban

Queremos probar una nueva combinación de colores.
We want to try a new color combination.

problema (el) [pro BLE ma] *n.* • problem
¿Tienes algún problema?
Do you have a problem?

profesional [pro fe syo NAL] *adj.* • professional
Diego es actor profesional.
Diego is a professional actor.

profesor, a (el, la) [pro fe SOR] *n.* • professor
El doctor Gracia es mi profesor de filosofía.
Dr. Gracia is my philosophy professor.

profundo, a [pro FUN do] *adj.* • deep
El río no es profundo aquí.
The river isn't deep here.

programa (el) [pro GRA ma] *n.* • program
¿Qué programas te gustan más?
What programs do you like best?

prohibir [pro ee BEER] *v.* • to forbid, to ban, to prohibit
prohibido estacionarse • no parking
prohibido fumar • no smoking
prohibida la entrada • do not enter
La maestra nos prohibe hablar en la clase.
The teacher forbids us to talk in class.

prometer [pro me TER] *v.* • to promise
No me gusta prometer lo que no puedo hacer.
I do not like to promise what I cannot do.

pronto [PRON to] *adv.* • soon, quickly
Manuel viene pronto.
Manuel is coming soon.

pronunciación (la) [pro nun sya SYON] n. • pronunciation
La pronunciación de las vocales es diferente en inglés y en español.
The pronunciation of vowels is different in English and in Spanish.

propina (la) [pro PEE na] *n.* • tip
Debemos dejar una buena propina.
We should leave a good tip.

propio, a [PRO pyo] *adj.* • own, one's own
Pago el viaje con mi propio dinero.
I'm paying for my trip with my own money.

proverbio (el) [pro BER byo] *n.* • proverb, saying
Tengo un libro con todos los proverbios españoles.
I have a book with all the Spanish proverbs.

próximo, a [PROKS ee mo] *adj.* • next
Los muchachos van al teatro el próximo domingo.
The boys are going to the theater next Sunday.

prueba (la) [pru E ba] *n.* • test, quiz
La maestra de biología nos da una prueba.
The biology teacher is giving us a quiz.

pueblo (el) [PWE blo] *n.* • town, village; people
Soy de un pueblo pequeño.
I'm from a small town.

El pueblo mexicano es muy amable.
The Mexican people are very friendly.

puente (el) [PWEN te] *n.* • bridge
Construyen un puente nuevo.
They are building a new bridge.

puerta (la) [PWER ta] *n.* • door
Las puertas del teatro se cierran cuando empieza la función.
The doors of the theater close when the performance starts.

puerto (el) [PWER to] *n.* • port
Barcelona es un puerto de importancia comercial.
Barcelona is a port of commercial importance.

puesta del sol (la) [PWES ta del SOL] *n.* • sunset
Todos tenemos fotografías de puestas del sol.
We all have pictures of sunsets.

pulgada (la) [pul GA da] *n.* • inch
Una yarda tiene treinta y seis pulgadas.
A yard has thirty-six inches.

pulgar (el) [pul GAR] *n.* • thumb
Los bebés chupan el pulgar.
Babies suck their thumbs.

puma (el) [PU ma] *n.* • cougar
Un puma es la mascota de la Universidad de México.
A cougar is the mascot of the University of Mexico.

punto (el) [PUN to] *n.* • point; dot, period
El lápiz no tiene punto.
The pencil doesn't have a point.

pupitre (el) [pu PEE tre] *n.* • student desk
La escuela necesita más aulas y más pupitres.
The school needs more classrooms and more student desks.

puro, a [PU ro] *adj.* • pure
Este anillo es de oro puro.
This ring is made of pure gold.

Q

que [KE] *pron.* • who; that, which
La maestra que enseña español es de Guatemala.
The teacher who teaches Spanish is from Guatemala.

¿qué? [KE] *interr.* • what?, which?
¿Qué tenemos para mañana?
What do we have for tomorrow?

quedar [ke DAR] *v.* • to fit, to suit
quedarse *v.* • to stay, to remain
Durante las Pascuas nos quedaremos en la ciudad.
During Easter we will stay in the city.

Creo que a Rhonda el vestido azul le queda bien.
I think the blue dress suits Rhonda well.

quejarse [ke HAR se] *v.* • to complain
Cuando los vecinos tienen fiestas ruidosas nos quejamos a la policía.
When the neighbors have noisy parties, we complain to the police.

quemado, a [ke MA do] *adj.* • burned
La carne está quemada.
The meat is burned.

quemar [ke MAR] *v.* • to burn
Alano tiene que quemar la basura.
Alan has to burn the trash.

querer [ke RER] *v.* • to want, to love

yo	quiero
tú	quieres
usted	quiere
él, ella	quiere
nosotros, as	queremos
vosotros, as	queréis
ustedes	quieren
ellos, ellas	quieren

Los estudiantes quieren más actividades artísticas.
The students want more artistic activities.

querido, a [ke REE do] *adj.* • dear, beloved
Querido Kyle,
Espero que cuando recibas esta carta estés bien.....
Dear Kyle,
I hope that when you receive this leeter you are all right.....

quesadilla (la) [ke sa DEE ya] *n.* • folded tortilla with melted cheese and garnishes
Cuando estoy en México, me gusta comer quesadillas.
When I am in Mexico, I like to eat quesadillas.

queso (el) [KE so] *n.* • cheese
El queso es nutritivo pero tiene mucha grasa.
Cheese is nutritious, but it has a lot of fat.

quien [KYEN] *pron.* • who, whom
La maestra, quien no está, es muy amable.
The teacher, who isn't here, is very friendly.

Ella es la maestra de quien te hablo.
She is the teacher about whom I've been speaking to you.

¿quién? [KYEN] *interr.* • who?
¿Quién no está hoy?
Who isn't here today?

quieto, a [KYE to] *adj.* • quiet, calm
Nathan es un niño muy quieto.
Nathan is a very quiet child.

química (la) [KEE mee ca] *n.* • chemistry
La clase de química es difícil.
Chemistry class is difficult.

quitar [kee TAR] *v.* • to remove, to take away
quitarse *v.* • to take off one's clothing or make-up
¡Te voy a quitar ese juguete!
I'm going to take that toy away from you!

El actor se quita el maquillaje.
The actor takes off his makeup.

quizá, quizás [kee SA] *adv.* • perhaps, maybe
¿Vas commigo? Quizá.
Will you go with me? Perhaps.

R

radiador (el) [rra dya DOR] *n.* • radiator
No compro el automóvil; necesita un radiador nuevo.
I'm not buying the car; it needs a new radiator.

radio (la) [RRA dyo] *n.* • radio
Mi abuelita escucha la radio todos los días.
My grandmother listens to the radio every day.

rama (la) [RRA ma] *n.* • branch
Las ardillas hacen sus nidos en las ramas altas de los árboles.
Squirrels make their nests in the top branches of trees.

ramo de flores (el) [RRA mo DE FLO res] *n.* • bouquet
Quiero mandar un ramo de flores a mi tía por su nuevo bebé.
I want to send a bouquet to my aunt for her new baby.

rana (la) [RRA na] *n.* • frog
Las ranas son verdes.
Frogs are green.

rancho (el) [RRAN cho] *n.* • farm; ranch
Nuestra clase va a visitar un rancho mañana.
Our class is going to visit a farm tomorrow.

rápido, a [RRA pee do] *adj.* • quick, fast, rapid
Es un viaje corto y rápido.
It's a short, fast trip.

raro, a [RRA ro] *adj.* • rare, unusual
Es raro ver zorros en el bosque.
It is unusual to see foxes in the forest.

rascacielos (el) [rras ca SYE los] *n.* • skyscraper
El rascacielos más alto es la Torre Sears.
The tallest skyscraper is the Sears Tower.

rata (la) [RRA ta] *n.* • rat
Las ratas viven cerca del río.
Rats live near the river.

ratón (el) [rra TON] *n.* • mouse
Mi hermano tiene tres ratones blancos.
My brother has three white mice.

razón (la) [rra SON] *n.* • reason
No hay razón para salir tan temprano.
There is no reason to leave so early.

razonable [rra so NA ble] *adj.* • reasonable
Necesito comprar una cámara de precio razonable.
I need to buy a camera for a reasonable price.

realidad (la) [rre a lee DAD] *n.* • reality
No entiende la realidad de la situación.
He doesn't understand the reality of the situation.

recepción (la) [rre sep SYON] *n.* • reception; cocktail party
La recepción de bienvenida es en el Hotel Majestic.
The welcoming reception is at the Majestic Hotel.

recibir [rre see BEER] *v.* • to receive
Siempre recibo una tarjeta de cumpleaños de mis primos.
I always receive a birthday card from my cousins.

recoger [rre co HER] *v.* • to pick up, to retrieve
La carta es certificada; voy al correo a recogerla.
The letter is certified; I am going to the post office to pick it up.

recomendación (la) [rre co men da SYON] *n.* • recommendation
El maestro de matemáticas me da una carta de recomendación.
The math teacher is giving me a letter of recommendation.

recordar [rre cor DAR] *v.* • to remember

yo	recuerdo
tú	recuerdas
usted	recuerda
él, ella	recuerda
nosotros, as	recordamos
vosotros, as	recordáis
ustedes	recuerdan
ellos, ellas	recuerdan

A mi abuelo le gusta recordar su juventud.
My grandfather likes to remember his youth.

recreo (el) [rre CRE o] *n.* • recess; recreation
El recreo es a las once.
Recess is at eleven.

rectángulo (el) [rrec TAN gu lo] *n.* • rectangle
Primero dibujo un rectángulo, luego un círculo.
First I draw a rectangle, then a circle.

redondo, a [rre DON do] *adj.* • round
Emilia tiene la cara redonda.
Emilia has a round face.

reflejo (el) [rre FLE ho] *n.* • reflection
¿Puedes ver tu reflejo en el agua?
Can you see your reflection in the water?

refresco (el) [rre FRES co] *n.* • soft drink, refreshment
¿Quieres un refresco?
Do you want a soft drink?

refrigerador (el) [rre free he ra DOR] *n.* • refrigerator
Mañana vamos a comprar un refrigerador.
Tomorrow we're going to buy a refrigerator.

regalar [rre ga LAR] *v.* • to give (as a gift)
¿Me regalas un coche?
Are you giving me a car?

regalo (el) [rre GA lo] *n.* • gift, present
Compramos los regalos de Navidad.
We're buying the Christmas gifts.

regar [rre GAR] *v.* • to water

yo	riego
tú	riegas
usted	riega
él, ella	riega
nosotros, as	regamos
vosotros, as	regáis
ustedes	riegan
ellos, ellas	riegan

La señora Olivera riega su cacto cada año.
Mrs. Olivera waters her cactus every year.

región (la) [rre HYON] *n.* • region; zone
Andalucía es una región de España.
Andalusia is a region in Spain.

regla (la) [RRE gla] *n.* • ruler
Necesito una regla de centímetros.
I need a ruler in centimeters.

regresar [rre gre SAR] *v.* • to return
Podemos regresar a casa por la nueva autopista.
We can return home by way of the new expressway.

reina (la) [RRAY na] *n.* • queen
Doña Sofía es la reina de España.
Doña Sofía is the Queen of Spain

reír [rre EER] *v.* • to laugh
reírse de • to laugh at

yo	me	río
tú	te	ríes
usted	se	ríe
él, ella	se	ríe
nosotros, as	nos	reímos
vosotros, as	os	reís
ustedes	se	ríen
ellos, ellas	se	ríen

Reímos con el payaso.
We laugh with the clown.

relámpago (el) [rre LAM pa go] *n.* • lightning
Teresa tiene miedo a los relámpagos.
Teresa is afraid of lightning.

religioso, a [rre lee HYO so] *adj.* • religious
Hay muchos símbolos religiosos en la iglesia.
There are many religious symbols in the church.

reloj (el) [rre LO] *n.* • watch, clock
Mi reloj no anda.
My watch doesn't work.

relleno, a [rre YE no] *adj.* • stuffed
El menú ofrece pimientos rellenos con carne.
The menu offers peppers stuffed with meat.

remar [rre MAR] *v.* • to row
No puedo remar sola. Ayúdame por favor.
I can't row alone. Please help me.

remolacha (la) [rre mo LA cha] *n.* • beet
El azúcar puede extraerse de la remolacha.
Sugar can be extracted from beets.

repaso (el) [rre PA so] *n.* • review
La maestra no quiere darnos un repaso.
The teacher does not want to give us a review.

repetir [rre pe TEER] *v.* • to repeat

yo	repito
tú	repites
usted	repite
él, ella	repite
nosotros, as	repetimos
vosotros, as	repetís
ustedes	repiten
ellos, ellas	repiten

Los estudiantes repiten las respuestas.
The students repeat the answers.

resfriado (el) [rres free A d̲o] *n.* • cold (illnes)
No puedo hablar claramente porque tengo un resfriado.
I cannot speak clearly because I have a cold.

responsabilidad (la) [rres pon sa bee lee D̲AD] *n.* • responsibility
Los estudiantes tienen la responsabilidad de estudiar.
The students have the responsibility to study.

responsable [rres pon SA ble] *adj.* • responsible
Mis padres son responsables de la renta de la casa.
My parents are responsible for the rent of the house.

respuesta (la) [rres PWES ta] *n.* • answer, response, reply
En el examen tenemos que dar respuestas completas en español.
On the test we have to give complete answers in Spanish.

restaurante (el) [res tow RAN te] *n.* • restaurant
Este restaurante ofrece buenos precios.
This restaurant offers good prices.

resto (el) [RRES to] *n.* • rest, remainder
Leo el resto del libro mañana.
I will read the rest of the book tomorrow.

retrato (el) [rre TRA to] *n.* • picture (portrait)
Los retratos de la familia están en la sala.
The family portraits are in the living room.

reunión (la) [rre u NYON] *n.* • reunion; meeting
Los ex-alumnos asisten a la reunión de su clase.
The alumni attend their class reunion.

Tengo una reunión mañana.
I have a meeting tomorrow.

revelar [rre be LAR] *v.* • to reveal; to develop (a photograph)
Ella no revela el secreto.
She won't reveal the secret.

Aprendemos a revelar fotos en la clase de fotografía.
We learn to develop photos in the photography class.

revista (la) [rre BEES ta] *n.* • magazine
Los pacientes leen revistas mientras esperan al médico.
The patients read magazines while they wait for the doctor.

revuelto, a [rre BWEL to] *adj.* • scrambled
Hay huevos revueltos para el desayuno.
There are scrambled eggs for breakfast.

rey (el) [RRAY] *n.* • king
El rey vive en el castillo.
The king lives in the castle.

rico, a [RREE co] *adj.* • rich
Tengo un tío muy rico.
I have a very rich uncle.

río (el) [RREE o] *n.* • river
El río Misisipí es muy largo.
The Mississippi River is very long.

risa (la) [RREE sa] *n.* • laughter
La risa es una buena medicina.
Laughter is a good medicine.

ritmo (el) [RREET mo] *n.* • rhythm
Estudiamos el ritmo en la clase de música.
We're studying rhythm in music class.

rizado, a [rree SA do] *adj.* • curly
Araceli tiene el pelo rizado.
Araceli has curly hair.

robar [rro BAR] *v.* • to steal, to rob
Roban esa tienda por lo menos una vez al año.
That store is robbed at least once a year.

robo (el) [RRO bo] *n.* • theft, robbery
Los ladrones planean un robo.
The thieves are planning a robbery.

rodilla (la) [rro DEE ya] *n.* • knee
No puede jugar por la rodilla.
He can't play because of his knee.

rojizo, a [rro HEE so] *adj.* • reddish
El cielo es rojizo de madrugada.
The sky is reddish early in the morning.

rojo, a [RRO ho] *adj.* • red
Quiero comprar un coche rojo.
I want to buy a red car.

romper [rrom PER] *v.* • to break
¡Cuidado! Vas a romper la ventana.
Careful! You're going to break the window.

ropa (la) [RRO pa] *n.* • clothes
Durante el verano usamos ropa ligera.
During summer we wear light clothes.

ropero (el) [rro PE ro] *n.* • closet
Por favor guarda tu ropa en el ropero.
Please keep your clothes in the closet.

rosa (la) *n.* [RRo-sa] • rose
Mi novio siempre me regala rosas.
My boyfriend always gives me roses.

rosado, a [RRO sa d̲o] *adj.* • pink
Las rosas pueden ser rosadas, blancas, rojas o amarillas.
Roses can be pink, white, red or yellow

rubio, a [RRU byo] *adj.* • blond, blonde
Adela es rubia.
Adela is blonde.

rueda (la) [ru E d̲a] *n.* • wheel
La rueda es una invención prehistórica.
The wheel is a prehistoric invention.

ruido (el) [rru EE d̲o] *n.* • noise
No puedo dormir con mucho ruido.
I cannot sleep with a lot of noise.

ruina (la) [rru EE na] *n.* • ruin
Vamos a visitar las ruinas romanas este verano.
We're going to visit the Roman ruins this summer.

rural [rru RAL] *adj.* • rural
La vida rural es tranquila.
Rural life is quiet.

ruso, a [RRU so] *adj.* • Russian
ruso (el) *n.* • Russian (language)
ruso, a (el, la) *n.* • Russian (person)
El Kremlin está en la capital rusa.
The Kremlin is in the Russian capital.

Miguel puede hablar ruso.
Miguel can speak Russian.

rutina (la) [rru TEE na] *n.* • routine
La rutina de quehaceres domésticos es muy aburrida.
The routine of housework is very boring.

S

sábado (el) [SA ba do] *n.* • Saturday
Limpiamos la casa los sábados.
We clean the house on Saturdays.

sábana (la) [SA ba na] *n.* • sheet
Los niños tienen sábanas blancas en su cama.
The children have white sheets on their bed.

sabelotodo (el, la) [sa be lo TO do] *n.* • know-it-all

Es molesto hablar con un sabelotodo.
It's annoying to talk with a know-it-all.

saber [sa BER] v. • to know (facts or information)
saber + infinitive • to know how to do something

yo	sé
tú	sabes
usted	sabe
él, ella	sabe
nosotros, as	sabemos
vosotros, as	sabéis
ustedes	saben
ellos, ellas	saben

Todavía no sabemos nuestras calificaciones.
We still do not know our grades.

Sé nadar.
I know how to swim.

sabio, a [SA byo] *adj.* • wise
sabio, a (el, la) *n.* • wise person

Mi abuela es muy sabia.
My grandmother is very wise.

El sabio del pueblo tiene ochenta años.
The wise man of the town is eighty years old

sacar [sa CAR] *v.* • to obtain, to get, to take out
sacar fotos *v.* • to take pictures

Juan siempre saca buenas notas.
Juan always gets good grades.

saco (el) [SA co] *n.* • sports coat, jacket; sack
El restaurante exige saco y corbata.
The restaurant requires a jacket and tie.

sal (la) [SAL] *n.* • salt
A mi tío no le gusta la sal.
My uncle doesn't like salt.

sala (la) [SA la] *n.* • living room
sala de clase (la) *n.* • classroom
La familia se reune en la sala a platicar.
The family gets together in the living room to chat.

salchicha (la) [sal CHEE cha] *n.* • sausage
El bratwurst es un tipo de salchicha.
Bratwurst is a type of sausage.

salida (la) [sa LEE da] *n.* • exit
¿Dónde está la salida?
Where is the exit?

salir [sa LEER] *v.* • to leave, to exit

yo	salgo
tú	sales
usted	sale
él, ella	sale
nosotros, as	salimos
vosotros, as	salís
ustedes	salen
ellos, ellas	salen

Necesito pasaporte para salir del país.
I need a passport to leave the country.

saltamontes (el) [sal ta MON tes] *n.* • grasshopper
Los saltamontes viven en el jardín.
Grasshoppers live in the garden.

saltar [sal TAR] *v.* • to jump, to leap
La bailarina salta con gracia.
The ballerina leaps with grace.

salud (la) [sa LUD] *n.* • health
Gozo de muy buena salud.
I am in very good health.

saludar [sal u DAR] *v.* • to greet
El jefe saluda a los empleados.
The boss greets the employees.

salvar [sal BAR] *v.* • to save, to rescue
Los trabajadores de rescate salvan a la niña.
The rescue workers save the little girl.

salvavidas (el) [sal ba BEE das] *n.* • lifesaver, life jacket
La ley requiere el uso de salvavidas en la lancha.
The law requires the use of a life jacket in the boat.

sandalia (la) [san DA lya] *n.* • sandal
Usamos sandalias en la playa.
We wear sandals on the beach.

sandía (la) [san DEE a] *n.* • watermelon
La sandía es una fruta jugosa.
Watermelon is a juicy fruit.

sangre (la) [SAN gre] *n.* • blood
Pablo dona sangre dos veces al año.
Pablo donates blood twice a year.

sano y salvo [SA no EE SAL bo] *col.* • safe and sound
Los alpinistas regresan sanos y salvos.
The mountain climbers are returning safe and sound.

sapo (el) [SA po] *n.* • toad
El sapo del cuento es un príncipe encantado.
The toad of the story is an enchanted prince.

sardina (la) [sar DEE na] *n.* • sardine
Me gustan las sardinas en salsa de mostaza.
I like sardines in mustard sauce.

sartén (la) [sar TEN] *n.* • frying pan
Freímos los huevos en la sartén.
We fry eggs in the frying pan.

sastre (el) [SAS tre] *n.* • tailor
El sastre hace los trajes de mi padre.
The tailor makes my father's suits.

secadora (la) [se ca DO ra] *n.* • dryer
No uso secadora de pelo durante el verano.
I don't use a hair dryer during the summer.

secar [se CAR] *v.* • to dry
secarse *v.* • to dry oneself
Durante el verano me gusta secar la ropa al sol.
In summer I like to dry clothes in the sun.

seco, a [SE co] *adj.* • dry
Nevada tiene un clima seco.
Nevada has a dry climate.

secretario, a (el, la) [se cre TA ryo] *n.* • secretary
Antonia es una secretaria muy eficiente.
Antonia is a very efficient secretary.

secreto (el) [se CRE to] *n.* • secret
Un secreto no se debe repetir.
A secret should not be repeated.

secundario, a [se cun DA ryo] *adj.* • secondary
efecto secundario (el) *n.* • side effect
Tenemos que explicar los efectos secundarios de este producto.
We have to explain the side effects of this product.

sed (la) [SED] *n.* • thirst
El agua es lo mejor para calmar la sed.
Water is the best thing for quenching thirst.

seguir [se GEER] *v.* • to follow

yo	sigo
tú	sigues
usted	sigue
él, ella	sigue
nosotros, as	seguimos
vosotros, as	seguís
ustedes	siguen
ellos, ellas	siguen

Tomás siempre sigue a su hermano mayor.
Tomás is always following his big brother.

según [se GUN] *prep.* • according to
Según la información que tengo, salimos a las ocho.
According to the information I have, we're leaving at eight.

segundo, a [se GUN do] *adj.* • second
segundo (el) *n.* • second
Alfredo vive en el segundo piso.
Alfredo lives on the second floor.

Una hora tiene tres mil seiscientos segundos.
An hour has thirty-six hundred seconds.

seguro, a [se GU ro] *adj.* • safe, sure
Estoy segura que Juan viene hoy.
I'm sure Juan is coming today.

selva (la) [SEL ba] *n.* • jungle
selva tropical *n.* • rain forest
Los monos viven en la selva.
Monkeys live in the jungle.

sello (el) [SE yo] *n.* • stamp; seal
La carta a Puerto Rico necesita un sello de veintineuve centavos.
The letter to Puerto Rico needs a twenty-nine cent stamp.

semáforo (el) [se MA fo ro] *n.* • traffic light
Hay un semáforo en la esquina.
There is a traffic light on the corner.

semana (la) [se MA na] *n.* • week
Una semana tiene siete días.
A week has seven days.

sencillo, a [sen SEE yo] *adj.* • simple; easy
Es una casa sencilla.
It's a simple house.

Esta lección es muy sencilla.
This lesson is very easy.

sendero (el) [sen DE ro] *n.* • path, trail
Los senderos están en el mapa del parque.
The paths are on the park map.

sentado, a [sen TA do] *adj.* • seated
La secretaria está sentada todo el día.
The secretary sits all day.

sentarse [sen TAR se] *v.* • to sit down

yo	me siento
tú	te sientas
usted	se sienta
él, ella	se sienta
nosotros, as	nos sentamos
vosotros, as	os sentáis
ustedes	se sientan
ellos, ellas	se sientan

Nos sentamos después de caminar tanto.
We sit down after walking so much.

sentimiento (el) [sen tee MYEN to] *n.* • feeling, emotion

Nunca expresas tus sentimientos.
You never express your feelings.

sentir [sen TEER] *v.* • to feel; to regret
sentirse *v.* • to feel (be)

yo	me siento
tú	te sientes
usted	se siente
él, ella	se siente
nosotros, as	nos sentimos
vosotros, as	os sentís
ustedes	se sienten
ellos, ellas	se sienten

Puedo sentir el calor de la máquina.
I can feel the heat from the machine.

Teresa no se siente bien hoy.
Teresa doesn't feel good today.

señalar [se nya LAR] *v.* • to point, to indicate

Las flechas señalan el camino a la conferencia.
The arrows indicate the way to the conference.

señor (el) [se NYOR] *n.* • Mr.; gentleman
El señor García es maestro de historia.
Mr. García is a history teacher.

señora (la) [se NYO ra] *n.* • Mrs.; lady
La señora López es de Managua.
Mrs. López is from Managua.

señorita (la) [se nyo REE ta] *n.* • Miss; young lady
La señorita Pérez es la maestra de español.
Miss Pérez is the Spanish teacher.

septiembre (el) [sep TYEM bre] *n.* • September
Regresamos a las clases en septiembre.
We return to classes in September.

ser [SER] *v.* • to be

yo	soy
tú	eres
usted	es
él, ella	es
nosotros, as	somos
vosotros, as	sois
ustedes	son
ellos, ellas	son

Felipe es fotógrafo.
Felipe is a photographer.

serio, a [SE ryo] *adj.* • serious
Jaime es un chico muy serio.
Jaime is a very serious guy.

serpiente (la) [ser PYEN te] *n.* • snake, serpent
Algunas serpientes son venenosas.
Some snakes are poisonous.

servicio (el) [ser BEE syo] *n.* • service
Este proyecto es un gran servicio a la comunidad.
This project is a great service to the community.

servilleta (la) [ser bee YE ta] *n.* • napkin
Quiero usar las servilletas azules con el mantel blanco.
I want to use the blue napkins with the white tablecloth.

servir [ser BEER] *v.* • to serve

yo	sirvo
tú	sirves
él, ella	sirve
usted	sirve
nosotros, as	servimos
vosotros, as	servís
ellos, ellas	sirven
ustedes	sirven

La cafetería sirve el almuerzo al mediodía.
The cafeteria serves lunch at noon.

si [SEE] *conj.* • if
sí *adv.* • yes
Sí, podemos ir al concierto si conseguimos boletos.
Yes, we can go to the concert if we get tickets.

siempre [SYEM pre] *adv.* • always
Siempre votamos durante las elecciones.
We always vote during elections.

sierra (la) [SYE rra] *n.* • sierra, mountain range
España es muy montañoso; tiene varias sierras.
Spain is very mountainous; it has several mountain ranges.

siglo (el) [SEE glo] *n.* • century
Estos libros son del siglo XV.
These books are from the fifteenth century.

siguiente [see GYEN te] *adj.* • next (following)
Contesta la siguiente pregunta.
Answer the next question.

silbar [seel BAR] *v.* • to whistle
No puedo silbar cuando como.
I cannot whistle when I eat.

silencio (el) [see LEN syo] *n.* • silence
Los estudiantes trabajan en silencio.
The students work in silence.

silencioso, a [see len SYO so] *adj.* • quiet, silent
El músico necesita un lugar silencioso para practicar la flauta.
The musician needs a quiet place to practice the flute.

silla (la) [SEE ya] *n.* • chair
  silla de montar *n.* • saddle
Alquilamos sillas para la fiesta.
We are renting chairs for the party.

sillón (el) [see YON] *n.* • armchair
La sala de espera tiene dos sillones.
The waiting room has two armchairs.

símbolo (el) [SEEM bo lo] *n.* • symbol; emblem
Un Mercedes Benz es un símbolo de éxito económico.
A Mercedes Benz is a symbol of economic success.

simpático, a [seem PA tee co] *adj.* • nice, pleasant
Los meseros en este restaurante son muy simpáticos.
The waiters in this restaurant are very pleasant.

sin [SEEN] *prep.* • without
Compro el coche sin aire acondicionado.
I'm buying the car without air conditioning.

sitio (el) [SEE tyo] *n.* • place, site
¿Es éste el sitio del nuevo edificio?
Is this the site of the new building?

situación (la) [see tu a SYON] *n.* • situation
Tenemos una situación difícil aquí.
We have a difficult situation here.

sobre [SO bre] *prep.* • on, on top of
sobre (el) *n.* • envelope
sobre todo *coll.* • above all
El sobre está sobre la mesa.
The envelope is on the table.

sobrino (el) [so BREE no] *n.* • nephew
sobrina (la) *n.* • niece
Mis sobrinos y sobrinas nos visitan en el verano.
My nieces and nephews visit us during the summer.

sofá (el) [so FA] *n.* • couch
El invitado puede dormir en el sofá.
The guest can sleep on the couch.

sol (el) [SOL] *n.* • sun
El sol es muy importante en las culturas antiguas.
The sun is very important in ancient cultures.

solamente [so la MEN te] *adv.* • only
Tomamos el examen final solamente una vez.
We take the final test only once.

soldado (el) [sol DA do] *n.* • soldier
Los soldados viven en el cuartel.
The soldiers live in the barracks.

solo, a [SO lo] *adj.* • alone
sólo *adv.* • only
Mi hermano vive solo.
My brother lives alone.

Sólo necesito recoger mi abrigo y podemos irnos.
I only need to pick up my coat and we can leave.

sombra (la) [SOM bra] *n.* • shadow, shade
Preferimos asientos en la sombra.
We prefer seats in the shade.

sombrero (el) [som BRE ro] *n.* • hat
Usamos sombreros para protegernos del sol.
We wear hats to protect us from the sun.

sombrilla (la) [som BREE ya] *n.* • parasol; beach umbrella
No debes olvidar la sombrilla.
You should not forget the beach umbrella.

sonar [so NAR] *v.* • to ring, to sound

yo	sueno
tú	suenas
usted	suena
él, ella	suena
nosotros, as	sonamos
vosotros, as	sonáis
ustedes	suenan
ellos, ellas	suenan

El timbre está descompuesto y no suena.
The doorbell is broken and it does not ring.

sonreír [son rre EER] *v.* • to smile

yo	sonrío
tú	sonríes
usted	sonríe
él, ella	sonríe
nosotros, as	sonreímos
vosotros, as	sonreís
ustedes	sonríen
ellos, ellas	sonríen

Sonreímos en la fotografía.
We are smiling in the photograph.

soñar [so NYAR] *v.* • to dream
soñar despierto, a *v.* • to daydream
soñar con *v.* • to dream about

yo	sueño
tú	sueñas
usted	sueña
él, ella	sueña
nosotros, as	soñamos
vosotros, as	soñáis
ustedes	sueñan
ellos, ellas	sueñan

Dicen que soñamos todas las noches.
They say we dream every night.

sopa (la) [SO pa] *n.* • soup
La sopa de tomate es mi favorita.
Tomato soup is my favorite.

sordo, a [SOR do] *adj.* • deaf
sordo, a (el, la) *n.* • deaf person
Después de un concierto, los jóvenes están sordos por un rato.
After a concert the young people are deaf for a while.

Muchos sordos usan lenguaje por señas.
Many deaf people use sign language.

sorprendente [sor pren DEN te] *adj.* • surprising
El fin del cuento es sorprendente.
The end of the story is surprising.

sorprender [sor pren DER] *v.* • to surprise
sorprenderse • to be surprised
Sorprendemos a Pedro mañana.
We'll surprise Pedro tomorrow.

sorpresa (la) [sor PRE sa] *n.* • surprise
¡Qué sorpresa! Muchas gracias.
What a surprise! Thanks a lot.

sótano (el) [SO ta no] *n.* • basement
La secadora de ropa está en el sótano.
The clothes dryer is in the basement.

su [SU] *adj.* • your, his, her, its, their
Su libro está en el escritorio.
Your book is on the desk.

suave [SWA be] *adj.* • smooth, soft
Esta crema mantiene la piel suave.
This lotion keeps the skin soft.

suavemente [swa be MEN te] *adv.* • softly, smoothly
Ella canta suavemente al niño.
She sings softly to the little boy.

subibaja (el) [su bee BA ha] *n.* • seesaw
Los niños juegan en el subibaja.
The children play on the seesaw.

subir [su BEER] *v.* • to go up, to climb
No podemos subir a la montaña sin guía.
We cannot climb the mountain without a guide.

sucio, a [SU syo] *adj.* • dirty
Nadie quiere lavar los platos sucios.
Nobody wants to wash the dirty dishes.

suegro (el) [SWE gro] *n.* • father-in-law
suegra (la) *n.* • mother-in-law
suegros (los) *n.* • in-laws
Mis suegros viven en Arizona.
My in-laws live in Arizona.

suelo (el) [SWE lo] *n.* • floor
Prefiero sentarme en el suelo.
I prefer to sit on the floor.

suerte (la) [SWER te] *n.* • luck
¡Buena suerte en el examen!
Good luck on the exam!

suéter (el) [SWE ter] *n.* • sweater
Usamos suéteres cuando hace frío.
We wear sweaters when it is cold.

sumar [su MAR] *v.* • to add
Los niños aprenden a sumar en la escuela.
The children learn to add in school.

supermercado (el) [su per mer CA d̲o] *n.* • supermarket
Necesito ir al supermercado.
I need to go to the supermarket.

sur (el) [SUR] *n.* • south
La gente habla español y portugués en la América del Sur.
People speak Spanish and Portuguese in South America.

T

tabaco (el) [ta BA co] *n.* • tobacco
El tabaco no es bueno para la salud.
Tobacco is not good for your health.

tacaño, a [ta CA nyo] *adj.* • stingy, cheap
Alfredo es tacaño.
Alfredo is stingy.

tal vez [tal BES] *adv.* • maybe, perhaps
Tal vez vienen más tarde.
Maybe they are coming later.

talento (el) [ta LEN to] *n.* • talent
Hay un concurso de talento este fin de semana.
There is a talent contest this weekend.

talla (la) [TA ya] *n.* • size (clothing)
Mi hermana usa la misma talla que yo.
My sister wears the same size as I.

tamaño (el) [ta MA nyo] *n.* • size, dimension
El tamaño de la casa influye el precio.
The size of the house affects the price.

también [tam BYEN] *adv.* • also, too, as well
También necesito escribirle a mi tía.
I also need to write to my aunt.

tambor (el) [tam BOR] *n.* • drum
El soldado toca el tambor.
The soldier plays the drum.

tampoco [tam PO co] *adv.* • neither, not either
Juan no quiere café; yo tampoco.
Juan doesn't want coffee; neither do I.

tanque (el) [TAN ke] *n.* • tank
tanque de gasolina *n.* • gas tank
Me cuesta $20 llenar el tanque de gasolina.
It costs me $20 to fill the gas tank.

tanto, a [TAN to] *adj.* • so much; so many (*pl*)
¡Ese señor tiene tanto dinero y tantos criados!
That gentleman has so much money—and so many servants!

tapa (la) [TA pa] *n.* • lid, top
Ponemos la tapa en la olla.
We put the lid on the pot.

taquilla (la) [ta KEE ya] *n.* • box office, ticket office
La taquilla se abre media hora antes de la función.
The ticket office opens half an hour before the performance.

tarde [TAR de] *adv.* • late
tarde (la) *n.* • afternoon
El conferencista no llega tarde.
The lecturer does not arrive late.

Tengo clase por la tarde.
I have class in the afternoon.

tarjeta (la) [tar HE ta] *n.* • card
tarjeta postal *n.* • postcard
Recibo varias tarjetas de cumpleaños.
I receive several birthday cards.

taxi (el) [TAKS ee] *n.* • cab
Llamamos un taxi cuando no tenemos automóvil.
We call a cab when we do not have a car.

taxista (el, la) [taks EES ta] *n.* • taxi driver
El taxista nos lleva al aeropuerto.
The taxi driver takes us to the airport.

taza (la) [TA sa] *n.* • cup
La anfitriona nos ofrece una taza de café.
The hostess offers us a cup of coffee.

té (el) [TE] *n.* • tea
Los ingleses toman el té a las cinco.
The English drink tea at five.

teatro (el) [te A tro] *n.* • theater
Nos encontramos en el teatro.
We'll meet at the theater.

techo (el) [TE cho] *n.* • ceiling, roof
Mis hermanos pintan el techo.
My brothers are painting the ceiling.

tejer [te HER] *v.* • to knit, to weave
Tejo un suéter para el invierno.
I'm knitting a sweater for winter.

tejido, a [te HEE do] *adj.* • knitted, woven
tejido (el) *n.* • weaving, woven or knitted piece
Ana tiene un suéter tejido.
Ana has a knitted sweater.

Hay una exhibición de tejidos de Guatemala.
There is an exhibit of Guatemalan weavings.

telar (el) [te LAR] *n.* • loom
Hay un telar antiguo en el museo.
There is an ancient loom in the museum.

teléfono (el) [te LE fo no] *n.* • telephone, phone
Buscamos el número de teléfono en el directorio.
We look up the phone number in the phone book.

televisión (la) [te le bee SYON] *n.* • television
Vemos películas viejas en la televisión.
We watch old movies on television.

tema (el) [TE ma] *n.* • theme, subject, topic
El tema de la conferencia es "El arte oriental".
The lecture's topic is "Oriental Art."

temer [te MER] *v.* • to fear
Luisa teme las consecuencias de su acción.
Luisa fears the consequences of her action.

temperatura (la) [tem pe ra TU ra] *n.* • temperature
La enfermera toma la temperatura del paciente.
The nurse takes the patient's temperature.

tempestad (la) [tem pes TAD] *n.* • storm, tempest
Prefiero estar en mi casa durante una tempestad.
I prefer to be in my house during a storm.

temporada (la) [tem po RA da] *n.* • season, period
¿Cuándo es la temporada de ópera?
When is the opera season?

temprano [tem PRA no] *adv.* • early
Tenemos que salir temprano.
We have to leave early.

tendero (el) [ten DE ro] *n.* • shopkeeper; grocer
El tendero nos dice los precios de la mercancía.
The grocer tells us the prices of the merchandise.

tenedor (el) [te ne DOR] *n.* • fork
Cortamos el pescado con el tenedor.
We cut the fish with the fork.

tener [te NER] *v.* • to have, to own

yo	tengo
tú	tienes
usted	tiene
él, ella	tiene
nosotros, as	tenemos
vosotros, as	tenéis
ustedes	tienen
ellos, ellas	tienen

La profesora tiene cuatro gatos.
The teacher has four cats.

tenis (el) [TE nees] *n.* • tennis
Me gusta jugar al tenis con mi padre.
I like to play tennis with my father.

tensión (la) [ten SYON] *n.* • tension, stress
Hago ejercicio para aliviar la tensión.
I exercise to relieve stress.

terminar [ter mee NAR] *v.* • to finish, to end
Los estudiantes terminan su tarea.
The students finish their homework.

ternera (la) [ter NE ra] *n.* • veal
Mi mamá prepara ternera para cenar.
My mother is fixing veal for dinner.

terrible [te RREE ble] *adj.* • terrible
Hay un accidente terrible en la carretera.
There is a terrible accident on the highway.

tesoro (el) [te SO ro] *n.* • treasure
Un dragón guarda el tesoro.
A dragon guards the treasure.

texto (el) [TEKS to] *n.* • text
Compramos los textos para nuestras clases.
We buy the texts for our classes.

tiempo (el) [TYEM po] *n.* • time; weather
a tiempo *coll.* • on time
Hace buen tiempo hoy.
The weather is nice today.

No tengo tiempo para estudiar.
I don't have time to study.

tienda (la) [TYEN da] *n.* • store, shop
La tienda tiene una liquidación anual.
The store has an annual sale.

tierra (la) [TYE rra] *n.* • earth; land, soil
La Tierra es el planeta más bello.
The Earth is the most beautiful planet.

tigre (el) [TEE gre] *n.* • tiger (male)
tigresa (la) [tee GRE sa] *n.* • tiger (female)
Podemos ver los tigres en el zoológico.
We can see the tigers in the zoo.

tijeras (las) [tee HE ras] *n.* • scissors
Los niños pequeños no usan tijeras.
Small children do not use scissors.

timbre (el) [TEEM bre] *n.* • doorbell
Las visitas tocan el timbre.
The guests ring the doorbell.

tío (el) [TEE o] *n.* • uncle
tía (la) *n.* • aunt
Mi tío nos visita los domingos.
My uncle visits us on Sundays.

La tía da dulces a los niños.
The aunt gives candies to the children.

tiovivo (el) [tee o BEE bo] *n.* • merry-go-round
Hay un tiovivo en el parque.
There is a merry-go-round in the park.

típico, a [TEE pee co] *adj.* • typical; traditional
Paella es un plato típico de España.
Paella is a traditional Spanish dish.

tipo (el) [TEE po] *n.* • type, kind
Hay varios tipos de rosas.
There are several kinds of roses.

tirar [tee RAR] *v.* • to throw
Los chicos tiran piedras en la calle.
The boys are throwing stones in the street.

tiza (la) [TEE sa] *n.* • chalk
El maestro usa tizas de diferentes colores.
The teacher uses chalk of different colors.

toalla (la) [to A ya] *n.* • towel
Traemos toallas a la playa.
We bring towels to the beach.

tobillo (el) [to BEE yo] *n.* • ankle
Eduardo tiene el tobillo roto.
Eduardo has a broken ankle.

tocadiscos (el) [to ca DEES cos] *n.* • record player
Tocamos el disco en el tocadiscos.
We play the record on the record player.

tocador (el) [to ca DOR] *n.* • dresser
Pongo la ropa limpia en el tocador.
I put the clean clothes in the dresser.

tocar [to CAR] *v.* • to play; to touch
La profesora de música toca el piano.
The music teacher plays the piano.

No debes tocar la computadora sin permiso.
You shouldn't touch the computer without permission.

tocino (el) [to SEE no] *n.* • bacon
Me gustan los huevos fritos con tocino.
I like fried eggs with bacon.

todavía [to da BEE a] *adv.* • still, yet
Todavía están en clase.
They are still in class.

todo, a [TO do] *adj.* • all, whole, entire
todo (el) *n.* • all everything
Toda la familia está aquí.
The whole family is here.

Todo está bien.
Everything is fine.

tomar [to MAR] *v.* • to take; to drink
Manuel toma el libro ahora.
Manuel is taking the book now.

¿Qué quieres tomar?
What do you want to drink?

tomate (el) [to MA te] *n.* • tomato
Compramos tomates en el mercado.
We buy tomatoes at the market.

tormenta (la) [tor MEN ta] *n.* • storm
La tormenta viene del lago.
The storm is coming from the lake.

toro (el) [TO ro] *n.* • bull
El toro es un animal fuerte.
The bull is a strong animal.

toronja (la) [to RON ha] *n.* • grapefruit
El jugo de toronja tiene vitamina C.
Grapefruit juice has vitamin C.

torre (la) [TO rre] *n.* • tower
El castillo tiene cuatro torres.
The castle has four towers.

tortilla (la) [tor TEE ya] *n.* • tortilla (Mexico), omelette (Spain)
En México la tortilla se hace de maíz; en España se hace de huevos.
In Mexico the tortilla is made of corn; in Spain it is made of eggs.

tortuga (la) [tor TU ga] *n.* • turtle
La tortuga es un animal lento.
Turtles are slow animals.

tos (la) [TOS] *n.* • cough
La enfermera nos da medicina para la tos.
The nurse gives us cough medicine.

toser [to SER] *v.* • to cough
Ella tose porque tiene un resfriado.
She's coughing because she has a cold.

tostado, a [tos TA do] *adj.* • toasted; tan
tostada (la) *n.* • toast
Comemos tostadas con mermelada.
We eat toast with marmalade.

Pepe está muy tostado.
Pepe is very tan.

tostadora (la) [tos ta DO ra] *n.* • toaster
La tostadora no funciona.
The toaster isn't working.

tostar [tos TAR] *v.* • to toast

yo	tuesto
tú	tuestas
usted	tuesta
él, ella	tuesta
nosotros, as	tostamos
vosotros, as	tostáis
ustedes	tuestan
ellos, ellas	tuestan

Tostamos el pan en la tostadora.
We toast the bread in the toaster.

trabajador, a (el, la) [tra ba ha DOR] *n.* • worker
trabajador, a social *n.* • social worker
Esa fábrica tiene muchos trabajadores.
That factory has a lot of workers.

trabajar [tra ba HAR] *v.* • to work
Los estudiantes trabajan en el verano.
The students work during the summer.

trabajo (el) [tra BA ho] *n.* • work, job
La descripción del trabajo está en el periódico.
The job description is in the newspaper.

trabalenguas (el) [tra ba LEN gwas] *n.* • tongue twister
Es difícil repetir los trabalenguas.
It's difficult to repeat tongue twisters.

tractor (el) [trac TOR] *n.* • tractor
El granjero usa el tractor durante la cosecha.
The farmer uses the tractor during the harvest.

tradición (la) [tra dee SYON] *n.* • tradition
¿Tiene su familia muchas tradiciones?
Does your family have many traditions?

traer [tra ER] *v.* • to bring

yo	traigo
tú	traes
usted	trae
él, ella	trae
nosotros, as	traemos
vosotros, as	traéis
ustedes	traen
ellos, ellas	traen

Traemos recuerdos de nuestro viaje.
We bring souvenirs from our trip.

tráfico (el) [TRA fee co] *n.* • traffic
Para evitar el tráfico salimos temprano.
To avoid the traffic we leave early.

traje (el) [TRA he] *n.* • suit
traje de baño *n.* • swimsuit
Los empleados de la oficina usan traje.
The office employees wear suits.

tranquilamente [tran kee la MEN te] *adv.* • calmly
El bebé duerme tranquilamente.
The baby sleeps calmly.

tranquilo, a [tran KEE lo] *adj.* • calm
Juan es una persona tranquila.
Juan is a calm person.

tránsito (el) [TRAN see to] *n.* • traffic
El tránsito en el centro de la ciudad me pone de mal humor.
The traffic downtown puts me in a bad mood.

trapeador (el) [tra pe a DOR] *n.* • mop
Compramos un trapeador para limpiar la casa.
We buy a mop to clean the house.

trapo (el) [TRA po] *n.* • rag
Limpio el coche con un trapo viejo.
I clean the car with an old rag.

tratar [tra TAR] *v.* • to try; to handle; to treat
Trata de llegar a tiempo.
Try to arrive on time.

Debemos tratar la situación con cuidado.
We should handle the situation carefully.

tren (el) [TREN] *n.* • train
Viajamos a California en tren.
We're traveling to California by train.

triciclo (el) [tree SEE clo] *n.* • tricycle
La niña juega con su triciclo.
The girl plays with her tricycle.

trigal (el) [tree GAL] *n.* • wheat field
El trigal es de color dorado.
The wheat field is a golden color.

trigo (el) [TREE go] *n.* • wheat
Este pan está hecho de harina de trigo.
This bread is made of wheat flour.

triste [TREES te] *adj.* • sad
No queremos ver películas tristes.
We do not want to see sad movies.

tristemente [trees te MEN te] *adv.* • sadly
¿Por qué llora la heroína tan tristemente?
Why is the heroine crying so sadly?

trofeo (el) [tro FE o] *n.* • trophy
El trofeo es para el ganador del concurso.
The trophy is for the winner of the contest.

trompeta (la) [trom PE ta] *n.* • trumpet
El soldado toca la trompeta.
The soldier plays the trumpet.

tropical [tro pee CAL] *adj.* • tropical
Panamá es un país tropical.
Panama is a tropical country.

truco (el) [TRU co] *n.* • trick
El mago muestra algunos trucos.
The magician shows some tricks.

trueno (el) [tru E no] *n.* • thunder
A Luis le da miedo el trueno.
Luis is afraid of thunder.

tubo (el) [TU bo] *n.* • tube
La pasta de dientes viene en tubos.
Toothpaste comes in tubes.

turismo (el) [tu REES mo] *n.* • tourism
Las Vegas depende del turismo.
Las Vegas depends on tourism.

turista (el, la) [tu REES ta] *n.* • tourist
Los turistas sacan fotos.
The tourists take pictures.

turno (el) [TUR no] *n.* • turn
En el juego de cartas cada jugador tiene su turno.
In the card game each player has his turn.

U

último, a [UL tee mo] *adj.* • last
  último, a (el, la) *n.* • last one
Siempre llegas en el último minuto.
You always arrive at the last minute.

Juan es el último en salir.
Juan is the last one to leave.

un [UN] *art.* • a, an (m.)
una *art.* • a, an (f.)
Necesito un libro para mañana.
I need a book for tomorrow.

Quiero tener una casa grande.
I want to have a big house.

único, a [U nee co] *adj.* • only
hijo, a único, a *n.* • only child
Eres mi única amiga.
You are my only friend.

Roberto es hijo único.
Roberto is an only child.

unido, a [u NEE do] *adj.* • united
Tenemos una familia unida.
We have a united family.

uniforme (el) [u nee FOR me] *n.* • uniform
En la escuela no usamos uniforme.
We do not wear uniforms in school.

universidad (la) [u nee ber see DAD] *n.* • college, university
José estudia en la Universidad de México.
José studies at the University of Mexico.

usual [u SUAL] *adj.* • usual, customary
¿Cuánto es la propina usual?
How much is the usual tip?

usualmente [u sual MEN te] *adv.* • usually
Me levanto temprano usualmente.
I usually get up early.

usar [u SAR] *v.* • to use; to wear
Usamos abrigos durante el invierno.
We wear coats during winter.

útil [U teel] *adj.* • useful
Un diccionario es un libro útil.
A dictionary is a useful book.

uva (la) [U ba] *n.* • grape
El vino está hecho de uvas.
Wine is made from grapes.

V

vaca (la) [BA ca] *n.* • cow
Hay más de doscientas vacas en la granja.
There are more than 200 cows on the farm.

vacaciones (las) [ba ca SYO nes] *n.* • vacation, holidays
Tomamos vacaciones en verano.
We take a vacation in summer.

vaciar [ba SYAR] *v.* • to empty; to pour out
Vaciamos el refrigerador para limpiarlo.
We empty the refrigerator to clean it.

vacunar [ba cu NAR] *v.* • to vaccinate
La enfermera vacuna a los niños.
The nurse vaccinates the children.

vagón (el) [ba GON] *n.* • car (in a train)
El comedor está en el tercer vagón.
The dining room is in the third car.

vainilla (la) [bi NEE ya] *n.* • vanilla
La tía Juana hace helado de vainilla.
Aunt Juana makes vanilla ice cream.

valiente [ba LYEN te] *adj.* • courageous
Mi hermano es un hombre valiente.
My brother is a courageous man.

valle (el) [BA ye] *n.* • valley
La ciudad de México está en un valle.
Mexico City is in a valley.

vamos [BA mos] *coll.* • let's go
Vamos. Es tarde.
Let's go. It's late.

vaquero, a (el, la) [ba KE ro] *n.* • cowboy, cowgirl
Los vaqueros trabajan en el rodeo.
Cowboys work at the rodeo.

variado, a [ba ree A do] *adj.* • varied
La cocina sudamericana es variada.
South American cuisine is varied.

variedad (la) [ba ree e DAD] *n.* • variety
Latinoamérica tiene una gran variedad de climas.
Latin America has a great variety of climates.

varios, as [BA ryos] *adj.* • several
Varios profesores van al simposio.
Several professors are going to the symposium.

vaso (el) [BA so] *n.* • glass (drinking)
El vaso está medio lleno.
The glass is half full.

vecino, a (el, la) [be SEE no] *n.* • neighbor
Mi vecino va a muchas fiestas.
My neighbor goes to a lot of parties.

vegetación (la) [be he ta SYON] *n.* • vegetation
La vegetación tropical es hermosa.
Tropical vegetation is beautiful.

vegetal (el) [be he TAL] *n.* • vegetable
Compramos vegetales para la ensalada.
We buy vegetables for the salad.

vehículo (el) [be EE cu lo] *n.* • vehicle
El vehículo más común en Holanda es la bicicleta.
The most common vehicle in Holland is the bicycle.

vela (la) [BE la] *n.* • candle
Julieta apaga las velas de su pastel de cumpleaños.
Julieta blows out the candles of her birthday cake.

venado (el) [be NA do] *n.* • deer
Los venados viven en el bosque.
Deer live in the forest.

vendedor, a (el, la) [ben de DOR] *n.* • salesperson, clerk
Los vendedores ayudan a sus clientes.
Salespeople help their clients.

vender [ben DER] *v.* • to sell
Harry vende su automóvil por un precio razonable.
Harry sells his car for a reasonable price.

venir [be NEER] *v.* • to come

yo	vengo
tú	vienes
usted	viene
él, ella	viene
nosotros, as	venimos
vosotros, as	venís
ustedes	vienen
ellos, ellas	vienen

Venimos a la escuela todos los días.
We come to school every day.

ventana (la) [ben TA na] *n.* • window
La ventana necesita cortinas nuevas.
The window needs new curtains.

ventanilla (la) [ben ta NEE ya] *n.* • (counter) window, (car) window
El banco tiene veinte ventanillas de servicio.
The bank has twenty service windows.

ventilador (el) [ben tee la DOR] *n.* • fan
Prendemos el ventilador cuando hace calor.
We turn on the fan when it is hot.

ver [BER] *v.* • to see

yo	veo
tú	ves
usted	ve
él, ella	ve
nosotros, as	vemos
vosotros, as	veis
ustedes	ven
ellos, ellas	ven

Te veo mañana.
I'll see you tomorrow.

verano (el) [ve RA no] *n.* • summer
El verano es mi estación favorita.
Summer is my favorite season.

verbo (el) [BER bo] *n.* • verb
Conjugamos los verbos en español.
We conjugate the verbs in Spanish.

verdad (la) [ber DAD] *n.* • truth
¿verdad? *coll.* • isn't that right?, right?
Los niños deben decir la verdad.
Children should tell the truth.

Vamos al cine, ¿verdad?
We're going to the movies, right?

verde [BER de] *adj.* • green
Los aguacates son verdes.
Avocados are green.

vestido (el) [bes TEE do] *n.* • dress
Necesito comprar un vestido y unos zapatos.
I need to buy a dress and some shoes.

vestir [bes TEER] *v.* • to dress (someone)
vestirse *v.* • to get dressed, to dress (oneself)

yo	me	visto
tú	te	vistes
usted	se	viste
él, ella	se	viste
nosotros, as	nos	vestimos
vosotros, as	os	vestís
ustedes	se	visten
ellos, ellas	se	visten

Nos vestimos de prisa por la mañana.
We get dressed in a hurry in the morning.

veterinario, a (el, la) [be te ree NA ryo] *n.* • veterinarian
El veterinario cura los animales.
The veterinarian cures the animals.

vez (la) [BES] *n.* • time; turn
La próxima vez te enseño las fotos de mi familia.
Next time I will show you my family pictures.

viajar [bya HAR] *v.* • to travel
Viajamos a Barcelona durante las vacaciones.
We travel to Barcelona during the holidays

viaje (el) [BYA he] *n.* • travel; trip
El libro de los viajes de Cristóbal Colón es muy interesante.
The book about the travels of Columbus is very interesting.

viajero, a (el, la) [bya HE ro] *n.* • traveler
cheque de viajero *n.* • traveler's check
Los viajeros visitan países extranjeros.
The travelers visit foreign countries.

¿Puedo pagar con cheque de viajero?
May I pay with a traveler's check?

víbora (la) [VEE bo ra] *n.* • snake
Las víboras de cascabel son venenosas.
Rattlesnakes are poisonous.

vida (la) [BEE da] *n.* • life
Una biografía es un libro sobre la vida de una persona.
A biography is a book about somebody's life.

vidrio (el) [VEE dryo] *n.* • glass (other than drinking glass)
El florero es de vidrio tallado.
The vase is made of cut glass.

viejo, a [BYE ho] *adj.* • old
viejo, a (el, la) *n.* • old person
Mi abuela es muy vieja.
My grandmother is very old.

Ese viejo tiene cien años.
That old man is a hundred years old.

viento (el) [BYEN to] *n.* • wind
El viento es del norte.
The wind is from the north.

viernes (el) [BYER nes] *n.* • Friday
El viernes vamos a un concierto.
On Friday we're going to a concert.

vigilar [bee hee LAR] *v.* • to watch, to guard; to take care of
La policía vigila la tienda.
The police woman watches the store.

vino (el) [BEE no] *n.* • wine
vino blanco • white wine
vino rosado • rosé
vino tinto • red wine
Tomamos vino tinto con la carne.
We drink red wine with meat.

violencia (la) [bee o LEN sya] *n.* • violence
La gente protesta la violencia en la televisión.
People protest the violence on television.

violeta [bee o LE ta] *adj.* • violet
violeta (la) *n.* • violet
Las violetas africanas son bonitas.
African violets are pretty.

violín (el) [bee o LEEN] *n.* • violin
El violín es un instrumento de cuerdas.
The violin is a string instrument.

visitar [bee see TAR] *v.* • to visit
Los turistas visitan el museo.
The tourists visit the museum.

vista (la) [BEES ta] *n.* • sight, view
La vista de las montañas es espectacular.
The view of the mountains is spectacular.

vitamina (la) [bee ta MEE na] *n.* • vitamin
La mamá les da vitaminas a los niños.
The mother gives vitamins to the children.

viudo (el) [BYU do] *n.* • widower
viudo a (la) *n.* • widow
La señora Pérez es viuda.
Mrs. Pérez is a widow.

vivir [bee BEER] *v.* • to live
El presidente vive en la Casa Blanca.
The president lives in the White House.

vivo, a [BEE bo] *adj.* • alive, living
Ese animal no está muerto, está vivo.
That animal isn't dead, it's alive.

vocabulario (el) [bo ca bu LA ryo] *n.* • vocabulary
Aprendemos el vocabulario en español.
We are learning the vocabulary in Spanish.

vocal (la) [bo CAL] *n.* • vowel
Las vocales son a, e, i, o, u.
The vowels are a, e, i, o, u.

volar [bo LAR] *v.* • to fly

yo	vuelo
tú	vuelas
usted	vuela
él, ella	vuela
nosotros, as	volamos
vosotros, as	voláis
ustedes	vuelan
ellos, ellas	vuelan

Volamos al Ecuador mañana.
We're flying to Ecuador tomorrow.

volcán (el) [bol CAN] *n.* • volcano
Hay muchos volcanes en Hawai.
There are many volcanoes in Hawaii.

volver [bol BER] *v.* • to return
volverse • to become

yo	me	vuelvo
tú	te	vuelves
usted	se	vuelve
él, ella	se	vuelve
nosotros, as	nos	volvemos
vosotros, as	os	volvéis
ustedes	se	vuelven
ellos, ellas	se	vuelven

Volvemos contentos del campamento.
We return happy from camping.

Al final del cuento el hombre se vuelve loco.
At the end of the tale the man goes crazy.

voz (la) [BOS] *n.* • voice
en voz alta • in a loud voice
en voz baja • quietly
La cantante tiene una voz bella.
The singer has a beautiful voice.

vuelo (el) [BWE lo] *n.* • flight
Salimos en el vuelo 893.
We leave on flight 893.

vuelta (la) [BWEL ta] *n.* • turn; walk
Tomamos la vuelta en la carretera.
We take the turn in the road.

Vamos a dar una vuelta por el parque.
Let's take a walk through the park.

Y

ya no [YA no] *adv.* • no longer
Ya no trabajo allí.
I no longer work there.

yate (el) [YA te] *n.* • yacht
La fiesta es en el yate.
The party is on the yacht.

yegua (la) [YE gwa] *n.* • mare
La yegua tiene dos potrillos.
The mare has two colts.

yerno (el) [YER no] *n.* • son-in-law
Su yerno trabaja en un hospital.
His son-in-law works in a hospital.

yo [YO] *pron.* • I
Yo no sé hablar alemán.
I do not know how to speak German.

yodo (el) [YO do] *n.* • iodine
Usamos yodo para desinfectar.
We use iodine to disinfect.

yogur (el) [yo GUR] *n.* • yogurt
¿Te gusta el yogur?
Do you like yogurt?

Z

zanahoria (la) [san a O rya] *n.* • carrot
Las zanahorias tienen vitamina A.
Carrots have vitamin A.

zapatería (la) [sa pa te REE a] *n.* • shoe store
Hay varias zapaterías en el centro de la ciudad.
There are several shoe stores downtown.

zapatero, a (el, la) [sa pa TE ro] *n.* • shoemaker
El zapatero repara los zapatos.
The shoemaker repairs shoes.

zapato (el) [sa PA to] *n.* • shoe
Necesito limpiar mis zapatos.
I need to clean my shoes.

zoológico (el) [so o LO hee co] *n.* • zoo
El zoológico tiene animales exóticos.
The zoo has exotic animals.

zorro, a (el, la) [SO rro] *n.* • fox
El zorro es un animal muy astuto.
The fox is a very cunning animal.

Illustrations/*Ilustraciones*

la chaqueta
jacket

las gafas de sol
sunglasses

el delantal
apron

el cinturón
belt

los pendientes
earrings

el collar
necklace

la bufanda
scarf

el vestido
dress

el traje de baño
swimsuit

la blusa
blouse

Clothing—La ropa

el impermeable
raincoat
el calcetín
sock
las sandalias
sandals
el bolso
purse
el hilo
thread
el botón
button
la falda
skirt
la camiseta
T-shirt
el zapato
shoe
el paraguas
umbrella
la corbata
tie
los pantalones
pants

Clothing—La ropa

la grapadora
stapler
el mapa
map
la regla
ruler
el borrador
eraser
la tiza
chalk
el libro
book
el bolígrafo
ball-point pen
la tarjeta postal
post card
el sobre
envelope
DICIEMBRE
1 2 3 4 5
6 7 8 9 10 11 12
13 14 15 16 17 18 19
20 21 22 23 24 25 26
27 28 29 30 31
el cuaderno
notebook
la estampilla
postage stamp
el calendario
calendar
el lápiz
pencil
la hoja de papel
sheet of paper

Office Supplies—Artículos de oficina

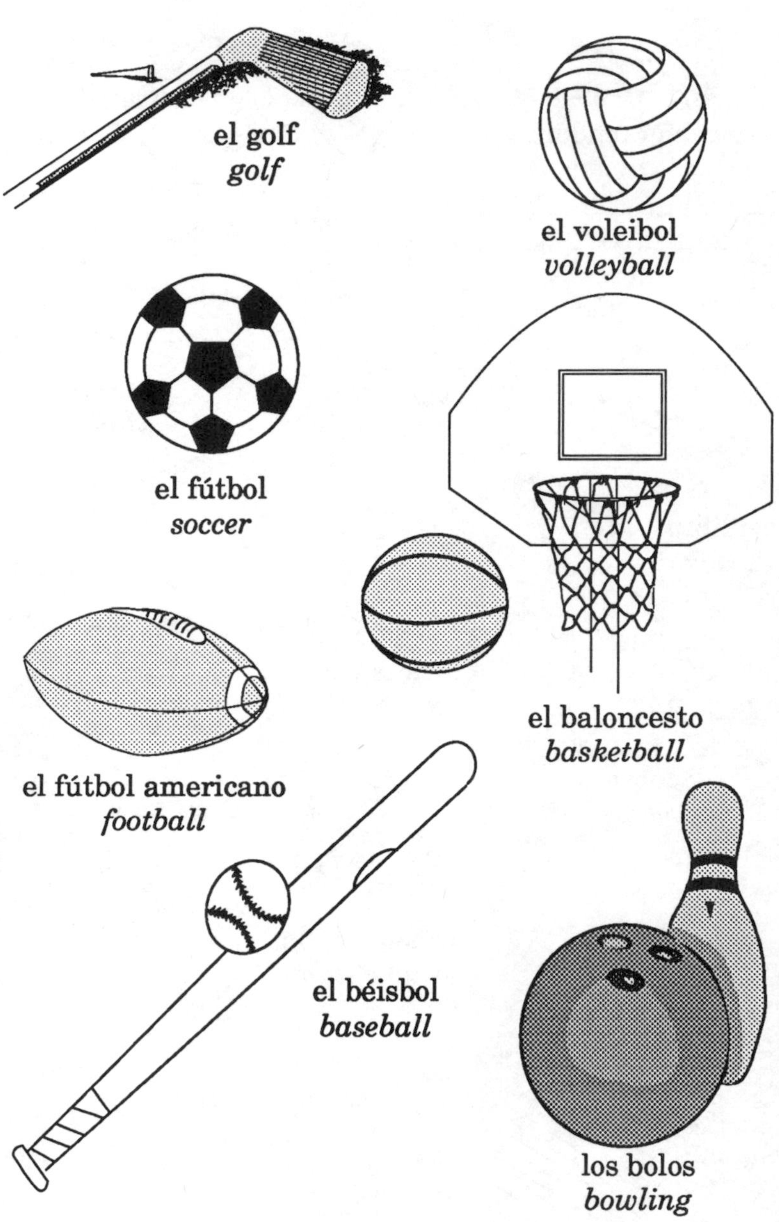

Sports—Los deportes

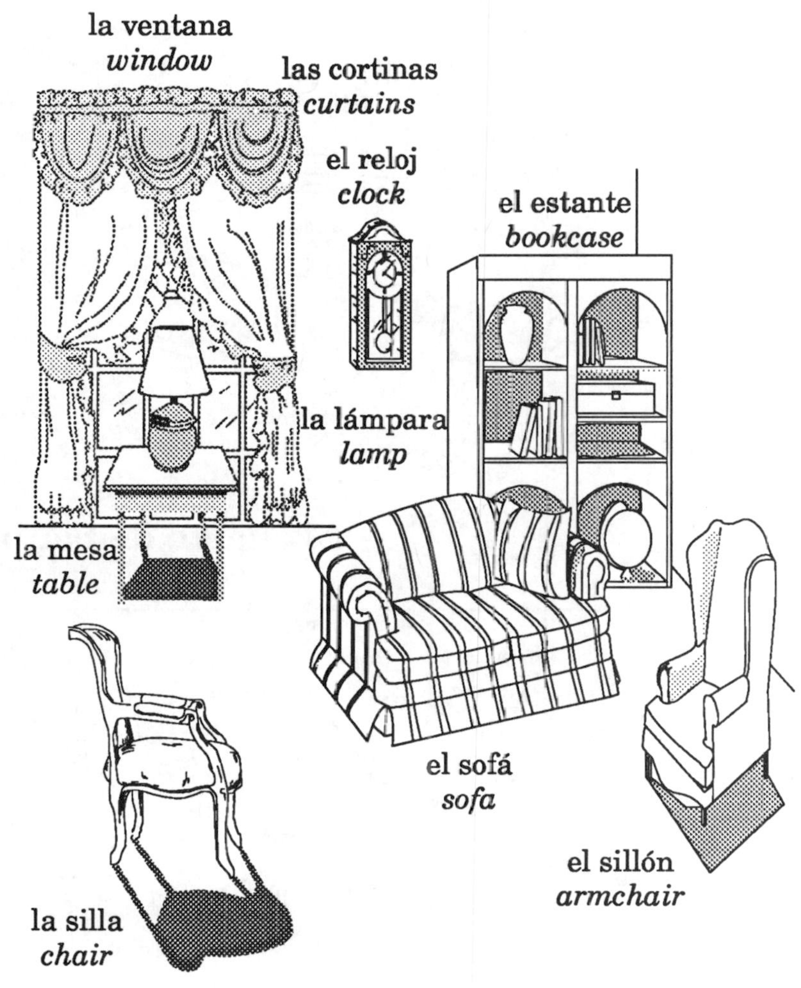

Living Room—La sala

Bathroom—
El cuarto de baño

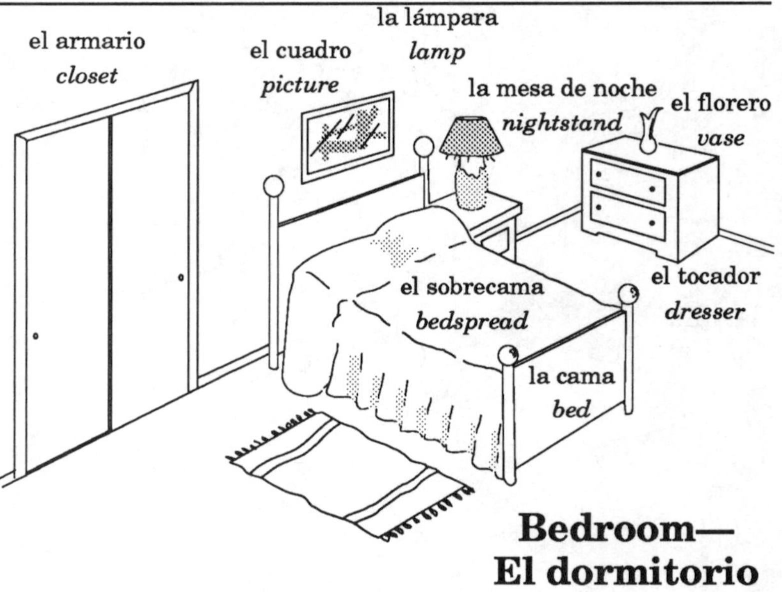

Bedroom—
El dormitorio

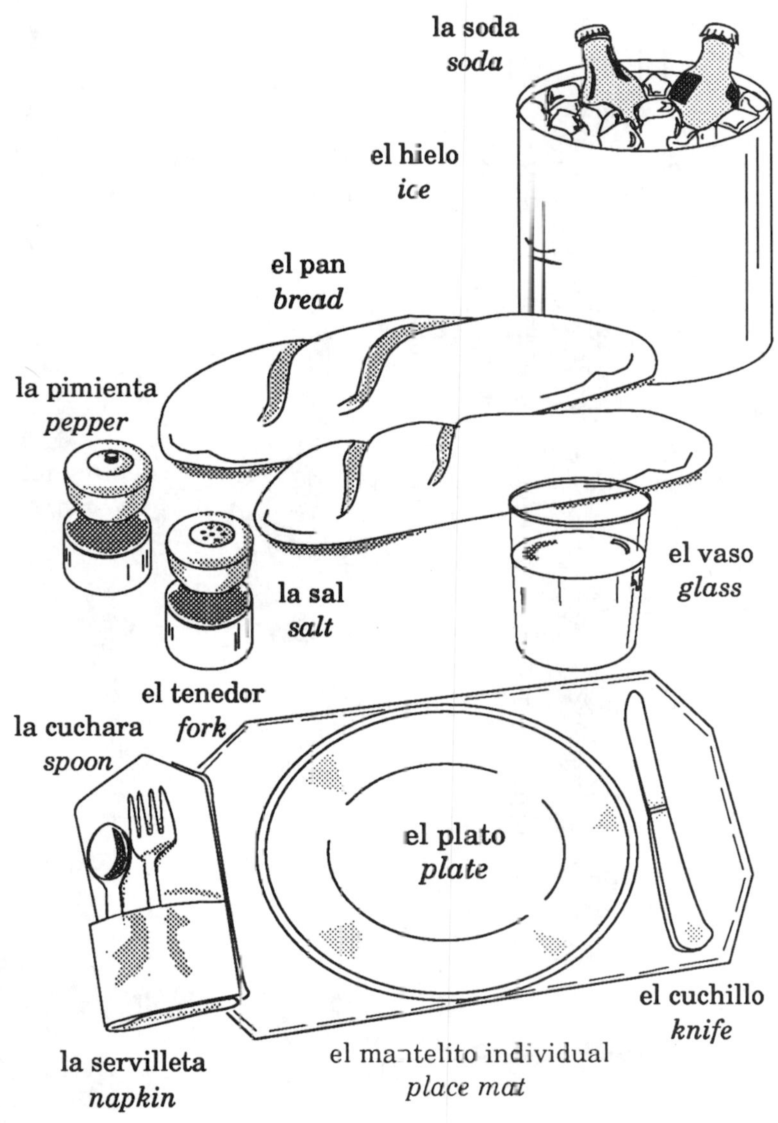
la soda
soda
el hielo
ice
el pan
bread
la pimienta
pepper
la sal
salt
el vaso
glass
el tenedor
fork
la cuchara
spoon
el plato
plate
el cuchillo
knife
la servilleta
napkin
el mantelito individual
place mat

Table—La mesa

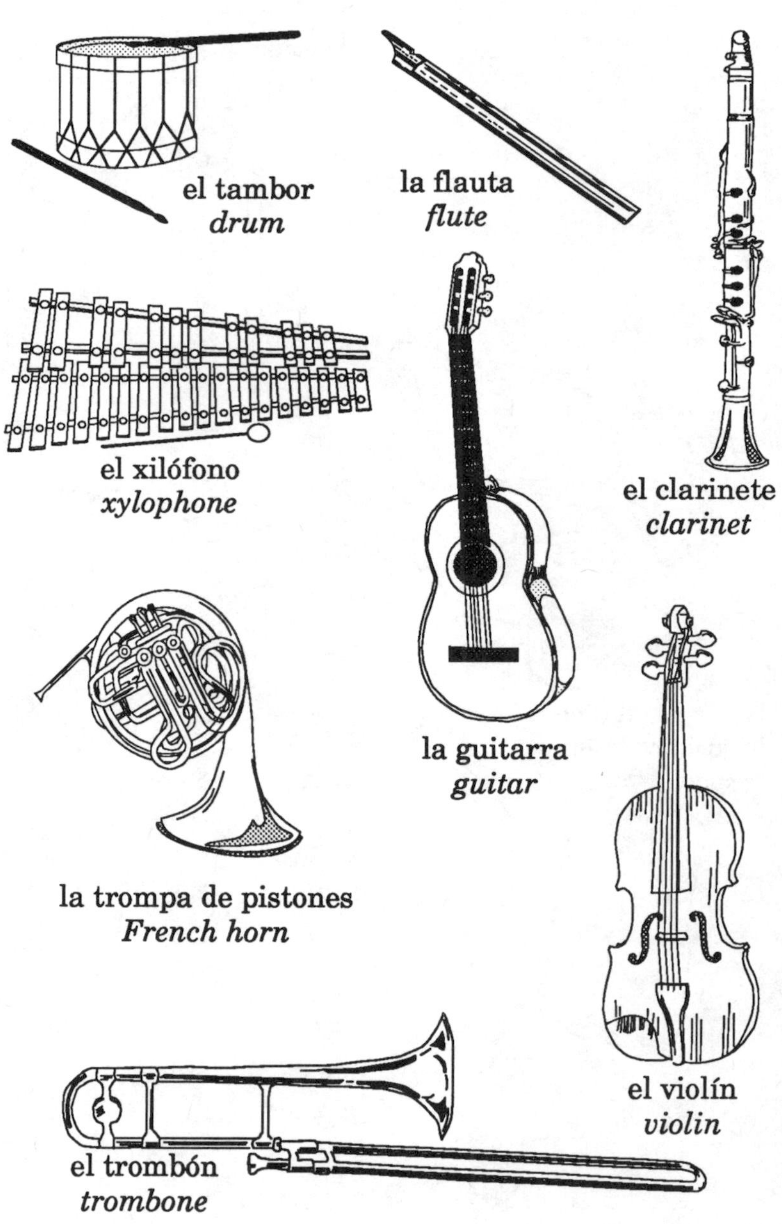

Musical Instruments—
Los instrumentos musicales

Flowers—Las flores

Vegetables—Las legumbres

la manzana
apple
la sandía
watermelon
el plátano
banana
la fresa
strawberry
las cerezas
cherries
las uvas
grapes
el limón
lemon
las frambuesas
raspberries
el durazno
peach
la pera
pear

Fruit—La fruta

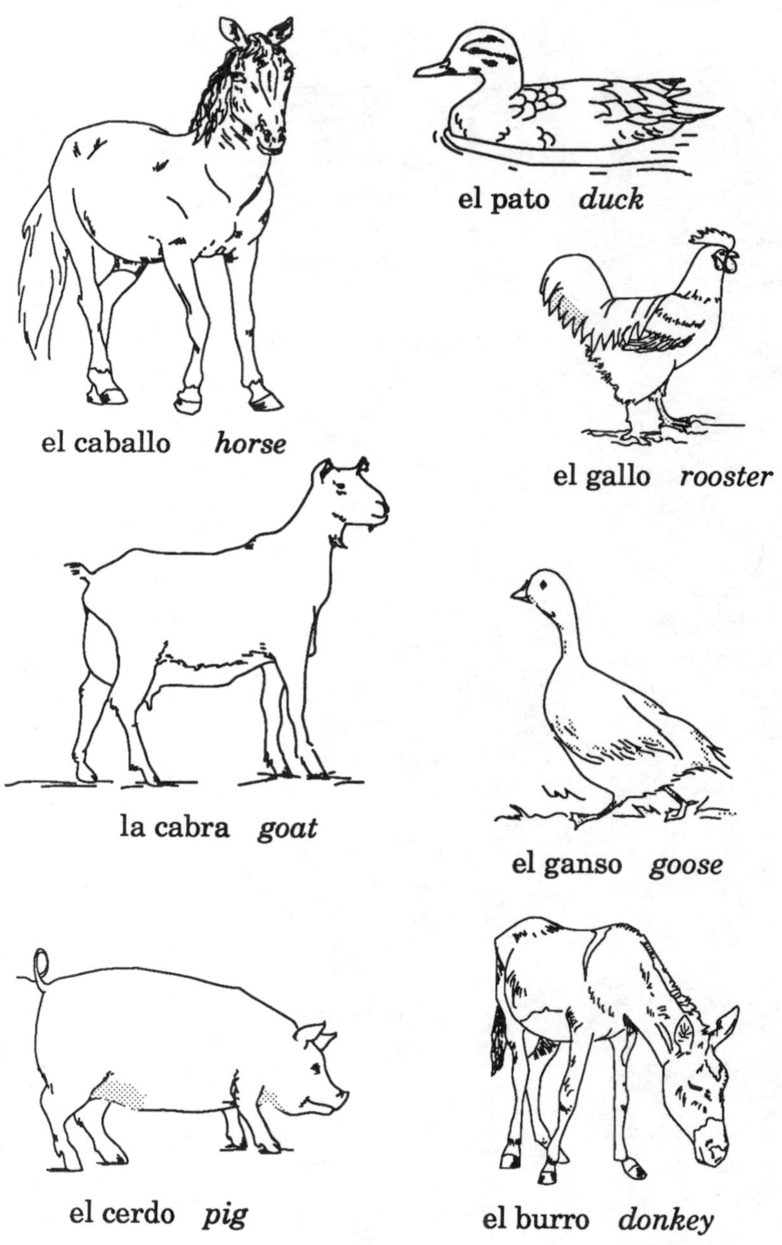

el caballo *horse*

el pato *duck*

el gallo *rooster*

la cabra *goat*

el ganso *goose*

el cerdo *pig*

el burro *donkey*

Farm animals—Animales de la granja

Birds—Las aves

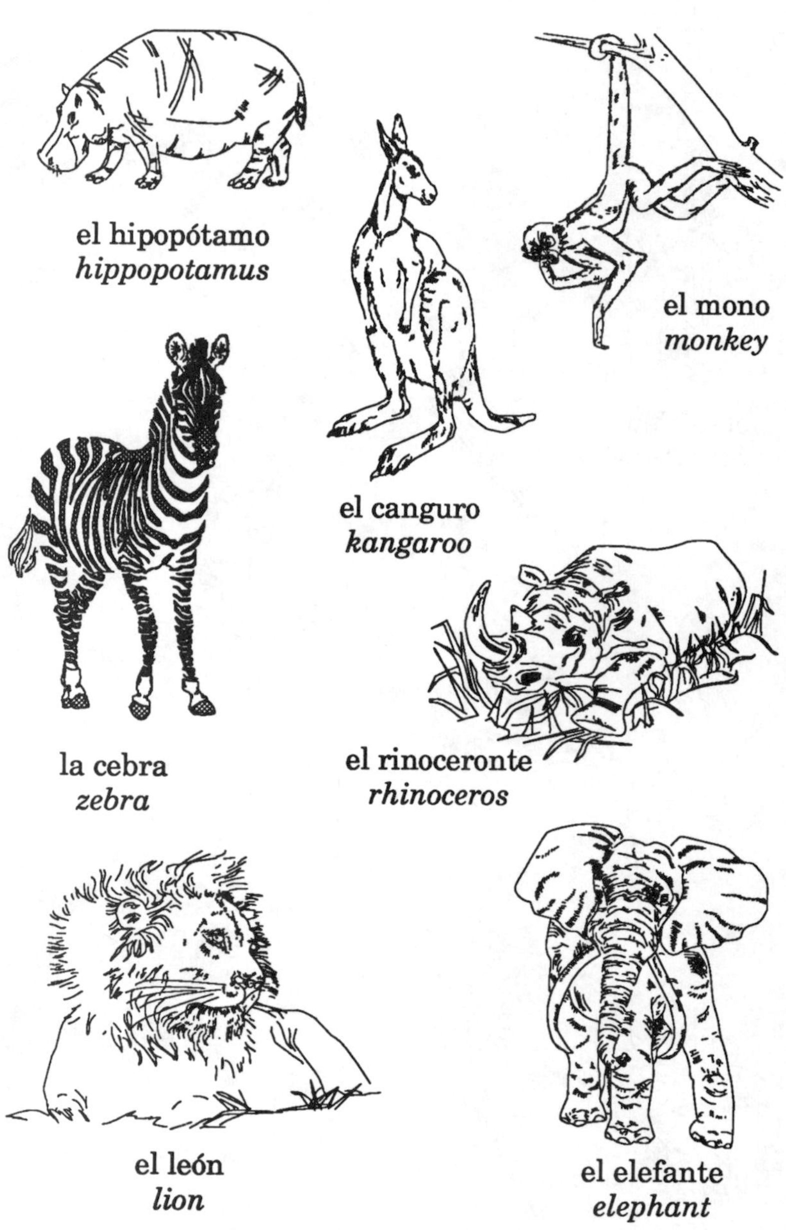

Zoo Animals—Animales del zoológico

Wild Animals—Los animales salvajes

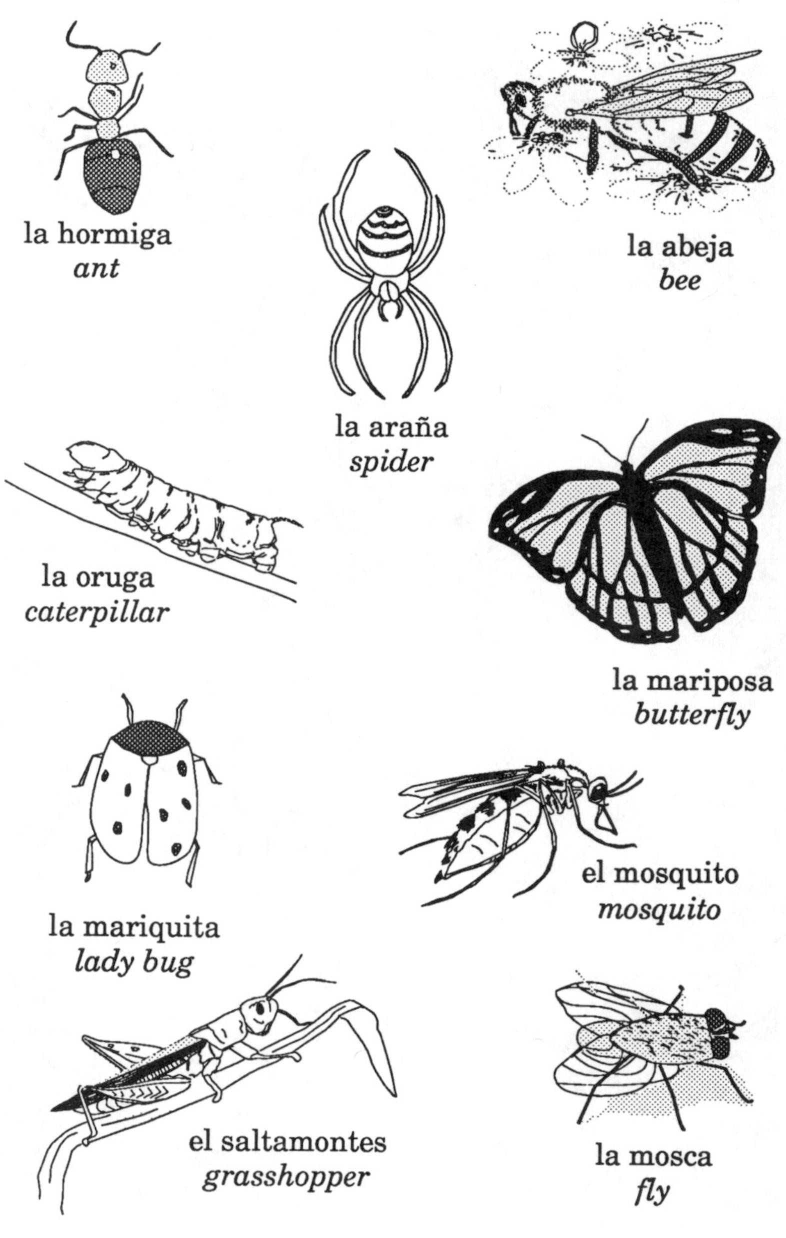

Insects—Los insectos

Pets—Animales domésticos

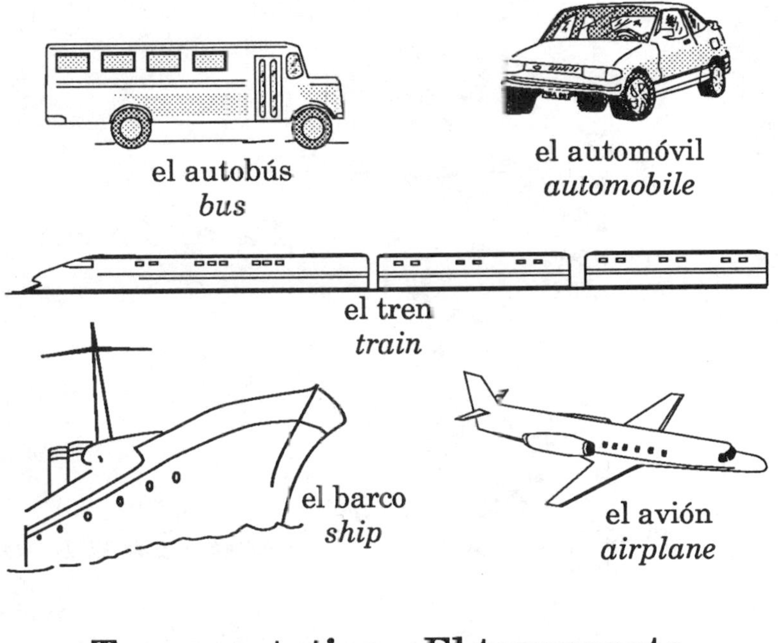

Transportation—El transporte

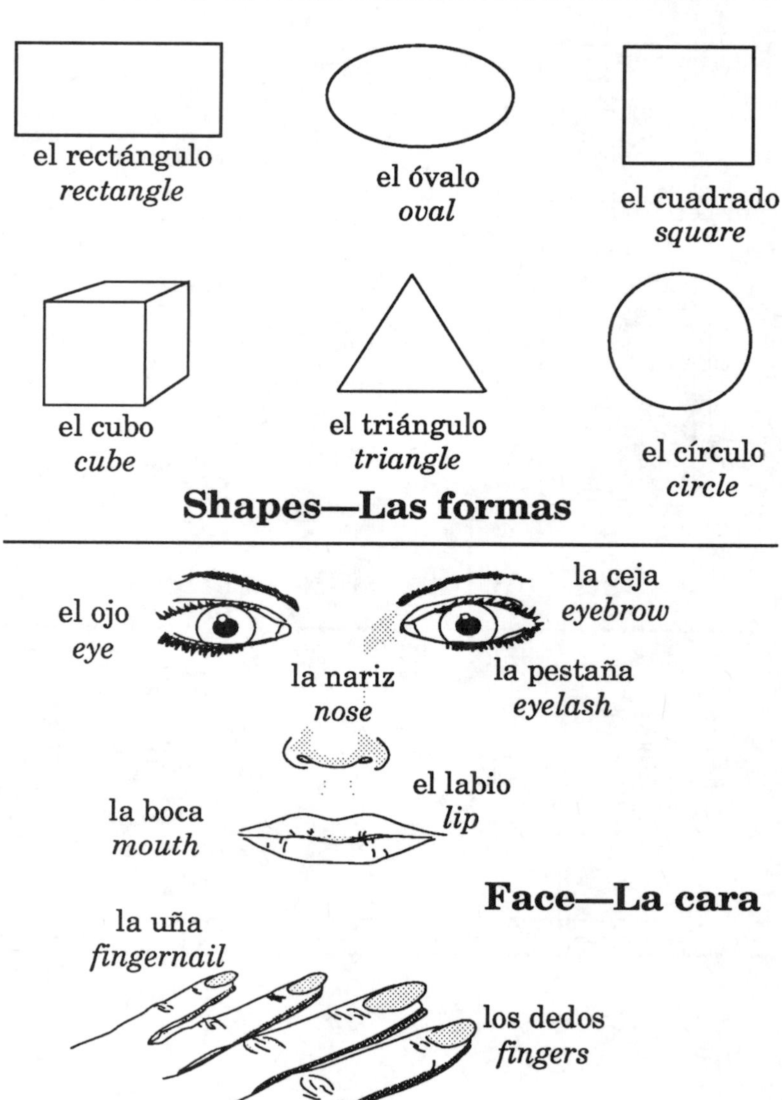

Shapes—Las formas

Face—La cara

la uña
fingernail

los dedos
fingers

el pulgar
thumb

Hand—La mano

English—Spanish/*Inglés—Español*

A

a [ä] *art.* • un, una
There is a new film at the movie theater.
Hay una nueva película en el cine.

I need to buy a notebook.
Necesito comprar un cuaderno.

abandon, to [ä BAN dän] *v.* • abandonar
abandoned *adj.* • abandonado, a
I have to abandon the project.
Tengo que abandonar el proyecto.

We found an abandoned kitten.
Encontramos un gatito abandonado.

able, to be [EIBL] *v.* • poder, ser capaz (de)
My aunts and uncles are able to come to the party.
Mis tíos pueden venir a la fiesta.

I am not able to run a marathon.
No soy capaz de correr un maratón.

about [ä BAUT] *prep.* • sobre, acerca de
I like stories about animals.
Me gustan los cuentos sobre animales.

above [ä BÄV] *adv.* • encima, arriba
prep. • encima de, sobre
above all *coll.* • sobre todo
She lives above the store.
Ella vive encima de la tienda.

Above all it is important to be honest
Sobre todo es importante ser honesto.

absent [AB sent] *adj.* • ausente
absent-minded *adj.* • distraído, a
John is absent today.
John está ausente hoy.

The teacher is absent-minded.
La maestra es distraída.

absurd [ab SËRD] *adj.* • absurdo, a
It is absurd to think of a planet without forests.
Es absurdo pensar en un planeta sin bosques.

accident [AX i dent] *n.* • accidente (el)
The ambulance arrives at the site of the accident.
La ambulancia llega al lugar del accidente.

according to [ä COR ding tu] *prep.* • según
According to Greek mythology the gods live on Mount Olympus.
Según la mitología griega los dioses viven en el monte Olimpo.

acquainted, to be [ä KWEIN ted] *v.* • conocer
The principal is acquainted with the students.
El director conoce a los estudiantes.

act, to [ACT] *v.* • actuar
We learn to act in theater class.
Aprendemos a actuar en la clase de teatro.

actor [AC tër] *n.* • actor (el)
The hero is a famous actor.
El héroe es un actor famoso.

actress [AC tres] *n.* • actriz (la)
The actress works at the theater.
La actriz trabaja en el teatro.

add, to [AD] *v.* • sumar
We do not need a calculator to add these numbers.
No necesitamos una calculadora para sumar estos números.

address, to [ä DRES] *v.* • dirigir (una carta); atender (un tema)
address *n.* • dirección (la)
The letter is addressed to me.
La carta está dirigida a mí.

My address is 2020 Main.
Mi dirección es 2020 Main.

adjective [AD gec tiv] *n.* • adjetivo (el)
An adjective describes a noun.
Un adjetivo describe un sustantivo.

admire, to [ad MAIR] *v.* • admirar
The child admires his father.
El niño admira a su papá.

adult [ä DÄLT] *n.* • adulto (el)
Adults can decide where they go on vacation.
Los adultos pueden decidir adonde van de vacaciones.

adventure [ad VEN chër] *n.* • aventura (la)
Indiana Jones has many adventures.
Indiana Jones tiene muchas aventuras.

advice [ad VAIS] *n.* • consejo (el)
Parents give advice to their children.
Los padres dan consejos a sus hijos.

advise, to [ad VAIZ] *v.* • aconsejar
Ann Landers advises her readers.
Ann Landers aconseja a sus lectores.

affection [ä FEC shän] *n.* • cariño (el)
My mother always ends her letters "With affection."
Mi mamá siempre termina sus cartas "Con cariño".

afraid, to be [ä FREID] *v.* • tener miedo, temer
I am afraid to fly.
Tengo miedo de volar.

The child is afraid of darkness.
El niño teme la oscuridad.

after [AF tër] *prep.* • después de
There is a dance after dinner.
Hay un baile después de la cena.

afternoon [af tër NUN] *n.* • tarde (la)
We study in the afternoon.
Estudiamos por la tarde.

again [ä GEN] *adv.* • otra vez
I have to take my exam again.
Tengo que tomar mi examen otra vez.

against [ä GENST] *prep.* • en contra de, contra
We should be against air pollution.
Debemos estar en contra de la contaminación del aire.

age [EIG] *n.* • edad (la)
Aunt Jane doesn't want to reveal her age.
La tía Jane no quiere revelar su edad.

agreement [ä GRI ment] *n.* • acuerdo (el)
The presidents have an agreement.
Los presidentes tienen un acuerdo.

ahead [ä JED] *adv.* • adelante
The captain always walks ahead.
El capitán siempre camina adelante.

aid, to [EID] *v.* • ayudar
aid *n.* • socorro (el), ayuda (la)
first aid *n.* • primeros auxilios (los)
The financial aid office is open.
La oficina de ayuda financiera está abierta.

air [ER] *n.* • aire (el)
air *adj.* • aéreo, a
airmail *n.* • correo aéreo (el)
airplane *n.* • avión (el), aeroplano (el)
air pollution *n.* • contaminación del aire (la)
airport *n.* • aeropuerto (el)
The letter to Spain goes airmail.
La carta a España va por correo aéreo.

The airport is close to home.
El aeropuerto está cerca de casa.

air conditioning [ER cän di shän ing] *n.* • aire acondicionado (el)
We use air conditioning in summer.
Usamos el aire acondicionado en el verano.

alarm clock [ä LARM clac] *n.* • despertador (el)
This alarm clock is electric.
Este despertador es eléctrico.

alike [ä LAIC] *adj.* • igual, parecido, a
to look like *v.* • ser parecido, a (a)
Juan looks like his father.
Juan es parecido al padre.

The colors are alike.
Los colores son parecidos.

all [OL] *adj.* • todo, a
The child wants all the cake.
El niño quiere todo el pastel.

almost [OL most] *adv.* • casi
It is almost five.
Son casi las cinco.

alone [ä LON] *adj.* • solo, a
Julia lives alone.
Julia vive sola.

along [ä LONG] *prep.* • a lo largo
The mountains extend along the coast.
Las montañas se extienden a lo largo de la costa.

aloud [ä LAUD] *adv.* • en voz alta
My grandfather reads the story aloud.
Mi abuelo lee el cuento en voz alta.

alphabet [AL fä bet] *n.* • alfabeto (el)
The Russian language is written with the Cyrillic alphabet.
El idioma ruso se escribe con el alfabeto cirílico.

already [ol REDI] *adv.* • ya
It's already time to leave.
Ya es hora para salir.

also [OL so] *adv.* • también
I also need to buy shoes and socks.
También necesito comprar zapatos y calcetines.

always [OL weis] *adv.* • siempre
The sun always rises in the east.
El sol siempre sale por el este.

ambulance [AM byu läns] *n.* • ambulancia (la)
The ambulance has a siren.
La ambulancia tiene una sirena.

American [ä ME ri cän] *adj.* • americano, a
n. • americano, a (el, la); (USA) norteamericano, a (el, la)
John is American.
John es norteamericano.

amusing [ä MYU zing] *adj.* • divertido, a
He is an amusing man.
Él es un hombre divertido.

an [AN] *art.* • un, una
An hour has sixty minutes.
Una hora tiene sesenta minutos

There is an egg in the refrigerator.
Hay un huevo en la nevera.

and [AND] *conj.* • y
We buy apples and oranges.
Compramos manzanas y naranjas.

angry [ANG gri] *adj.* • enojado, a; enfadado, a
My dad is angry with me.
Mi papá está enojado conmigo.

animal [A ni mäl] *n.* • animal (el)
We visit the farm and see the animals.
Visitamos la granja y vemos los animales.

ankle [AN cäl] *n.* • tobillo (el)
The X-rays show her ankle is all right.
Los rayos-X muestran que el tobillo está bien.

anniversary [an ni VER sä ri] *n.* • aniversario (el)
Tomorrow is our anniversary.
Mañana es nuestro aniversario.

announcer [ä NAUN ser] *n.* • locutor,a (el, la)
The announcer is bilingual.
El locutor es bilingüe.

annoy, to [ä NOY] *v.* • molestar
Mosquitoes annoy me.
Los mosquitos me molestan.

another [ä NÖTH ër] *adj.* • otro, a
Lorena is buying another book.
Lorena compra otro libro.

answer, to [AN sër] *v.* • contestar
Aunt Jane always answers her letters.
La tía Jane siempre contesta sus cartas.

ant [ANT] *n.* • hormiga (la)
Ants work hard.
Las hormigas trabajan duro.

antenna [an TE nä] *n.* • antena (la)
The TV antenna is new.
La antena de la televisión es nueva.

apartment [ä PÄRT ment] *n.* • apartamento (el)
María has an apartment in Madrid.
María tiene un apartamento en Madrid.

appearance [ä PIR äns] *n.* • apariencia (la)
Is physical appearance important?
¿Es importante la apariencia física?

appetite [A pe tait] *n.* • apetito (el)
Right now I have no appetite.
Ahora no tengo apetito.

applaud, to [ä PLOD] *v.* • aplaudir
The public applauds the actors.
El público aplaude a los actores.

apple [APL] *n.* • manzana (la)
The market sells apples in October.
El mercado vende manzanas en octubre.

apricot [AP ri cat] *n.* • albaricoque (el)
Apricots are delicious.
Los albaricoques son deliciosos.

April [EI pril] *n.* • abril
Tulips bloom in April.
Los tulipanes florecen en abril.

apron [EI prän] *n.* • delantal (el)
I use an apron in the kitchen.
Uso delantal en la cocina.

aquarium [ä KWER iäm] *n.* • acuario (el)
The restaurant has a beautiful aquarium.
El restaurante tiene un hermoso acuario.

arm [ARM] *n.* • brazo (el)
Conan has strong arms.
Conan tiene los brazos fuertes.

armchair [ARM cher] *n.* • sillón (el)
The lawyer has a leather armchair in his office.
El abogado tiene un sillón de cuero en su oficina.

army [AR mi] *n.* • ejército (el)
The U.S. has a big army.
Los Estados Unidos tiene un ejército grande.

around [ä RAUND] *prep.* • alrededor de
We're planting flowers around the patio.
Plantamos flores alrededor del patio.

arrange, to [ä REING] *v.* • arreglar
Silvia is arranging the party.
Silvia arregla la fiesta.

arrest, to [ä rest] *v.* • arrestar
The detective arrests the thief.
El detective arresta al ladrón.

arrival [ä RAI vël] *n.* • llegada (la)
The arrival of flight 893 is at 2:00 p.m.
La llegada del vuelo 893 es a las dos de la tarde.

arrive, to [ä RAIV] *v.* • llegar
The passengers arrive at gate A.
Los pasajeros llegan a la puerta A.

art [ART] *n.* • arte (el)
The art museum is downtown.
El museo de arte está en el centro.

artist [AR tist] *n.* • artista (el, la)
Leonardo da Vinci is a well-known artist.
Leonardo da Vinci es un artista bien conocido.

as [AS] *conj.* • como
as.....as *adv.* • tan....como
Do as you wish.
Haz como quieras.

The Empire State Building is not as tall as the Sears Tower.
El edificio Empire State no es tan alto como la torre Sears.

ashamed, to be [ä SHEIMD] *v.* • avergonzarse
They are ashamed of their behavior.
Ellos se avergüenzan de su comportamiento.

ask, to [ASC] *v.* • preguntar
ask for, to *v.* • pedir
We ask the price.
Preguntamos el precio.

We ask for the bill.
Pedimos la cuenta.

asleep [ä SLIP] *adj.* • dormido, a
The boss is asleep in his office.
El jefe está dormido en su oficina.

astronaut [AS tro not] *n.* • astronauta (el, la)
There are astronauts from many countries.
Hay astronautas de muchos países.

at [AT] *prep.* • en, a
We are at home.
Estamos en casa.

He is leaving at two o'clock.
El sale a las dos.

athlete [ATH lit] *n.* • atleta (el, la)
An athlete can win scholarships.
Un atleta puede ganar becas.

athletic [ath LET ic] *adj.* • atlético, a
The athletic club has 700 members.
El club atlético tiene 700 miembros.

attend, to [ä TEND] *v.* • asistir (a)
Sue attends her classes.
Sue asiste a sus clases.

attic [A tic] *n.* • ático (el)
My grandmother has an attic full of photographs.
Mi abuela tiene un ático lleno de fotografías.

auditorium [o di TO ri äm] *n.* • auditorio (el)
The debate is in the auditorium.
El debate es en el auditorio.

August [o gäst] *n.* • agosto
August is a warm month.
Agosto es un mes caluroso.

aunt [ANT] *n.* • tía (la)
Aunt Lisa lives in Spain.
La tía Lisa vive en España.

autumn [O täm] *n.* • otoño (el)
Halloween is in autumn.
La víspera de Todos los Santos es en el otoño.

avenue [A ve nu] *n.* • avenida (la)
New York's Fifth Avenue is very famous.
La Quinta Avenida de Nueva York es muy famosa.

B

baby [BEI bi] *n.* • bebé (el)
The baby plays with his toys.
El bebé juega con sus juguetes.

back [BAC] *n.* • espalda (la)
My back aches.
Me duele la espalda.

bad [BAD] *adj.* • malo, a
bad-mannered *adj.* • mal educado, a
That book is very bad.
Ese libro es muy malo.

The boy is bad-mannered.
El muchacho es mal educado.

badly [BAD li] *adv.* • mal
The child behaves badly with the babysitter.
El niño se porta mal con la niñera.

bag [BAG] *n.* • bolsa (la)
Do you need a bag for the fruit?
¿Necesitas una bolsa para la fruta?

baggage [BAG äg] *n.* • equipaje (el)
Carmen does not carry baggage on her business trip.
Carmen no lleva equipaje en su viaje de negocios.

baker [BEI kër] *n.* • panadero, a (el, la)
The baker makes delicious bread.
El panadero hace panes deliciosos.

bakery [BEI cri] *n.* • panadería (la)
There is a bakery at the supermarket.
Hay una panadería en el supermercado.

balcony [BAL cä ni] *n.* • balcón (el)
Many Spanish houses have a balcony.
Muchas casas españolas tienen balcón.

ball [BOL] *n.* • pelota (la)
The little boy has a red ball.
El niño tiene una pelota roja.

balloon [bä LUN] *n.* • globo (el)
We need lots of balloons for the party.
Necesitamos muchos globos para la fiesta.

banana [bä NA nä] *n.* • banana (la), plátano (el)
These bananas are from Honduras.
Estas bananas son de Honduras.

bank [BANC] *n.* • banco (el)
bank teller *n.* • cajero, a (el, la)
The bank teller gives me my money.
El cajero me da mi dinero.

My uncle works in a bank.
Mi tío trabaja en un banco.

baseball [BEIS bol] *n.* • béisbol (el)
Baseball is a popular sport in Puerto Rico.
El béisbol es un deporte popular en Puerto Rico.

basement [BEIS ment] *n.* • sótano (el)
The pool table is in the basement.
La mesa de billar está en el sótano.

basket [BAS ket] *n.* • canasta (la)
basketball *n.* • baloncesto (el), basquetbol (el)
We take the basket to the market.
Llevamos la canasta al mercado.

They play basketball.
Ellos juegan al baloncesto.

bath [BATH] *n.* • baño (el)
bathroom *n.* • baño (el)
bathtub *n.* • bañera (la)
bathing suit *n.* • traje de baño (el)
The bathtub is in the bathroom.
La bañera está en el baño.

We wear bathing suits at the beach.
Llevamos trajes de baño en la playa.

bathe, to [BEITH] *v.* • bañar (tran.); bañarse (intran.)
Cathy bathes after working in the garden.
Cathy se baña después de trabajar en el jardín.

We bathe the dog frequently.
Bañamos al perro frecuentemente.

be, to [BI] *v.* • ser; estar
to be acquainted • conocer (a una persona)
to be afraid • tener miedo
to be against • oponerse a, estar en contra
to be at fault • tener la culpa
to be careful • tener cuidado
to be cold • tener frío (personas); hacer frío (tiempo)
to be curious • ser curioso, a
to be happy • estar contento, a
to be hot • tener calor (personas); hacer calor (tiempo)
to be hungry • tener hambre
to be in a hurry • tener prisa, estar de prisa
to be jealous • tener celos
to be lucky • tener suerte
to be patient • tener paciencia
to be successful • tener éxito
to be thirsty • tener sed
to be tired • estar cansado, a

beach [BICH] *n.* • playa (la)
They make a sand castle at the beach.
Ellos hacen un castillo de arena en la playa.

beak [BIC] *n.* • pico (el)
The bird has a broken beak.
El pájaro tiene el pico roto.

bear [BER] *n.* • oso (el)
Black bears can be dangerous.
Los osos negros pueden ser peligrosos.

beard [BIRD] *n.* • barba (la)
Do you like Alan's beard?
Te gusta la barba de Alan?

beast [BIST] *n.* • bestia (la)
The tiger is a wild beast.
El tigre es una bestia salvaje.

beat [BIT] *n.* • ritmo (el)
beat (to have a) *v.* • tener ritmo
beat (to listen to the) *v.* • escuchar el ritmo
I like to listen to the beat.
Me gusta escuchar el ritmo.

That song has a good beat.
Esa canción tiene buen ritmo.

beautiful [BIU ti fäl] *adj.* • bello, a, hermoso, a
It is a beautiful day.
Es un día hermoso.

My mother is a beautiful woman.
Mi madre es una mujer bella.

beaver [BI vër] *n.* • castor (el)
Beavers live in the forests.
Los castores viven en el bosque.

because [bi CQZ] *conj.* • porque
because of *prep.* • a causa de
I study Spanish because I am going to Ecuador.
Estudio español porque voy al Ecuador.

The factory is closed because of the strike.
La fábrica está cerrada a causa de la huelga.

become, to [bi CÄM] *v.* • hacerse, convertirse, volverse
Paul is becoming famous.
Pablo se está haciendo famoso.

Carlos would like to become a millionaire.
A Carlos le gustaría convertirse en millonario.

bed [BED] *n.* • cama (la)
bedroom *n.* • dormitorio (el), alcoba (la)
I make my bed every morning.
Hago mi cama todas las mañanas.

bee [BI] *n.* • abeja (la)
Bees make honey.
Las abejas hacen miel.

beef [BIF] *n.* • carne de res (la)
Vegetarians do not eat beef.
Los vegetarianos no comen carne de res.

beer [BIR] *n.* • cerveza (la)
You can buy beer in the store if you are 21 years old.
Puedes comprar cerveza en la tienda si tienes 21 años.

before [bi FOR] *adv.* • antes; delante
prep. • antes de, delante de
Lorri goes to the bank before she goes to the store.
Lorri va al banco antes de ir a la tienda.

We should leave at 7, not before.
Debemos salir a las siete, no antes.

begin, to [bi GIN] *v.* • comenzar, empezar
Classes begin at 7 a.m.
Las clases empiezan a las 7 de la mañana

behave, to [bi JEIV] *v.* • portarse, comportarse
The students behave well.
Los estudiantes se portan bien.

behind [bi JAIND] *adv.* • detrás, atrás
prep. • detrás de
He is staying behind.
Él se queda detrás.

Dick sits behind Carl.
Dick se sienta detrás de Carl.

believe, to [bi LIV] *v.* • creer
Vanessa believes in a better world.
Vanessa cree en un mundo mejor.

bell [BEL] *n.* • campana (la)
doorbell *n.* • timbre (el)
The tower bell rings at noon.
La campana de la torre suena al mediodía.

The guests ring the doorbell.
Los invitados tocan el timbre.

belong, to [bi LONG] *v.* • pertenecer (a)
The yellow raincoat belongs to Dick Tracy.
El impermeable amarillo pertenece a Dick Tracy.

below [bi LO] *adv.* • *abajo, debajo*
prep. • *debajo de, bajo*
My office is downstairs.
Mi oficina está abajo.

The temperature is 5 below zero.
La temperatura es de 5 grados bajo cero.

belt [BELT] *n.* • cinturón (el)
seat belt *n.* • cinturón de seguridad (el)
The dress needs a belt.
El vestido necesita un cinturón.

best [BEST] *adj.* • (el, la) mejor
adv. • mejor
Best wishes.
Los mejores deseos.

Who is the best baseball player?
¿Quién es el mejor jugador de béisbol?

better [BE tër] *adj., adv.* • mejor
better than • mejor que
Which brand is better?
¿Cuál marca es mejor?

Do you think this movie is better than the one last week?
¿Tú crees que esta película es mejor que la de la semana pasada?

between [bi TWIN] *prep.* • entre
The situation between Jeff and Mary is not good.
La situación entre Jeff y Mary no es buena.

beverage [BEV ër äg] *n.* • bebida (la)
We bring our beverages to the party.
Traemos nuestras bebidas a la fiesta.

bicycle [BAI si cl] *n.* • bicicleta (la)
ride a bike, to *v.* • montar en bicicleta
Paul wants a cross-country bicycle.
Paul quiere una bicicleta de campo travieso.

Jim rides his bicycle to go to work.
Jim monta en su bicicleta para ir a trabajar.

big [BIG] *adj.* • grande
My apartment is not big.
Mi apartamento no es grande.

bike [BAIC] *n.* • bici (la)
Elena wants a red bike.
Elena quiere una bici roja.

bill (check) [BIL] *n.* • cuenta (la)
bill (paper) *n.* • billete (el)
The boss is paying the bill.
El jefe paga la cuenta.

There are no 2,000-dollar bills.
No hay billetes de dos mil.

binoculars [bin AC yu lërs] *n.* • prismáticos (los), binóculos (los)
We use the binoculars for bird watching.
Usamos los prismáticos para observar los pájaros.

bird (small) [BËRD] *n.* • pájaro (el)
bird (large) *n.* • ave (el) (f.)
The Blue Bird is an old movie.
El pájaro azul *es una película vieja.*

birthday [BERTH dei] *n.* • cumpleaños (el)
Happy birthday.
Feliz cumpleaños.

Teresa is preparing a birthday party for Frank.
Teresa prepara una fiesta de cumpleaños para Frank.

bite, to (with teeth) [BAIT] *v.* • morder
bite *n.* • mordisco (el)
to bite (insects, snakes) *v.* • picar
(insect) bite *n.* • picadura (la)
bite (mouthful) *n.* • bocado (el)
That dog won't bite you.
Ese perro no te muerde.

I have so many mosquito bites.
Tengo tantas picaduras de mosquito.

black [BLAC] *adj.* • negro, a
The piano is black.
El piano es negro.

blackboard [BLAC bord] *n.* • pizarra (la)
The teacher writes on the blackboard.
El maestro escribe en la pizarra.

blanket [BLAN ket] *n.* • manta (la), cobija (la)
The mother covers the baby with a blanket.
La mamá cubre al bebé con una manta.

blender [BLEND ër] *n.* • licuadora (la)
The blender is broken.
La licuadora está rota.

blind [BLAIND] *adj.* • ciego, a
n. • ciego, a (el, la)
My aunt is blind.
Mi tía está ciega.

Margarita trains dogs for the blind.
Margarita entrena perros para los ciegos.

block (street) [BLAC] *n.* • cuadra (la)
block (piece) *n.* • bloque (el)
The museum is three blocks from here.
El museo está a tres cuadras de aquí.

They are building the wall with concrete blocks.
Construyen la pared con bloques de concreto.

blond, blonde [BLAND] *adj.* • rubio, a
My cousin is blonde.
Mi prima es rubia.

blood [BLÄD] *n.* • sangre (la)
There are several blood types.
Hay varios tipos de sangre.

blouse [BLAUS] *n.* • blusa (la)
Cathy has fifty blouses in her closet.
Cathy tiene cincuenta blusas en su armario.

blow, to [BLO] *v.* • soplar
blow *n.* • golpe (el)
blow up, to (inflate) *v.* • inflar
You shouldn't blow on the soup!
¡No debes soplar en la sopa!

The accident is an emotional blow.
El accidente es un golpe emocional.

blue [BLU] *adj.* • azul
The sky is blue.
El cielo es azul.

body [BA di] *n.* • cuerpo (el)
The artist studies the human body.
El artista estudia el cuerpo humano.

book [BÜC] *n.* • libro (el)
bookcase *n.* • estante (el), estantería (la)
bookstore *n.* • librería (la)
You can buy those books at a bookstore.
Puedes comprar esos libros en una librería.

boot [BUT] *n.* • bota (la)
Rose wears boots.
Rose lleva botas.

bored, to get [BORD] *v.* • aburrirse
bored *adj.* • aburrido, a (with *estar*)
The children get bored on long trips.
Los niños se aburren durante viajes largos.

The children are bored because it's raining today.
Los niños están aburridos porque llueve hoy.

boring [BOR ing] *adj.* • aburrido, a (with *ser*)
That movie is boring.
Esa película es aburrida.

born, to be [BORN] *v.* • nacer
The baby is being born right now.
El niño nace ahora mismo.

borrow, to [BAR ro] *v.* • pedir prestado
May I borrow the book?
¿Puedo pedir prestado el libro?

boss [BOS] *n.* • jefe (el)
The boss has the big office.
El jefe tiene la oficina grande.

bottle [BATL] *n.* • botella (la)
Mr. Jones has a collection of bottles.
El señor Jones tiene una colección de botellas.

bowl [BOL] *n.* • tazón (el)
How many bowls do we need?
¿Cuántos tazones necesitamos?

bowl, to [BOL] *v.* • jugar a los bolos
bowling *n.* • bolos (los)
bowling alley *n.* • bolera (la)
We're going bowling today.
Jugamos a los bolos hoy.

box [BAX] *n.* • caja (la)
The books are in the boxes.
Los libros están en las cajas.

box, to [BAX] *v.* • boxear
boxing *n.* • boxeo (el)
The kids box at the gym.
Los muchachos boxean en el gimnasio.

The boxing championship is next week.
El campeonato de boxeo es la semana próxima.

boy (child) [BOI] *n.* • niño (el)
boy (teenager) *n.* • muchacho (el), chico (el)
That boy is a friend of my cousin.
Ese muchacho es amigo de mi primo.

boyfriend [BOI frend] *n.* • novio (el)
Her boyfriend is inviting her to a party.
Su novio la invita a una fiesta.

bracelet [BREIS let] *n.* • pulsera (la), brazalete (el)
I'm giving her a bracelet for Christmas.
Le voy a dar una pulsera para Navidad.

brakes [BREIKS] *n.* • frenos (los)
This car has good brakes.
Este carro tiene buenos frenos.

branch [BRANCH] *n.* • rama (la)
The bird is on the branch.
El pájaro está en la rama.

bread [BRED] *n.* • pan (el)
The bread comes from the bakery.
El pan viene de la panadería.

break, to [BREIC] *v.* • romper
The ball breaks the window.
La pelota rompe la ventana.

breakfast [BREC fäst] *n.* • desayuno (el)
There is orange juice and toast for breakfast.
Hay jugo de naranja y pan tostado para el desayuno.

bridge [BRIDg] *n.* • puente (el)
There are several Roman bridges in Spain.
Hay varios puentes romanos en España.

briefcase [BRIF keis] • *n.* • portafolio (el)
The manager carries his briefcase.
El gerente lleva su portafolio.

bring, to [BRING] *v.* • traer
She brings the plants to the office.
Ella trae las plantas a la oficina.

broad [BRO̱D] *adj.* • ancho, a
Juan has broad shoulders.
Juan tiene hombros anchos.

bronze [BRANZ] *n.* • bronce (el)
This sculpture is made of bronze.
Esta escultura es de bronce.

broom [BRUM] *n.* • escoba (la)
We need the broom to sweep.
Necesitamos la escoba para barrer.

brother [BRÄ thër] *n.* • hermano (el)
Ann's brother is not as tall as she is.
El hermano de Ann no es tan alto como ella.

brown [BRAUN] *adj.* • marrón, café
brown (hair) *adj.* • castaño
Where is my brown suit?
¿Dónde está mi traje marrón?

brush, to [BRUSH] *v.* • cepillarse
brush *n.* • cepillo (el)
hairbrush *n.* • cepillo (el)
toothbrush *n.* • cepillo de dientes (el)
Pauline brushes her hair every day.
Pauline se cepilla el pelo todos los días.

We carry a toothbrush on our trips.
Llevamos cepillo de dientes en nuestros viajes.

bucket [BÄC et] *n.* • cubeta (la)
He is bringing a bucket with water.
Trae una cubeta con agua.

build, to [BI̱LD] *v.* • construir
The company is building new offices.
La compañía construye nuevas oficinas.

bull [BÜL] *n.* • toro (el)
Bulls are big animals.
Los toros son animales grandes.

bump into, to • [BÄMP] *v., coll.* • encontrarse con
Miguel bumps into Juan every morning.
Miguel se encuentra con Juan cada mañana.

burglar [BËR glër] *n.* • ladrón (el)
The burglar is careful.
El ladrón es cuidadoso.

burn, to [BËRN] *v.* • quemar
They burn the trash.
Ellos queman la basura.

bus [BÄS] *n.* • autobús (el)
bus stop *n.* • parada de autobús (la)
The bus stop is in the shade.
La parada de autobús está en la sombra.

busy [BI̲ zi] *adj.* • ocupado, a
I am too busy to answer the phone.
Estoy demasiado ocupada para contestar el teléfono.

but [BÄT] *conj.* • pero
I like snow, but I do not like cold weather.
Me gusta la nieve, pero no me gusta el frío.

butcher [BÜT chër] *n.* • carnicero, a (el, la)
butcher shop *n.* • carnicería (la)
The butcher can do special cuts for you.
El carnicero puede hacer cortes especiales para ti.

butler [BÄT lër] *n.* • mayordomo (el)
The butler opens the door.
El mayordomo abre la puerta.

butter [BÄT tër] *n.* • mantequilla (la)
The butler brings the butter.
El mayordomo trae la mantequilla.

butterfly [BÄT tër flai] *n.* • mariposa (la)
Butterflies appear in the summer.
Las mariposas aparecen en el verano.

button [BÄT tän] *n.* • botón (el)
Shelly sews the buttons on the blouse.
Shelly cose los botones en la blusa.

buy, to [BAI] *v.* • comprar
My father wants to buy a new typewriter.
Mi padre quiere comprar una nueva máquina de escribir.

by (as agent, for transportation) [BAI] *prep.* • por
(for deadline) *prep.* • para
This book is written by Mark Twain.
Este libro es escrito por Mark Twain.

I prefer to travel by plane.
Prefiero viajar por avión.

He needs the book by tomorrow.
Necesita el libro para mañana.

C

cafeteria [caf e TIR iya] *n.* • cafetería (la), café (el)
We eat lunch at the cafeteria.
Comemos el almuerzo en la cafetería.

cake [KEIC] *n.* • pastel (el), torta (la)
The cake is delicious.
El pastel es delicioso.

calculator [CAL cyu lei tër] *n.* • calculadora (la)
This is a solar calculator.
Ésta es una calculadora solar.

calendar [CAL en dër] *n.* • calendario (el)
I need to write some appointments on the calendar.
Necesito anotar algunas citas en el calendario.

call, to [COL] *v.* • llamar
call *n.* • llamada (la)
called, to be (named) *v.* • llamarse
I have to call Sue.
Tengo que llamar a Sue.

Dr. Martínez has a phone call.
El Dr. Martínez tiene una llamada telefónica.

calm [CALM] *adj.* • tranquilo, a
María is a calm person.
María es una persona tranquila.

camera [CAM ër ä] *n.* • cámara (la)
I need to buy film for my camera.
Necesito comprar película para mi cámara.

camp [CAMP] *n.* • campamento (el)
The camp is next to the stream.
El campamento está junto al arroyo.

camping, to go [CAMP ing] *v.* • ir de camping
The group goes camping in the desert.
El grupo va de camping en el desierto.

can (to be able) [CAN] *v.* • poder
Can you speak Spanish?
¿Puedes hablar español?

can [CAN] *n.* • lata (la)
can opener *n.* • abrelatas (el)
canned goods *n.* • comida enlatada (la)
We need three empty cans for the project.
Necesitamos tres latas vacías para el proyecto.

candy [CAN di] *n.* • caramelo (el), dulce (el)
I have some candy for the children.
Tengo unos caramelos para los niños.

capital (city) [CAP i täl] *n.* • capital (la)
capital (money) *n.* • capital (el)
The capital of Venezuela is Caracas.
La capital de Venezuela es Caracas.

You need capital to start a new company.
Se necesita capital para empezar una empresa nueva.

car [CAR] *n.* • automóvil (el), carro (el), coche (el)
Henry has a new car.
Henry tiene un automóvil nuevo.

card [CARD] *n.* • tarjeta (la)
postcard *n.* • tarjeta postal (la)
Everybody is signing the birthday card for Sandra.
Todos firman la tarjeta de cumpleaños para Sandra.

Jon writes postcards during his trip.
Jon escribe tarjetas postales durante su viaje.

cardinal [CAR di näl] *n.* • cardenal (el)
cardinal point *n.* • punto cardinal (el)
Cardinals are red birds.
Los cardenales son pájaros rojos.

The cardinal points are north, south, east and west.
Los puntos cardinales son norte, sur, este y oeste.

care [KER] *n.* • cuidado (el)
Take care!
¡Ten cuidado!

career [cä RIR] *n.* • carrera (la), profesión (la)
Juanita has an interesting career.
Juanita tiene una carrera interesante.

careful [KER fäl] *adj.* • cuidadoso, a; prudente
Careful! *intj.* • ¡Cuidado!
Careful! The pot is hot!
¡Cuidado! ¡La olla está caliente!

The boy is very careful.
El muchacho es muy cuidadoso.

carefully [KER fäl li] *adv.* • cuidadosamente
The mother picks up the baby carefully.
La mamá levanta al bebé cuidadosamente.

careless [KER les] *adj.* • descuidado, a
The burglar is careless.
El ladrón es descuidado.

carpenter [CAR pen tër] *n.* • carpintero (el)
The carpenter does not have much work during winter.
El carpintero no tiene mucho trabajo durante el invierno.

carrot [CAR rät] *n.* • zanahoria (la)
The bunny eats the carrots.
El conejo come las zanahorias.

carry, to [CAR ri] *v.* • llevar
The student carries her books.
La estudiante lleva sus libros.

cassette [cä SET] *n.* • casete (la)
This cassette is of very good quality.
Esta casete es de muy buena calidad.

castle [CA̲S säl] *n.* • castillo (el)
The castle has several towers.
El castillo tiene varias torres.

cat [CA̲T] *n.* • gato, a (el, la)
My cat has seven kittens.
Mi gata tiene siete gatitos.

catch, to [KA̲CH] *v.* • capturar; coger
The police caught the thieves.
La policía capturó a los ladrones.

I always catch the bus at 8.
Siempro cojo el autobús a las 8.

ceiling [SIL i̲ng] *n.* • techo (el)
The ceiling is white.
El techo es blanco.

The lamp hangs from the ceiling.
La lámpara cuelga del techo.

celery [SEL ëri] *n.* • apio (el)
There is celery at the market.
Hay apio en el mercado.

cellar [SEL ër] *n.* • bodega (la)
basement *n.* • sótano (el)
The wines are in the cellar.
Los vinos están en la bodega.

My toys are in the basement now.
Mis juguetes están en el sótano ahora.

cereal [SIR i äl] *n.* • cereal (el)
My mother brings cereal from the supermarket.
Mi madre trae cereal del supermercado.

certain [SËR tän] *adj.* • seguro, a
I'm certain he's coming tomorrow.
Estoy segura que viene mañana.

chair [CHER] *n.* • silla (la)
That table has six chairs.
Esa mesa tiene seis sillas.

chalk [CHO̲LK] *n.* • tiza (la)
That chalk produces lots of dust.
Esa tiza produce mucho polvo.

change, to [CHEINg̲] *v.* • cambiar
change *n.* • cambio (el)
The teacher is changing our seats.
La maestra cambia nuestros asientos.

I have a ten dollar bill. Do you have change?
Tengo un billete de diez. ¿Tienes cambio?

cheap [CHIP] *adj.* • barato, a
Tomatoes are cheap in summer.
Los tomates son baratos en el verano.

check, to [CHEK] *v.* • (mechanical) revisar; (to make a mark) chequear
Please check the brakes of the car.
Por favor, revise los frenos del automóvil.

The teacher checks the homework.
La maestra chequea la tarea.

check [CHEK] *n.* • cheque (el)
check (bill) *n.* • cuenta (la)
Can I pay with a check?
¿Puedo pagar con cheque?

Waiter, will you please bring us the check?
Camarero, ¿nos trae la cuenta por favor?

cheek [CHIK] *n.* • mejilla (la)
My parents dance cheek to cheek.
Mis padres bailan mejilla a mejilla.

cheerful [CHIR fäl] *adj.* • alegre
I need to read something cheerful.
Necesito leer algo alegre.

cheese [CHIZ] *n.* • queso (el)
Pizza without cheese?
¿Pizza sin queso?

chef [CHEF] *n.* • jefe de cocina (el)
The new chef wants to change the menu.
El nuevo jefe de cocina quiere cambiar el menú.

cherry [CHE ri] *n.* • cereza (la)
Fresh cherries are delicious.
Las cerezas frescas son deliciosas.

chess [CHES] *n.* • ajedrez (el)
Chess is an ancient game.
El ajedrez es un juego antiguo.

chest (body) [CHEST] *n.* • pecho (el)
chest (trunk) *n.* • baúl (el)
The general wears his medals on his chest.
El general lleva sus medallas en el pecho.

The blankets are in the chest.
Las mantas están en el baúl.

chicken [CHI ken] *n.* • pollo (el)
We frequently eat chicken.
Comemos pollo frecuentemente.

child [CHAILD] *n.* • niño, a (el, la)
childhood *n.* • niñez (la)
The children want to play now.
Los niños quieren jugar ahora.

Can you remember your childhood?
¿Puedes recordar tu niñez?

chimney [CHIM ni] *n.* • chimenea (la)
The cabin has a chimney.
La cabaña tiene una chimenea.

chin [CHIN] *n.* • barbilla (la)
His beard covers his chin.
Su barba cubre la barbilla.

chocolate [CHOC ä lät] *n.* • chocolate (el)
I like chocolate.
Me gusta el chocolate.

choose, to [CHUZ] *v.* • escoger
Consuelo chooses the red shoes.
Consuelo escoge los zapatos rojos.

church [CHËRCH] *n.* • iglesia (la)
We pray in the church.
Rezamos en la iglesia.

cigar [si GAR] *n.* • cigarro (el)
cigarette *n.* • cigarrillo (el)
That store sells cigarettes.
Esa tienda vende cigarrillos.

circle [SËR cl] *n.* • círculo (el)
A circle is a geometric figure.
El círculo es una figura geométrica.

circus [SËR cäs] *n.* • circo (el)
The clowns come with the circus.
Los payasos vienen con el circo.

city [SI ti] *n.* • ciudad (la)
The city has three museums.
La ciudad tiene tres museos.

city hall [SI ti jol] *n.* • ayuntamiento (el)
The city hall is downtown.
El ayuntamiento está en el centro de la ciudad.

clap, to [CLAP] *v.* • aplaudir
We clap with enthusiasm.
Aplaudimos con entusiasmo.

clarinet [CLER i net] *n.* • clarinete (el)
Lisa plays the clarinet in the school band
Lisa toca el clarinete en la banda de la escuela.

class [CLAS] *n.* • clase (la)
class (graduation year) *n.* • promoción (la)
Astronomy class is very interesting.
La clase de astronomía es muy interesante.

The class of '69 gave a plaque to the school.
La promoción del '69 dio una placa a la escuela.

classmate [CLAS meit] *n.* • compañero, a de clase (el, la)
My classmate lends me her notes.
Mi compañera de clase me presta sus notas.

classroom [CLAS rum] *n.* • sala de clase (la)
The students are in the classroom.
Los estudiantes están en la sala de clase.

clean, to [CLIN] *v.* • limpiar
clean *adj.* • limpio, a
My father cleans the kitchen.
Mi papá limpia la cocina.

Is this shirt clean?
¿Está limpia esta camisa?

clear [CLÏR] *adj.* • claro, a
The sound of her voice is very clear.
El sonido de su voz es muy claro.

clever [CLE ver] *adj.* • listo, a; inteligente,
The students in that class are very clever.
Los estudiantes en esa clase son muy listos.

climb, to (a mountain, a cliff) [CLAIM] *v.* • escalar
climb, to (a ladder, a building) *v.* • ascender, subir
The expedition climbs the mountain.
La expedición escala la montaña.

The cat climbs the ladder easily.
El gato sube la escalera fácilmente.

clock [CLAC] *n.* • reloj (el)
There is a clock in the kitchen.
Hay un reloj en la cocina.

close, to [CLOZ] *v.* • cerrar
She closes the door.
Ella cierra la puerta.

close to [CLOZ] *prep.* • cerca de
The school is close to the movie theater.
La escuela está cerca del cine.

closed [CLOZD] *adj.* • cerrado, a
The doors are closed.
Las puertas están cerradas.

closet [CLA zet] *n.* • armario (el), ropero (el)
This house has ten closets.
Esta casa tiene diez armarios.

clothes [CLOZ] *n.* • ropa (la)
  clothes store *n.* • tienda de ropa (la)
My winter clothes are in the closet.
Mi ropa de invierno está en el armario.

The clothes store is closed.
La tienda de ropa está cerrada.

cloud [CLAUD] *n.* • nube (la)
The clouds cover the sun.
Las nubes cubren el sol.

cloudy [CLAU di] *adj.* • nublado, a
The sky is cloudy today.
El cielo está nublado hoy.

clown [CLAUN] *n.* • payaso, a (el, la)
I have more than 100 clowns in my collection.
Tengo más de cien payasos en mi colección.

coat [COT] *n.* • abrigo (el)
A wool coat is expensive.
Un abrigo de lana es caro.

cod [CAD] *n.* • bacalao (el)
My mother cooks cod for Christmas.
Mi mamá cocina bacalao para la Navidad.

coffee [CO fi] *n.* • café (el)
This coffee is cold.
Este café está frío.

coin [COYN] *n.* • moneda (la)
Juan collects antique coins.
Juan colecciona monedas antiguas.

cold [COLD] *adj.* • frío, a
The beer is cold.
La cerveza está fría.

cold (weather) [COLD] *n.* • frío (el)
cold (sickness) *n.* • resfriado (el)
to have a cold *v.* • estar resfriado, a
Michigan has very cold winters.
Michigan tiene los inviernos muy fríos.

I do not go out because I have a cold.
No salgo porque estoy resfriado.

collect, to [cäl LECT] *v.* • coleccionar
to collect (pick up) *v.* • recoger
Michelle collects stamps.
Michelle colecciona estampillas.

The city collects the trash on Sunday.
La ciudad recoge la basura los domingos.

collection [cäl LEC shän] *n.* • colección (la)
That museum has a large collection of pottery.
Ese museo tiene una colección grande de cerámica.

color [CÄ lër] *n.* • color (el)
Red is my favorite color.
El rojo es mi color favorito.

color, to [CÄ lër] *v.* • colorear, pintar
The children color their drawings.
Los niños colorean sus dibujos.

comb, to [COM] *v.* • peinarse
comb *n.* • peine (el)
The boy combs his hair.
El niño se peina.

The comb is on the dresser.
El peine está en la cómoda.

come, to [CÄM] *v.* • venir
to come across • encontrarse con
to come again • volver
to come back • regresar
to come between • interponerse entre
to come down • bajar
to come down with • caer enfermo, a con
to come in • entrar
to come up • subir
to come up with • proponer
His brother comes to the party.
Su hermano viene a la fiesta.

comfortable [CÄM fër tä bl] *adj.* • cómodo, a
The bed is comfortable.
La cama es cómoda.

compact disc [CAM pact disc] n. • disco compacto (el)
That album comes only as a compact disc.
Ese álbum viene sólo como disco compacto.

company [CÄM pä ni] *n.* • compañía (la)
That company manufactures toys.
Esa compañía fabrica juguetes.

complain, to [cäm PLEIN] *v.* • quejarse
The customer complains about a bad product.
El cliente se queja de un producto malo.

complete [cäm PLIT] *adj.* • completo, a
How much is the complete set?
¿Cuánto cuesta el juego completo?

computer [cäm PYU tër] *n.* • computadora (la), ordenador (el) (Spain)
My aunt sells computers.
Mi tía vende computadoras.

concert [CAN sërt] *n.* • concierto (el)
Do you want to go to the concert with me?
¿Quieres ir al concierto conmigo?

conductor (music) [cän DÄC tër] *n.* • director, a (el, la)
conductor (vehicle) n. • conductor, a (el, la)
Emilio Ruiz is the symphony conductor.
Emilio Ruiz es el director de la sinfónica.

The conductor announces the stops.
El conductor anuncia las paradas.

confused [cän FYUZD] *adj.* • confuso, a
Are you confused?
¿Estás confuso?

continue, to [cän TI̲N yu] *v.* • continuar
We can continue the project tomorrow.
Podemos continuar el proyecto mañana.

cook, to [CÜC] *v.* • cocinar
cook *n.* • cocinero, a (el, la)
Do you like to cook?
¿Te gusta cocinar?

My mom is a good cook.
Mi mamá es buena cocinera.

cookie [CÜ ci] *n.* • galleta (la)
Where is the cookie jar?
¿Dónde está el jarro de galletas?

cool [CUL] *adj.* • fresco, a
The water is cool.
El agua está fresca.

copy, to [CA pi] *v.* • copiar
The secretary copies the documents.
El secretario copia los documentos.

corn [CORN] *n.* • maíz (el)
We eat corn with butter.
Comemos maíz con mantequilla.

corner [CORN ër] *n.* • esquina (la)
Marisa is waiting for us on the corner.
Marisa nos espera en la esquina.

correct [co RECT] *adj.* • correcto, a
We need thirty correct answers to pass the test.
Necesitamos treinta respuestas correctas para aprobar el examen.

correct, to [co RECT] *v.* • corregir
The teacher corrects the tests.
El maestro corrige los exámenes.

cost, to [CQST] *v.* • costar
How much do these boots cost?
¿Cuánto cuestan estas botas?

costume [CAS tum] *n.* • disfraz (el)
I need a costume for Elena's party.
Necesito un disfraz para la fiesta de Elena.

cotton [CA tän] *n.* • algodón (el)
This fabric is cotton.
Esta tela es de algodón.

couch [CAUCH] *n.* • sofá (el)
The couch is comfortable.
El sofá es cómodo.

cough [CQF] *n.* • tos (la)
cough medicine *n.* • medicina para la tos (la)
Dorothy has a horrible cough.
Dorothy tiene una tos horrible.

count, to [CAUNT] *v.* • contar
Do you know how to count in Spanish?
¿Sabes contar en español?

country [CÄN tri] *n.* • país (el)
countryside *n.* • campo (el)
They want to travel through the countries of Central America.
Quieren viajar por los países de Centroamérica.

They like to spend their vacations in the country.
Les gusta pasar sus vacaciones en el campo.

courageous [Kë REI gäs] *adj.* • valiente
She is a courageous woman.
Ella es una mujer valiente.

cousin [CÄ sän] *n.* • primo, a (el, la)
My cousins live in Mexico.
Mis primos viven en México.

cover, to [CÄ vër] *v.* • cubrir
covered *adj.* • cubierto, a
The tablecloth does not cover the table; it's too small.
El mantel no cubre la mesa; es demasiado pequeño.

The bed is covered with a blanket
La cama está cubierta con una manta.

cow [CAU] *n.* • vaca (la)
Cows live on farms.
Las vacas viven en granjas.

cradle [CREI däl] *n.* • cuna (la)
The baby sleeps in the cradle.
El bebé duerme en la cuna.

crayon [CREI on] *n.* • creyón (el)
I need a red crayon.
Necesito un creyón rojo.

crazy [CREI zi] *adj.* • loco, a
crazy about • loco, a por
It's a crazy idea!
¡Es una idea loca!

He is crazy about her.
Él está loco por ella.

cream [CRIM] *n.* • crema (la)
There are strawberries with cream for dessert.
Hay fresas con crema para postre.

criticize, to [cri ti SAIZ] *v.* • criticar
He criticizes everybody.
Él critica a todos.

cross, to [CROS] *v.* • cruzar, atravesar
The children cross the street at the corner.
Los niños cruzan la calle en la esquina.

The boat crosses the river.
La lancha atraviesa el río.

cry, to [CRAI] *v.* • llorar
The baby cries loudly.
El bebé llora fuerte.

cucumber [CU cäm bër] *n.* • pepino (el)
There are cucumbers at the market.
Hay pepinos en el mercado.

cup [CÄP] *n.* • taza (la)
cupboard *n.* • aparador (el)
The cups are in the cupboard.
Las tazas están en el aparador.

curious [CYUR i äs] *adj.* • curioso, a
curious (unique, odd) *adj.* • raro
The cat is curious and playful
El gato es curioso y juguetón.

His behavior is very odd.
Su comportamiento es muy raro.

curly [KËR li] *adj.* • rizado, a
She wants a wig with curly hair.
Ella quiere una peluca con el pelo rizado.

curtain [KËR tän] *n.* • cortina (la)
Martha is making new curtains for her house.
Martha hace cortinas nuevas para su casa.

cut, to [KÄT] *v.* • cortar
Michael cuts his birthday cake.
Michael corta su pastel de cumpleaños.

cute [CYUT] *adj.* • gracioso, a; simpático, a
The baby is cute.
El bebé es gracioso.

cutlet [KÄT let] *n.* • chuleta (la)
She never eats veal cutlets.
Ella nunca come chuleta de ternera.

D

dad [DAD] *n.* • papá (el)
Peter's dad works at the factory.
El papá de Peter trabaja en la fábrica.

daily [DEI li] *adv.* • diariamente
daily *adj.* • diario, a
I call my grandmother daily.
Llamo a mi abuela diariamente.

She has a daily routine.
Tiene una rutina diaria.

dairy product [DA ri PRA däct] *n.* • producto lácteo (el)
dairy (store) *n.* • lechería (la)
I can't eat dairy products.
No puedo comer productos lácteos

Do you need anything from the dairy?
¿Necesitas algo de la lechería?

daisy [DEI si] *n.* • margarita (la)
The daisies are for my mother.
Las margaritas son para mi mamá.

damp [DAMP] *adj.* • húmedo, a
The cellar is damp.
La bodega es húmeda.

dance, to [DANS] *v.* • bailar
dance *n.* • baile (el)
Shall we dance?
¿Bailamos?

The dance begins at eight.
El baile empieza a las ocho.

dancer [DAN sër] *n.* • bailarín (el); bailarina (la)
That dancer practices eight hours a day.
Esa bailarina practica ocho horas al día.

danger [DEIN gër] *n.* • peligro (el)
Many animals are in danger of extinction.
Muchos animales están en peligro de extinción.

dangerous [DEIN ge räs] *adj.* • peligroso, a
What is the most dangerous sport?
¿Cuál es el deporte más peligroso?

dare, to [DER] *v.* • atreverse
She doesn't dare climb that mountain.
Ella no se atreve a escalar esa montaña.

dark [DARC] *adj.* • oscuro, a
She likes to wear dark colors.
A ella le gusta usar colores oscuros.

darling [DAR ling] *adj.* • encantador, a; precioso, a
The puppy is darling.
El cachorro es encantador.

date [DEIT] *n.* • cita (la); fecha (la)
They have a date tonight.
Ellos tienen una cita esta noche.

What is today's date?
¿Cuál es la fecha hoy?

dear [DIR] *adj.* • querido, a
She is our dear friend.
Es nuestra querida amiga.

deceive, to [di SIV] *v.* • engañar
The student does not deceive the professor.
El estudiante no engaña al profesor.

December [di SEM bër] *n.* • diciembre
December is the last month of the year.
Diciembre es el último mes del año.

decorate, to [de co REIT] *v.* • decorar
They want to decorate in an Arabic style.
Ellos quieren decorar en un estilo árabe.

deep [DIP] *adj.* • hondo, a; profundo, a
That well is not very deep.
Ese pozo no es muy hondo.

deer [DIR] *n.* • venado (el)
The deer runs in the forest.
El venado corre en el bosque.

delicious [di LI shäs] *adj.* • delicioso, a
The cake is delicious.
El pastel es delicioso.

delight, to [di LAIT] *v.* • encantar
delighted [di LAIT ed] *adj.* • encantado, a
I am delighted to be here.
Me encanta estar aquí.

They are delighted with the baby.
Están encantados con el bebé.

dentist [DEN tist] *n.* • dentista (el, la)
The dentist is very friendly.
El dentista es muy amable.

department store [di PART ment stor] *n.* • almacén (el)
There are several department stores downtown.
Hay varios almacenes en el centro.

departure [di PART chër] *n.* • salida (la)
The departure is at 5:30.
La salida es a las 5:30.

desk [DESC] *n.* • escritorio (el)
I need a larger desk.
Necesito un escritorio más grande.

dessert [de ZËRT] *n.* • postre (el)
Fruit is a healthy dessert.
La fruta es un postre sano.

detest, to [di TEST] *v.* • detestar, odiar
She detests spinach soup.
Ella detesta la sopa de espinacas.

dictionary [DI̱C shän er i] *n.* • diccionario (el)
The dictionary is at the library.
El diccionario está en la biblioteca.

different [DI̱F rent] *adj.* • diferente
These books are different.
Estos libros son diferentes.

difficult [DI̱ fi cält] *adj.* • difícil
The lesson is very difficult.
La lección es muy difícil.

dining room [DAIN i̱ng RUM] *n.* • comedor (el)
We're eating in the dining room.
Comemos en el comedor.

dinner [DI̱ nër] *n.* • comida (la), cena (la)
There is meat for dinner.
Hay carne para la cena.

direct, to [dër ECT] *v.* • dirigir
direct *adj.* • directo, a
She directs the school choir.
Ella dirige el coro de la escuela.

It is a direct flight.
Es un vuelo directo.

dirty [DËR ti] *adj.* • sucio, a
They are dirty after working in the shop.
Están sucios después de trabajar en el taller.

dish [DI̱SH] *n.* • plato (el)
dishwasher *n.* • lavaplatos (el)
Elena puts the dishes in the dishwasher.
Elena pone los platos en el lavaplatos.

do, to [DU] *v.* • hacer
They like to do the housework on the weekends.
Les gusta hacer los quehaceres los fines de semana.

doctor (medical) [DAC tër] *n.* • médico, a (el, la)
doctor (Ph. D.) *n.* • doctor, a (el, la)
Juan is going to the doctor because he is sick.
Juan va al médico porque está enfermo.

My psychology professor is Dr. García.
Mi profesor de psicología es el doctor García.

dog [DO̲G] *n.* • perro, a (el, la)
The dog is very playful.
El perro es muy juguetón.

doll [DAL] *n.* • muñeca (la)
dollhouse *n.* • casa de muñecas (la)
The girl plays with her doll.
La niña juega con su muñeca.

dollar [DAL ër] *n.* • dólar (el)
I change my dollars at the border.
Cambio mis dólares en la frontera.

done [DÄN] *adj.* • hecho, a
well done! *intj.* • ¡bien hecho!
Everything is done.
Todo está hecho.

My father says, "Well done!" when I get good grades.
Mi padre dice —— ¡bien hecho! —— cuando saco buenas notas.

donkey [DO̲N ki] *n.* • burro, a (el, la)
The donkey is not very smart.
El burro no es muy inteligente.

door [DOR] *n.* • puerta (la)
doorbell *n.* • timbre (el)
doorknob *n.* • perilla (la)
The doorbell is on the side of the door.
El timbre está al lado de la puerta.

The doorknob is broken.
La perilla está rota.

downtown [DAUN taun] *n.* • centro (el), centro de la ciudad (el)
There are many stores downtown.
Hay muchas tiendas en el centro.

dozen [DÄ zen] *n.* • docena (la)
A dozen roses are expensive during winter.
Una docena de rosas es cara durante el invierno.

drag, to [DRA̲G] *v.* • arrastrar
The baby drags the blanket.
El bebé arrastra la manta.

draw, to [DRO̲] *v.* • dibujar
He likes to draw.
A él le gusta dibujar.

drawer [DRO̲ ër] *n.* • cajón (el)
I keep my magazines in this drawer.
Guardo mis revistas en este cajón.

dream, to [DRIM] *v.* • soñar
dream about, to *v.* • soñar con
They say we dream every night.
Dicen que soñamos todas las noches.

I dream about winning the lottery.
Sueño con ganar la lotería.

dress, to [DRES] v. • vestir
to get dressed v. • vestirse
The mother dresses the baby.
La madre viste al bebé.

Miguel gets dressed in five minutes
Miguel se viste en cinco minutos.

dress [DRES] *n.* • vestido (el)
She buys a new dress.
Ella compra un vestido nuevo.

dresser [DRES ër] *n.* • tocador (el), cómoda (la)
The dresser is full.
El tocador está lleno.

drink, to [DRINC] *v.* • beber
She drinks eight glasses of water a day.
Ella bebe ocho vasos de agua al día.

drive, to [DRAIV] *v.* • manejar
driver *n.* • chofer (el), conductor, a (el, la)
The driver doesn't like to drive in the snow.
Al chofer no le gusta manejar en la nieve.

drugstore [DRÄG stor] *n.* • farmacia (la)
The drugstore is open twenty-four hours a day.
La farmacia está abierta veinticuatro horas al día.

drum [DRÄM] *n.* • tambor (el)
Richard plays the drum.
Richard toca el tambor.

dry, to [DRAI] *v.* • secar
dry *adj.* • seco, a
Please dry the fruit.
Por favor seca la fruta.

The towel is dry now.
La toalla está seca ahora.

during [DËR ing] *prep.* • durante
They sing during the party.
Ellos cantan durante la fiesta.

E

each [ICH] *adj.* • cada
each one *pron.* • cada uno
Each player plays once.
Cada jugador juega una vez.

Each one plays only once.
Cada uno juega sólo una vez.

ear [IR] *n.* • oreja (la)
Rabbits have big ears.
Los conejos tienen las orejas grandes.

early [ËR li] *adv.* • temprano
They always arrive early.
Siempre llegan temprano.

earn, to [ËRN] *v.* • ganar
He earns a lot of money at his job.
Él gana mucho dinero en su trabajo.

earth [ËRTH] *n.* • tierra (la)
Miguel is planting the seeds in the earth.
Miguel siembra las semillas en la tierra.

easily [I zi li] *adv.* • fácilmente
She learns dancing easily.
Ella aprende a bailar fácilmente.

east [IST] *n.* • este (el)
Georgia is east of Alabama.
Georgia está al este de Alabama.

easy [I zi] *adj.* • fácil
This lesson is easy.
Esta lección es fácil.

eat, to [IT] *v.* • comer
They like to eat Indian food.
Les gusta comer comida india.

egg [EG] *n.* • huevo (el)
She does not like eggs for breakfast.
A ella no le gustan los huevos para el desayuno.

elbow [EL bo] *n.* • codo (el)
Her elbow is better now.
El codo está mejor ahora.

electric [e LEC tric] *adj.* • eléctrico, a
electric stove *n.* • estufa eléctrica (la)
electric train *n.* • tren eléctrico (el)
electrician *n.* • electricista (el, la)
The electrician fixes the electric stove.
El electricista compone la estufa eléctrica.

The typewriter is not electric.
La máquina de escribir no es eléctrica.

elephant [EL ä fänt] *n.* • elefante (el)
The elephant likes peanuts.
Al elefante le gustan los cacahuates.

empty [EM ti] *adj.* • vacío, a
The theater is empty today.
El teatro está vacío hoy.

end [END] *n.* • fin (el)
The end of the book is very romantic.
El fin del libro es muy romántico.

engineer [en gi NIR] *n.* • ingeniero, a (el, la)
The engineer is here.
El ingeniero está aquí.

enough [i NÄF] *adj.* • bastante, suficiente
adv. • suficientemente, bastante
Is there enough fruit?
¿Hay bastante fruta?

Are you eating enough?
¿Comes suficientemente?

enter, to [EN tër] *v.* • entrar (en)
They enter the restaurant.
Entran en el restaurante.

envelope [AN ve lop] *n.* • sobre (el)
The envelopes need stamps.
Los sobres necesitan estampillas.

equal [I kwäl] *adj.* • igual
The recipe asks for equal amounts of milk and sugar.
La receta pide cantidades iguales de leche y azúcar.

erase, to [i REIS] *v.* • borrar
eraser *n.* • borrador (el)
Please erase the board.
Por favor borra la pizarra.

The eraser is in that box.
El borrador está en esa caja.

error [E rër] *n.* • error (el)
I think there is an error.
Creo que hay un error.

especially [es PE shäl li] *adv.* • especialmente
I like coffee, especially when I am tired.
Me gusta el café, especialmente cuando estoy cansado.

even [I ven] *adv.* • aun, hasta
not even *adv.* • ni siquiera
Even he knows it.
Aun él lo sabe.

They do not even know I am here.
Ni siquiera saben que estoy aquí.

evening [IV ning] *n.* • noche (la)
The evening is quiet.
La noche es tranquila.

every [EV ri] *adj.* • cada
everybody *pron.* • todo el mundo
everywhere *adv.* • en todas partes
I put every book in its place.
Pongo cada libro en su lugar.

Everybody is coming to the party.
Todo el mundo viene a la fiesta.

There is snow everywhere.
Hay nieve en todas partes.

exam [ex AM] *n.* • examen (el)
When is the math exam?
¿Cuándo es el examen de matemáticas?

excellent [EX ä länt] *adj.* • excelente
The book is excellent.
El libro es excelente.

excuse me [ex CYUZ mi] *coll.* • discúlpeme, perdón (to ask forgiveness or to get someone's attention); con permiso (to request permission to pass by)
Excuse me, what time is it?
Discúlpeme, ¿qué hora es?

Excuse me, I need to get through.
Con permiso, necesito pasar.

expensive [ex PEN siv] *adj.* • caro, a
They think the car is too expensive.
Ellos piensan que el automóvil es demasiado caro.

explain, to [ex PLEIN] *v.* • explicar
She explains the lesson to me.
Ella me explica la lección.

extraordinary [ex TROR di na ri] *adj.* • extraordinario, a
She has an extraordinary collection of pottery.
Ella tiene una colección extraordinaria de cerámica.

eye [AI] *n.* • ojo (el)
She has beautiful green eyes.
Ella tiene hermosos ojos verdes.

F

face, to [FEIS] *v.* • estar frente a
face *n.* • cara (la)
The theater faces the park.
El teatro está frente al parque.

She has a beautiful face.
Ella tiene una cara hermosa.

factory [FAC tä ri] *n.* • fábrica (la)
The factory has eight hundred workers.
La fábrica tiene ochocientos empleados.

fair [FER] *n.* • feria (la)
fair *adj.* • justo, a
The county fair is in June.
La feria del distrito es en junio.

They think it is fair.
Ellos creen que es justo.

fairy [FER i] *n.* • hada (el) (f.)
fairy godmother *n.* • hada madrina (el) (f.)
What is the fairy's name in the tale?
¿Cómo se llama el hada en el cuento?

fall [FOL] *n.* • otoño (el)
School starts in the fall.
Las clases comienzan en el otoño.

fall, to [FQL] *v.* • caerse
You're going to fall!
¡Te vas a caer!

fall asleep, to [FQL ä SLIP] *v.* • dormirse
Jane falls asleep at the movie theater.
Jane se duerme en el cine.

family [FA mi li] *n.* • familia (la)
Judy's family lives in California.
La familia de Judy vive en California.

famous [FEI mäs] *adj.* • famoso, a
The restaurant is famous for its coffee.
El restaurante es famoso por su café.

fan (paper) (FAN) *n.* • abanico (el)
fan (admirer) *n.* • admirador, a (el, la)
fan (electric) *n.* • ventilador (el)
My grandmother has a collection of fans.
Mi abuela tiene una colección de abanicos.

That singer does not have many fans.
Ese cantante no tiene muchos admiradores.

fantastic [fan TAS tic] *adj.* • fantástico, a
Marco has fantastic adventures.
Marco tiene aventuras fantásticas.

far [FAR] *adv.* • lejos
The Smiths do not live very far.
Los Smith no viven muy lejos.

farewell [FER wel] *n.* • despedida (la)
There is a farewell party for Professor Smith.
Hay una fiesta de despedida para el profesor Smith.

farm [FARM] *n.* • granja (la)
farmer *n.* • granjero, a (el, la)
There are several types of animals on the farm.
Hay varios tipos de animales en la granja.

He comes from a family of farmers.
Él viene de una familia de granjeros.

fast [FAST] *adj.* • rápido, a
adv. • rápidamente
A car is faster than a bicycle.
Un coche es más rápido que una bicicleta.

María reads fast.
María lee rápidamente.

fasten, to [FAS en] *v.* • abrocharse
Please fasten your seat belts.
Por favor, abróchense los cinturones de seguridad.

fat [FAT] *adj.* • gordo, a
fat *n.* • grasa (la)
That lady is very fat.
Esa mujer es muy gorda.

Carrots do not have fat.
Las zanahorias no tienen grasa.

father [FATH ër] *n.* • padre (el)
father-in-law *n.* • suegro (el)
Charles' father is a mechanic.
El padre de Charles es mecánico.

Bill and his father-in-law get along well.
Bill y su suegro se llevan bien.

favorite [FEIV ër it] *adj.* • favorito, a
What is your favorite book?
¿Cuál es tu libro favorito?

fear, to [FIR] *v.* • temer
I fear you are wrong.
Temo que no tengas razón.

feather [FETH ër] *n.* • pluma (la)
Ostrich feathers are very big.
Las plumas de avestruz son muy grandes

February [FEB ru eri] *n.* • febrero
February has only twenty-eight days.
Febrero tiene sólo veintiocho días.

feel, to [FIL] *v.* • sentir (tran.); sentirse (intran.)
I can feel the heat from the machine.
Puedo sentir el calor de la máquina.

Theresa does not feel well today.
Theresa no se siente bien hoy.

feelings [FIL ings] *n.* • sentimientos (los)
The letter expresses my feelings.
La carta expresa mis sentimientos.

feet [FIT] *n.* • pies (los)
My feet are tired.
Los pies están cansados.

ferocious [fe RO shäs] *adj.* • feroz
Tigers are ferocious.
Los tigres son feroces.

fever [FI vër] *n.* • fiebre (la)
She has a fever.
Ella tiene fiebre.

field [FILD] *n.* • campo (el)
The farmer is in the cornfield.
El granjero está en el campo de maíz.

My brother is interested in track and field.
A mi hermano le interesa la pista y campo.

fierce [FIRS] *adj.* • feroz
The lion is a fierce animal.
El león es un animal feroz.

fight, to [FAIT] *v.* • luchar
We have to fight against pollution.
Tenemos que luchar contra la contaminación.

fill, to [FIL] *v.* • llenar
Please fill the glasses on the table.
Por favor, llena los vasos en la mesa.

film [FILM] *n.* película (la)
I like dramatic films.
Me gustan las películas dramáticas.

I have to buy film for my camera.
Tengo que comprar película para mi cámara.

finally (at last) [FAI nä li] *adv.* • por fin
She finally wants to learn geography!
¡Por fin ella quiere aprender la geografía!

find, to [FAIND] *v.* • encontrar
The professor cannot find her keys.
La profesora no puede encontrar sus llaves.

fine [FAIN] *adv.* • bien
I 'm fine, thanks. And you?
Estoy bien, gracias. ¿Y tú?

finger [FIN gër] *n.* • dedo (el)
fingernail *n.* • uña (la)
Rosario has long fingers and plays the piano.
Rosario tiene dedos largos y toca el piano.

What fingernail polish do you prefer?
¿Qué esmalte de uñas prefieres?

finish, to [FIN ish] *v.* • terminar, acabar
finished (of an object) *adj.* • acabado, a
We are going to finish the exam in an hour.
Vamos a terminar el examen en una hora.

Is the work finished?.
¿Está acabado el trabajo?

fire [FAIR] *n.* • fuego (el)
fire alarm *n.* • alarma de incendios (la)
fire extinguisher *n.* • extintor (el)
fire fighter *n.* • bombero, a (el, la)
fireplace *n.* • chimenea (la)
fire truck *n.* • camión de bomberos (el)
Fire fighters are very brave.
Los bomberos son muy valientes.

All houses need fire alarms.
Todas las casas necesitan una alarma de incendios.

first aid [fërst EID] *n.* • primeros auxilios (los)
The first aid team arrived moments after the accident.
El equipo de primeros auxilios llegó momentos después de accidente.

fish, to [FISH] *v.* • pescar
fishing *n.* • pesca (la)
fish tank *n.* • acuario (el)
The grandfather fishes with his grandson.
El abuelo pesca con su nieto.

Raúl's hobby is fishing.
El pasatiempo de Raúl es la pesca.

fish (alive) [FI̲SH] *n.* • pez (el)
fish (cooked) *n.* • pescado (el)
The fish in the tropics have many colors.
Los peces en los trópicos tienen muchos colores.

They eat a lot of fish in Spain.
En España comen mucho pescado.

fisherman [FI̲SH ër män] *n.* • pescador, a (el, la)
There are a lot of fishermen in Maine.
Hay muchos pescadores en Maine.

fix, to [FI̲X] *v.* • arreglar
The mechanic fixes the car at the shop.
El mecánico arregla el carro en el taller.

flag [FLA̲G] *n.* • bandera (la)
The first U.S. flag had thirteen stars.
La primera bandera de los Estados Unidos tenía trece estrellas.

flashlight [FLA̲SH lait] *n.* • linterna (la)
The boy wants a flashlight for his birthday.
El niño quiere una linterna para su cumpleaños.

flat [FLA̲T] *adj.* • llano, a
We live in the flatlands.
Vivimos en la tierra llana.

flight [FLAIT] *n.* • vuelo (el)
flight attendant *n.* • aeromozo, a (el, la), auxiliar de vuelo (el, la)
There are only two flights to Madrid.
Sólo hay dos vuelos a Madrid.

To call the flight attendant, press the button.
Para llamar al aeromozo, toca el botón.

floor [FLOR] *n.* • piso (el) (story); suelo (el)
That building has twelve floors.
Ese edificio tiene doce pisos.

Don't put your books on the floor!
¡No pongan sus libros en el suelo!

flower [FLAU ër] *n.* • flor (la)
You can buy flowers at the market.
Puedes comprar flores en el mercado.

flu [FLU] *n.* • influenza (la), gripe (la)
You have to rest when you have the flu.
Tienes que descansar cuando tienes la influenza.

fly, to [FLAI] *v.* • volar
Daniel doesn't like to fly.
A Daniel no le gusta volar.

fly (insect) [FLAI] *n.* • mosca (la)
There are flies in the trash.
Hay moscas en la basura.

fog [FOG] *n.* • niebla (la), neblina (la)
There is always a lot of fog in London.
Siempre hay mucha niebla en Londres.

follow, to [FA lo] *v.* • seguir
The spy follows the suspect.
El espía sigue al sospechoso.

football [FÜT bol] *n.* • fútbol americano (el)
The school football team is not very good.
El equipo de fútbol americano de la escuela no es muy bueno.

for [FOR] *prep.* • para; por
The blue box is for Pat.
La caja azul es para Pat.

The assignment is for Monday.
La tarea es para el lunes.

I'll give you $5.00 for the book.
Le doy cinco dólares por el libro.

Thanks for the watch!
¡Gracias por el reloj!

forbidden [for BI den] *adj.* • prohibido
It is forbidden to smoke in this building.
Es prohibido fumar en este edificio.

forehead [FOR jed] *n.* • frente (la)
Martin doesn't have any hair on his forehead.
Martin no tiene pelo en el frente.

foreign [FOR en] *adj.* • extranjero, a
Peggy's brother travels in foreign countries.
El hermano de Peggy viaja en países extranjeros.

forest [FOR est] *n.* • bosque (el)
They walk through the forest.
Ellos caminan por el bosque.

forever [for E vër] adv. • para siempre
Romeo loves Juliet forever.
Romeo ama a Julieta para siempre.

forget, to [for GET] *v.* • olvidar
I cannot forget that moment.
No puedo olvidar ese momento.

fortunate [FOR chu nät] *adj.* • afortunado, a
fortunate, to be (lucky) *v.* • tener suerte
Ellen has a Corvette. What a fortunate girl.
Elena tiene un Corvette. ¡Qué chica tan afortunada!

Jim is fortunate; he likes his job.
Jim tiene suerte; le gusta su trabajo.

fountain [FAUN tän] *n.* • fuente (la)
The fountain of youth is a legend.
La fuente de la juventud es una leyenda.

fox [FAX] *n.* • zorro, a (el, la)
Foxes are clever.
Los zorros son listos.

French [FRENCH] *adj.* • francés (el), francesa (la)
Joan prefers French cuisine.
Joan prefiere la cocina francesa.

frequently [FRI kwent li] *adv.* • frecuentemente
My grandparents visit us frequently.
Mis abuelos nos visitan frecuentemente.

fresh [FRESH] *adj.* • fresco, a
We want to eat fresh vegetables.
Queremos comer verduras frescas.

Friday [FRAI dei] *n.* • viernes (el)
Thank God it's Friday.
Gracias a Dios es viernes.

fried [FRAI d] *adj.* • frito, a
fry, to *v.* • freír
Gretel does not eat fried food.
Gretel no come comida frita.

Do you fry or bake the potatoes?
¿Fríes o horneas las papas?

friend [FREND] *n.* • amigo, a (el, la)
Edward and Ralph are good friends.
Edward y Ralph son buenos amigos.

friendship [FREND ship] *n.* • amistad (la)
Your friendship is very important.
Tu amistad es muy importante.

frog [FROG] *n.* • rana (la)
Frogs sing at night.
Las ranas cantan de noche.

from [FRÄM] *prep.* • de
This wine is from Spain.
Este vino es de España.

front of, (in) [FRÄNT äv] *prep.* • delante de
Jim is in front of Bill.
Jim está delante de Bill.

fruit [FRUT] *n.* • fruta (la)
There is a fruit salad in the refrigerator.
Hay ensalada de frutas en el refrigerador.

full [FÜL) *adj.* • lleno, a
The theater is full.
El teatro está lleno.

fun [FÄN] *adj.* • divertido, a
funny *adj.* • gracioso, a
It is fun to go to the fair.
Es divertido ir a la feria.

The clowns are funny.
Los payasos son graciosos.

furniture [FËR na chër] *n.* • muebles (los)
furniture store *n.* • mueblería (la)
The furniture needs to be changed.
Los meubles necesitan ser cambiados.

The furniture store has a warehouse.
La mueblería tiene un almacén.

future [FYU chër] *n.* • futuro (el)
We are going to visit other planets in the future.
Vamos a visitar otros planetas en el futuro.

G

game [GEIM] *n.* • juego (el)
Chess is an interesting game.
El ajedrez es un juego interesante.

garage [gä RAG] *n.* • garaje (el)
The house does not have a garage.
La casa no tiene garaje.

garden [GAR den] *n.* • jardín (el)
The garden has roses.
El jardín tiene rosas.

gas [GAS] *n.* • gasolina (la)
gas station *n.* • gasolinera (la)
Gas in Italy is not cheap.
La gasolina en Italia no es barata.

gelatin [GE lä tän] *n.* • gelatina (la)
The gelatin is in the refrigerator.
La gelatina está en la nevera.

generally [GE nä rä li] *adv.* • generalmente
I generally listen to the radio when I study.
Generalmente escucho la radio cuando estudio.

generous [GE nä räs] *adj.* • generoso, a
Mr. Schleider is a generous man.
El señor Schleider es un hombre generoso.

genius [GI nyäs] *n.* • genio (el)
The genius of Albert Einstein is impressive.
El genio de Albert Einstein es impresionante.

gentle [GEN täl] *adj.* • suave
It's hot, but there is a gentle breeze.
Hace calor, pero hay una brisa suave.

geography [gi AG rä fi] *n.* • geografía (la)
The maps are for the geography class.
Los mapas son para la clase de geografía.

get, to [GET] *v.* • obtener, conseguir
to get along with • llevarse bien con
to get away • irse
to get back something • recobrar
to get old • envejecerse
to get up • levantarse
Are you going to get the job?
¿Vas a conseguir el empleo?

Juan gets along with his cousins.
Juan se lleva bien con sus primos.

ghost [GOST] *n.* • fantasma (el)
Do you believe in ghosts?
¿Crees en fantasmas?

giant [GAI änt] *n.* • gigante (el)
The legend says a giant lives here.
La leyenda dice que un gigante vive aquí.

gift [GIFT] *n.* • regalo (el)
Ángela likes expensive gifts.
A Ángela le gustan los regalos caros.

girl (child) [GËRL] *n.* • niña (la)
girl (teenager) *n.* • muchacha (la), chica (la)
The girl is with her mother.
La niña está con su madre.

The girls prepare their science project.
Las chicas preparan su proyecto de ciencias.

girlfriend [GËRL frend] *n.* • novia (la)
His girlfriend is from Costa Rica.
Su novia es de Costa Rica.

give, to [GIV] *v.* • dar
give back, to *v.* • devolver
When I give my opinion, my parents listen to me.
Cuando doy mi opinión, mis padres me escuchan.

glad, to be [GLAD] *v.* • alegrarse (de)
I'm glad to hear the good news.
Me alegro de oír las buenas noticias.

glass (for drinking) [GLAS] *n* • vaso (el)
glass (material) *n.* • cristal (el)
A glass of milk, please!
¡Un vaso de leche, por favor!

The vase is made of glass.
El florero está hecho de cristal.

glasses [GLAS äs] *n.* • gafas (las); anteojos (los)
sunglasses *n.* • gafas de sol (las)
I'm always losing my glasses!
¡Siempre pierdo mis gafas!

glove [GLÄV] *n.* • guante (el)
These gloves are new.
Estos guantes son nuevos.

glue, to [GLU] *v.* • pegar
glue *n.* • cola (la)
The children glue pictures in their notebooks.
Los niños pegan fotos en sus cuadernos.

This glue is very sticky.
Esta cola es muy pegajosa.

go, to [GO] *v.* • ir
to go ahead • seguir adelante
to go around • circular
to go back • regresar
to go to bed • acostarse
to go out • salir
They are going to class now.
Van a clase ahora.

There is a rumor going around school.
Hay un rumor que circula por la escuela.

goal [GOL] *n.* • meta (la)
David's goal is to be an economist.
La meta de David es ser economista.

godchild [GAD chaild] *n.* • ahijado, a (el, la)
godfather *n.* • padrino (el)
godmother *n.* • madrina (la)
Her godmother is her aunt.
Su madrina es su tía.

gold [GOLD] *n.* • oro (el)
I have an ounce of gold dust.
Tengo una onza de oro en polvo.

golf [GALF] *n.* • golf (el)
Ana plays golf with her friends.
Ana juega al golf con sus amigas.

good [GÜD] *adj.* • bueno, a
It is a good book.
Es un buen libro.

grandchildren [GRAND chil drän] *n.* • nietos (los)
granddaughter *n.* • nieta (la)
grandfather *n.* • abuelo (el)
grandmother *n.* • abuela (la)
grandparents *n.* • abuelos (los)
grandson *n.* • nieto (el)
The grandchildren receive gifts from their grandfather.
Los nietos reciben regalos de su abuelo.

grape [GREIP] *n.* • uva (la)
Michigan produces grapes.
Michigan produce uvas.

grapefruit [GREIP frut] *n.* • toronja (la), pomelo (el)
There is grapefruit for breakfast.
Hay toronja para el desayuno.

grass, (lawn) [GRAS] *n.* • césped (el)
Ignacio has to mow the grass.
Ignacio tiene que cortar el césped.

grasshopper [GRAS jo për] *n.* • saltamontes (el)
Grasshoppers are insects.
Los saltamontes son insectos.

gray [GREI] *adj.* • gris
Jane buys a gray suit.
Jane compra un traje gris.

great [GREIT] *adj.* • magnífico, a
great! *intj.* • ¡fantástico!
Madrid is a great city!
¡Madrid es una ciudad magnífica!

Great! We are going to Acapulco.
¡Fantástico! Vamos a Acapulco.

green [GRIN] *adj.* • verde
Rachel has pretty geen eyes.
Rachel tiene bonitos ojos verdes.

greet, to [GRIT] *v.* • saludar
greeting *n.* • saludo (el)
They greet the new neighbors.
Ellos saludan a los nuevos vecinos.

Greetings to your family.
Saludos a tu familia.

grocer [GRO sër] *n.* • tendero, a (el, la)
The grocer doesn't have apples.
El tendero no tiene manzanas.

ground [GRAUND] *n.* • tierra (la), suelo (el)
playground *n.* • patio de recreo (el)
The ground is very dry this summer.
La tierra está muy seca este verano.

We sit on the ground during our picnic.
Nos sentamos en el suelo durante nuestra merienda.

The children are on the playground.
Los niños están en el patio de recreo.

grow, to [GRO] *v.* • crecer
My nephew is growing fast.
Mi sobrino crece rápidamente.

guard, to [GARD] *v.* • guardar
The dog guards the house.
El perro guarda la casa.

guess, to [GES] *v.* • adivinar
guess *n.* • conjetura (la)
Sonia guesses the answer.
Sonia adivina la respuesta.

guide, to [GAID] *v.* • guiar
guide *n.* • guía (el, la)
She guides the tourists around the city.
Ella guía a los turistas por la ciudad.

The guide explains the painting.
El guía explica la pintura.

guitar [gi TAR] *n.* • guitarra (la)
Isabel likes guitar music.
A Isabel le gusta la música de guitarra.

gum [GÄM] *n.* • chicle (el)
My grandmother does not like gum.
A mi abuela no le gusta el chicle.

gun [GÄN] *n.* • pistola (la)
Cowboys carry guns.
Los vaqueros llevan pistolas.

H

hair [JER] *n.* • pelo (el)
hair brush *n.* • cepillo (el)
Lucinda has blonde hair.
Lucinda tiene el pelo rubio.

half [JAF] *adj.* • medio, a
She wants half an orange.
Ella quiere media naranja.

hall [JOL] *n.* • pasillo (el)
The students talk in the halls.
Los estudiantes platican en los pasillos.

ham [JAM] *n.* • jamón (el)
Muriel does not eat ham.
Muriel no come jamón.

hamburger [JAM bër gër] *n.* • hamburguesa (la)
We eat hamburgers for lunch.
Comemos hamburguesas para el almuerzo.

hammer [JA mër] *n.* • martillo (el)
You can find a hammer in the box.
Puedes encontrar un martillo en la caja.

hand [JAND] *n.* • mano (la)
Mr. García shakes hands with the boss.
El señor García le da la mano al jefe.

handkerchief [JANC ër chif] *n.* • pañuelo (el)
This embroidered handkerchief is an antique.
Este pañuelo bordado es una antigüedad.

handsome [JAND säm] *adj.* • guapo, a; atractivo, a
Eduardo is very handsome.
Eduardo es muy guapo.

happy [JA pi] *adj.* • feliz
happy birthday *coll.* • feliz cumpleaños
Ana is very happy today.
Ana está muy feliz hoy.

Tom wishes Diana a happy birthday.
Tom le desea a Diana un feliz cumpleaños.

hard (difficult) [JARD] *adj.* • difícil
This test is hard!
¡Este examen es difícil!

hat [JAT] *n.* • sombrero (el)
We wear hats in winter.
Llevamos sombreros en el invierno.

hate, to [JEIT] *v.* • odiar
Jill hates the tropical climate.
Jill odia el clima tropical.

have, to [JAV] v. • tener
have to *v.* • tener que
I have five brothers.
Tengo cinco hermanos.

We have to study Spanish.
Tenemos que estudiar español.

hay [JEI] *n.* • heno (el)
Do sheep eat hay?
¿Comen heno las ovejas?

he [JI] *pron.* • él
He is so handsome!
¡Él es tan guapo!

head [JED] *n.* • cabeza (la)
My head hurts.
Me duele la cabeza.

headlight [JED lait] *n.* • faro (el)
Turn on the headlights.
Enciende los faros.

health [JELTH] *n.* • salud (la)
healthy *adj.* • sano, a; saludable
I run every day to improve my health.
Corro todos los días para mejorar la salud.

Running is a healthy activity.
Correr es una actividad sana.

hear, to [JIR] *v.* • oír
Grandmother does not hear well.
La abuela no oye bien.

heart [JART] *n.* • corazón (el)
  heart surgeon *n.* • cardiólogo, a (el, la)
My grandmother has a kind heart
Mi abuela tiene buen corazón.

Kathy is a heart surgeon.
Kathy es cardióloga.

heavy [JE vi] *adj.* • pesado, a
This box is heavy.
Esta caja es pesada.

helicopter [JE li cap tër] *n.* • helicóptero (el)
They fly in a helicopter to explore the area.
Ellos vuelan en un helicóptero para explorar el área.

hello [je LO] *intj.* • hola
Hello! My name is Adam.
¡Hola! Me llamo Adam.

help, to [JELP] *v.* • ayudar
  help *n.* • ayuda (la)
  help! *intj.* • ¡socorro!, ¡auxilio!
The boy helps his mother clean the house.
El niño ayuda a su mamá limpiar la casa.

her [JËR] *adj.* • su
  pron. • ella
Mrs. Lawson drives her car.
La señora Lawson maneja su automóvil.

The book is for her.
El libro es para ella.

here [JIR] *adv.* • aquí
We can have lunch here.
Podemos almorzar aquí.

hidden [JI dän] *adj.* • escondido, a
The treasure is hidden on the island.
El tesoro está escondido en la isla.

hide, to [JAID] *v.* • esconder
The girl hides her toys.
La niña esconde sus juguetes.

high [JAI] *adj.* • alto, a
The Sears Tower is very high.
La torre Sears es muy alta.

highway [JAI wei] *n.* • carretera (la)
That highway is dangerous in winter.
Esa carretera es peligrosa en el invierno.

his [JIS] *adj.* • su
His address is in the phone book.
Su dirección está en el directorio.

history [JIS tä ri] *n.* • historia (la)
The history of Egypt is fascinating.
La historia de Egipto es fascinante.

hit, to [JIT] *v.* • golpear
She hits the rug to clean it.
Ella golpea la alfombra para limpiarla.

hobby [JA bi] *n.* • pasatiempo (el)
What is your hobby?
¿Cuál es tu pasatiempo?

hole [JOL] *n.* • agujero (el)
The hole in the door needs to be repaired.
El agujero en la puerta necesita ser reparado.

holiday [JA li dei] *n.* • día festivo (el)
The Fourth of July is a holiday.
El cuatro de Julio es un día festivo.

home [JOM] *n.* • casa (la)
The Parkinsons want to buy a new home.
Los Parkinson quieren comprar una casa nueva.

homework [JOM wërc] *n.* • tarea (la)
I need to finish my homework.
Necesito terminar mi tarea.

honor [A nër] *n.* • honor (el)
The topic of this book is honor.
El tema de este libro es el honor.

hope, to [JOP] v. • esperar
Andy hopes to receive a scholarship.
Andy espera recibir una beca.

horse [JORS] *n.* • caballo (el)
Horses live on a farm.
Los caballos viven en una granja.

hospital [JAS pi täl] *n.* • hospital (el)
Tina is in the hospital.
Tina está en el hospital.

hot [JAT] *adj.* • caliente
The coffee is hot.
El café está caliente.

hotel [jo TEL] *n.* • hotel (el)
We're staying at the Plaza Hotel.
Nos alojamos en el Hotel Plaza.

The hotel calls a taxi for the client.
El hotel llama un taxi para el cliente.

I

I [AI] *pron.* • yo
I study Spanish.
Yo estudio español.

ice [AIS] *n.* • hielo (el)
ice cream *n.* • helado (el)
Do you want your water with ice?
¿Quieres tu agua con hielo?

I like ice cream.
Me gustan los helados.

idea [ai DI ä] *n.* • idea (la)
Your idea is good.
Tu idea es buena.

if [IF] *conj.* • si
If Wendy accepts the new job, she is going to live in New York.
Si Wendy acepta el nuevo trabajo, ella va a vivir en Nueva York.

ill [IL] *adj.* • enfermo, a
Julia is ill today.
Julia está enferma hoy.

immediately [im MI di ät li] *adv.* • inmediatamente
Please call your brother immediately.
Por favor, llama a tu hermano inmediatamente.

impatient [im PEI shänt] *adj.* • impaciente
Liana is nice but impatient.
Liana es agradable pero impaciente.

impolite [im po LAIT] *adj.* • descortés
It is impolite to ask certain questions.
Es decortés hacer ciertas preguntas.

important [im POR tänt] *adj.* • importante
The scientist makes an important discovery.
El científico hace un descrubrimiento importante.

impossible [im PA si bäl] *adj.* • imposible
It is impossible to travel faster than light.
Es imposible viajar más rápido que la luz.

in [IN] prep. • en
Her cousin lives in Madrid.
Su prima vive en Madrid.

information [in fër MEI shän] *n.* • información (la)
The information is in the almanac.
La información está en el almanaque.

insect [IN sect] *n.* • insecto (el)
Insects exist in all climates.
Los insectos existen en todos los climas.

inside [in SAID] *adv.* • adentro
It's cold; come inside.
Hace frío, ven adentro.

insist, to [in SIST] *v.* • insistir
Ana insists on leaving tomorrow.
Ana insiste en salir mañana.

intelligence [in TE li gents] *n.* • inteligencia (la)
intelligent *adj.* • inteligente
The results of the intelligence test are doubtful.
Los resultados de la prueba de inteligencia son dudosos.

Susie is very intelligent.
Susie es muy inteligente.

interesting [IN te res ting] *adj.* • interesante
The tour of the city is interesting.
La visita a la ciudad es interesante.

introduce, to [in tro DUS] *v.* • presentar
Daphne introduces her friends to her sister.
Daphne presenta sus amigos a su hermana.

invite, to [in VAIT] *v.* • invitar
Carmen invites her friends to the party.
Carmen invita a sus amigos a la fiesta.

iron, to [AIRN] *v.* • planchar
Cresencia irons her dress.
Cresencia plancha su vestido.

iron (appliance) *n.* • plancha (la)
iron (metal) *n.* • hierro (el)
The steam iron is in the closet.
La plancha de vapor está en el armario.

The old door is made of iron.
La vieja puerta está hecha de hierro.

irritable [IR itä bl] *adj.* • irritable
He can be very irritable when he is tired.
Él puede ser muy irritable cuando está cansado.

island [AI länd] *n.* • isla (la)
Puerto Rico is an island.
Puerto Rico es una isla.

its [ITS] *adj.* • su
The nightclub is popular for its music.
El club nocturno es popular por su música.

J

jacket [GA ket] *n.* • chaqueta (la)
The store has some jackets on sale.
La tienda tiene algunas chaquetas en liquidación.

jam [GAM] *n.* • mermelada (la)
This strawberry jam is delicious.
Esta mermelada de fresas es deliciosa.

January [GA nyu we ri] *n.* • enero
Dr. Martin Luther King, Jr.'s birthday is in January.
El cumpleaños del Dr. Martin Luther King, Jr., es en enero.

jealous [GE läs] *adj.* • celoso, a
to be jealous (of) *v.* • estar celoso, a (de)
He is jealous of his cousin.
Él está celoso de su primo.

jewel [GU el] *n.* • joya (la)
jeweler *n.* • joyero, a (el, la)
jewelry store *n.* • joyería (la)
Diamonds and sapphires are sold in the jewelry store.
Se venden diamantes y zafiros en la joyería.

joke [GOC] *n.* • broma (la)
Ann tells very bad jokes.
Ann dice muy malas bromas.

journalist [GËR nä list] *n.* • periodista (el, la)
That gentleman is a famous **journalist.**
Ese señor es un periodista famoso.

juice [GUS] *n.* • jugo (el)
Do you want some apple juice?
¿Quieres jugo de manzana?

July [GU lai] *n.* • julio
U.S. Independence Day is the 4th of July.
El día de la independencia de los Estados Unidos es el cuatro de julio.

jump, to [GÄMP] *v.* • saltar
We can jump the stream because it is very narrow.
Podemos saltar el arroyo porque es muy estrecho.

June [GUN] *n.* • junio
They will visit San Francisco in June.
Ellos van a visitar San Francisco en junio.

K

kangaroo [can gä RU] *n.* • canguro (el)
There are kangaroos at the zoo.
Hay canguros en el zoológico.

keep, to [KIP] *v.* • guardar
Lorie wants to keep the book.
Lorie quiere guardar el libro.

key [KI] *n.* • llave (la)
key chain *n.* • llavero (el)
The keys to the house are in my purse.
Las llaves de la casa están en mi bolsa.

kick, to [KIC] *v.* • patear
The soccer players kick the ball during the game.
Los jugadores de fútbol patean la pelota durante el juego.

kill, to [KIL] *v.* • matar
Pollution kills many animals.
La contaminación mata a muchos animales.

kilometer [kil A me tër] *n.* • kilómetro (el)
One mile is 1.6 kilometers.
Una milla es 1.6 kilómetros.

kind [CAIND] *adj.* • amable; bondadoso, a
Salvador is a kind man.
Salvador es un hombre amable.

king [KING] *n.* • rey (el)
The king is very wealthy.
El rey es muy rico.

kiss, to [KIS] *v.* • besar
kiss *n.* • beso (el)
The children greet the grandfather with a kiss.
Los niños saludan al abuelo con un beso.

kitchen [KITCH en] *n.* • cocina (la)
The kitchen is on the first floor.
La cocina está en el primer piso.

kite [CAIT] *n.* • cometa (la)
Michael has a beautiful kite.
Michael tiene una cometa bonita.

kitten [KIT än] *n.* • gatito, a (el, la)
The cat just had six kittens.
La gata acaba de tener seis gatitos.

L

ladder [LA dër] *n.* • escalera (la)
The ladder is in the basement.
La escalera está en el sótano.

lake [LEIC] *n.* • lago (el)
There are a lot of sailboats on the lake.
Hay muchos veleros en el lago.

lamb [LAM] *n.* • cordero (el)
They eat lamb on Easter.
Ellos comen cordero en Pascuas.

lamp [LAMP] *n.* • lámpara (la)
Please turn on the lamp.
Enciende la lámpara, por favor.

land, to [LAND] *v.* • aterrizar
land *n.* • tierra (la)
The plane lands at 4:30 p.m.
El avión aterriza a las 4:30 de la tarde.

The land here is very fertile.
La tierra aquí es muy fértil.

large [LARG] *adj.* • grande
She has a large house.
Ella tiene una casa grande.

last [LAST] *adj.* • último
last one *n.* • último, á (el, la)
You always wait until the last minute!
¡Siempre esperas hasta el último momento!

late [LEIT] *adv.* • tarde
They always come late.
Siempre llegan tarde.

laugh, to [LAF] *v.* • reírse
laugh *n.* • risa (la)
They laugh with the clown.
Ellos se ríen con el payaso.

She has a nice laugh.
Ella tiene una risa agradable.

lawyer [LOY ër] *n.* • abogado, a (el, la)
The lawyer talks with her client.
La abogada habla con su cliente.

lazy [LEI zi] *adj.* • perezoso, a
That child is very lazy.
Ese niño es muy perezoso.

lead, to [LID] *v.* • dirigir
leader *n.* • líder (el)
Kyle leads the group.
Kyle dirige el grupo.

The leader gives his speech.
El líder da su discurso.

leaf [LIF] *n.* • hoja (la)
Trees lose their leaves in the fall.
Los árboles pierden las hojas en el otoño.

learn, to [LËRN] *v.* • aprender
The baby learns to walk.
El bebé aprende a caminar.

leather [LE thër] *n.* • cuero (el)
The bag is made of leather.
La bolsa está hecha de cuero.

leave, to [LIV] *v.* • salir
The plane leaves at eight.
El avión sale a las ocho.

left [LEFT] *adj.* • izquierdo, a
My left arm hurts me.
Me duele el brazo izquierdo.

leg [LEG] *n.* • pierna (la)
Manuel has a broken leg.
Manuel tiene la pierna rota.

lemon [LE män] *n.* • limón (el)
She drinks her tea with lemon.
Ella bebe su té con limón.

lend, to [LEND] *v.* • prestar
My father lends me his car sometimes.
Mi padre me presta su automóvil algunas veces.

less [LES] *adj.* • menos
Alberto earns less money than José.
Alberto gana menos dinero que José.

lesson [LES än] *n.* • lección (la)
The lesson today is very important.
La lección hoy es muy importante.

letter [LET ër] *n.* • carta (la)
The letter just arrived.
La carta acaba de llegar.

lettuce [LET äs] *n.* • lechuga (la)
There is lettuce in my garden.
Hay lechuga en mi jardín.

library [LAI bre ri] *n.* • biblioteca (la)
I'll see you in the library.
Te veo en la biblioteca.

lie, to [LAI] *v.* • mentir
lie *n.* • mentira (la)
The child does not lie to his mother.
El niño no miente a su mamá.

You shouldn't tell lies.
No debes decir mentiras.

light [LAIT] *n.* • luz (la)
Please turn on the light.
Enciende la luz por favor.

lightning [LAIT ning] *n.* • relámpago (el)
There's a lot of thunder and lightning today.
Hay muchos truenos y relámpagos hoy.

like, to [LAIC] *v.* • gustar
I like fruit.
Me gusta la fruta.

lip [LIP] *n.* • labio (el)
lipstick *n.* • lápiz de labios (el)
The actress has very red lips.
La actriz tiene los labios muy rojos.

listen to , to [LI sän] *v.* • escuchar
I listen to the news on the radio.
Escucho las noticias en la radio.

little (size) [LI tl] *adj.* • pequeño, a
little (amount) *adj.* • poco, a
What a little house!
¡Qué casa tan pequeña!

There is little snow in these parts.
Hay poca nieve en estas regiones.

live, to [LIV] *v.* • vivir
They live in Peru.
Ellos viven en el Perú.

living room [LI̲V i̲ng rum] *n.* • sala (la)
The guests are in the living room.
Los invitados están en la sala.

long [LO̲NG] *adj.* • largo, a
no longer *adv.* • ya no
I have a long shopping list.
Tengo una larga lista de compras.

look, to [LÜC] *v.* • mirar
to look at oneself • mirarse
to look after • cuidar
to look for • buscar
Robert is looking at the map.
Robert mira el mapa.

They look for the answer in the library.
Buscan la respuesta en la biblioteca.

lose, to [LUZ] *v.* • perder
I don't want to lose my scholarship.
No quiero perder mi beca.

lot, a [LAT] *adj.* • mucho, a
adv. • mucho
There is a lot of food for the party.
Hay mucha comida para la fiesta.

They like strawberry ice cream a lot.
Les gusta mucho el helado de fresa.

loud [LAUD] *adj.* • fuerte (sound); ruidoso, a (noisy)
loudly *adv.* • fuerte, alto
She does not like loud noises.
A ella no le gustan los ruidos fuertes.

They play the radio very loudly.
Ellos tocan la radio muy fuerte.

love, to [LÄV] *v.* • amar, querer
  love *n.* • amor
Pedro loves me!
¡Pedro me ama!

Love is wonderful.
El amor es maravilloso.

low [LO] *adj.* • bajo, a
The baby has a low chair.
El bebé tiene una silla baja.

luck [LÄC] *n.* • suerte (la)
  good luck *coll.* • buena suerte
You need luck to win this game
Necesitas suerte para ganar este juego.

luggage [LÄG äg] *n.* • equipaje (el)
The luggage is in the car.
El equipaje está en el coche.

lunch, to eat [LÄNCH] *v.* • almorzar
  lunch *n.* • almuerzo (el)
They eat lunch in the cafeteria.
Ellos almuerzan en la cafetería.

María is preparing lunch for us.
María nos prepara el almuerzo.

M

machine [mä SHIN] *n.* • máquina (la)
That mechanic can fix this machine.
Ese mecánico puede arreglar esta máquina.

mad [MAD] *adj.* • enojado, a; enfadado, a
I'm mad at my brother.
Estoy enojado con mi hermano.

made (of) [MEID av] *adj.* • hecho, a (de)
The house is made of brick.
La casa está hecha de ladrillo.

magazine [MAG ä zin] *n.* • revista (la)
We have too many magazines in this house!
¡Tenemos demasiadas revistas en esta casa!

maid [MEID] *n.* • criada (la)
Our maid is named Soledad.
Nuestra criada se llama Soledad.

mail, to [MEIL] *v.* • echar al correo
mail *n.* • correo (el)
mailbox *n.* • buzón (el)
mail carrier *n.* • cartero, a (el, la)
We have to mail my father's gift.
Tenemos que echar al correo el regalo de mi padre.

make, to [MEIC] *v.* • hacer
The child likes to make castles on the beach.
Al niño le gusta hacer castillos en la playa.

makeup (facial) [MEIC äp] *n.* • maquillaje (el)
put on makeup, to *v.* • *maquillarse*
This type of makeup is good for your skin.
Este tipo de maquillaje es bueno para el cutis.

She puts on makeup before she goes out.
Ella se maquilla antes de salir.

mama [MA ma] *n.* • mamá (la)
mom *n.* • mamá (la)
My mom is from a big family.
Mi mamá es de una familia grande.

man [MAN] *n.* • hombre (el)
He is a nice man.
Él es un hombre agradable.

manager [MAN ä gër] *n.* • gerente (el)
He is the manager of the department.
Él es gerente del departamento.

manners [MAN nërs] *n.* • modales (los)
Good manners are very important.
Los buenos modales son muy importantes.

many (a lot) [MEN i] *adj.* • muchos, as
Jim has many friends.
Jim tiene muchos amigos.

map [MAP] *n.* • mapa (el)
A good map is an excellent aid.
Un buen mapa es una ayuda excelente.

marble [MAR bäl] *n.* • mármol (el)
Some of these statues are made of marble.
Algunas de estas estatuas están hechas de mármol.

March [MARCH] *n.* • marzo
Spring starts in March.
La primavera empieza en marzo.

margarine [MAR gë rin] *n.* • margarina (la)
Some people use margarine instead of butter.
Algunas personas usan margarina en vez de mantequilla.

market [MAR ket] *n.* • mercado (el)
I like to visit the open-air market.
Me gusta visitar el mercado al aire libre.

marmalade [MAR me leid] *n.* • mermelada (la)
Marmalade is not as sweet as jelly.
La mermelada no es tan dulce como la jalea.

marry, to [MER ri] *v.* • casarse con
married *adj.* • casado, a
Lucy is marrying Jack.
Lucy se casa con Jack.

Felipe is married.
Felipe está casado.

marvelous [MAR ve läs] *adj.* • maravilloso, a
What a marvelous party!
¡Qué fiesta tan maravillosa!

match (light) [MA̲TCH] *n.* • fósforo (el)
match (game) *n.* • partido (el)
We need a match to light the candles.
Necesitamos un fósforo para encender las velas.

mathematics [ma̲th MA̲T i̲cs] *n.* • matemáticas (las)
Mathematics is the basis of modern physics.
Las matemáticas es la base de la física moderna.

matter (subject) [MA̲T tër] *n.* • asunto (el)
it does not matter *coll.* • no importa
what's the matter? *coll.* • ¿qué pasa?; ¿qué hay?
How long do you need to arrange the matter?
¿Cuánto tiempo necesita para arreglar el asunto?

May [MEI] *n.* • mayo
My birthday is May 23rd.
Mi cumpleaños es el 23 de mayo.

may [MEI] *v.* • poder
May I help you?
¿Puedo ayudarte?

maybe [MEI bi] *adv.* • quizá, tal vez
Are you going to the movies tonight? Maybe.
¿Vas al cine esta noche? Quizá.

me [MI] *pron.* • me
He gives me the car keys.
Él me da las llaves del coche.

meal [MIL] *n.* • comida (la)
Breakfast is my favorite meal.
El desayuno es mi comida favorita.

meat [MIT] *n.* • carne (la)
Argentinians eat a lot of meat.
Los argentinos comen mucha carne.

mechanic [me CAN ic] *n.* • mecánico (el)
This mechanic has good tools.
Este mecánico tiene buenas herramientas.

medal [ME däl] *n.* • medalla (la)
He wants to win a medal at the Olympic Games.
Él quiere ganar una medalla en los Juegos Olímpicos.

medicine [MED i sin] *n* • medicina (la)
That medicine tastes sweet.
Esa medicina tiene un sabor dulce.

medium [MI dyum] *adj.* • mediano, a
He is of medium height.
Es de estatura mediana.

meet, to (a friend) [MIT] *v.* • encontrarse con
meet (for the first time) *v.* • conocer
meet (assemble) *v.* • reunirse
John is meeting Albert at the library.
John se encuentra con Albert en la biblioteca.

Do you want to meet my cousin?
¿Quieres conocer a mi prima?

The group meets tonight.
El grupo se reúne esta noche.

member [MEM bër] *n.* • miembro (el, la)
She is a member of many organizations.
Ella es miembro de muchas organizaciones.

menu [MEN yu] *n.* • menú (el)
There are many desserts on the menu.
Hay muchos postres en el menú.

merry-go-round [MER ri go RAUND] *n.* • tiovivo (el)
The children like the merry-go-round.
A los niños les gusta el tiovivo.

method [METH äd] *n.* • método (el)
Her method is effective.
Su método es efectivo.

microwave oven [MAI cro weiv Ä ven] *n.* • horno de microondas (el)
We do not have a microwave oven.
No tenemos un horno de microondas.

midday [MI̲D dei] *n.* • mediodía (el)
The midday sun is hot.
El sol de mediodía es caliente.

midnight [MI̲D nait] *n.* • medianoche (la)
At midnight her carriage turns into a pumpkin.
A la medianoche su carroza se convierte en calabaza.

mile [MAIL] *n.* • milla (la)
To run a mile is good exercise.
Correr una milla es buen ejercicio.

milk [MI̲LC] *n.* • leche (la)
Do you drink milk?
¿Bebes leche?

million [MIL yän] *n.* • millón (el)
The prize is a million dollars.
El premio es un millón de dólares.

minute [MIN et] *n.* • minuto (el)
I can be ready in a minute.
Puedo estar lista en un minuto.

mirror [MIR rër] *n.* • espejo (el)
The mirror is upstairs.
El espejo está arriba.

misbehave, to [mis bi JEIV] *v.* • portarse mal
Our child sometimes misbehaves.
Nuestro niño a veces se porta mal.

Miss [MIS] *n.* • señorita (la)
Miss Montes is the Spanish teacher.
La señorita Montes es la maestra de español.

mistake [mis TEIC] *n.* • error (el)
It is my mistake. I'm sorry.
Es mi error. Lo siento.

Mister, Mr. [MIS tër] *n.* • señor (el)
Mr. Thomas is my grandfather.
El Sr. Thomas es mi abuelo.

mix, to [MIX] *v.* • mezclar
Mix the eggs and the milk with the flour.
Mezcla los huevos y la leche con la harina.

modern [MAD ërn] *adj.* • moderno, a
His house is very modern.
Su casa es muy moderna.

moist [MOYST] *adj.* • húmedo, a
I need a moist cloth.
Necesito un trapo húmedo.

moment [MO ment] *n.* • momento (el)
Just a moment!
¡Un momento!

Monday [MÄN dei] *n.* • lunes (el)
We are going to visit the museum on Monday.
Vamos a visitar el museo el lunes.

money [MÄN i] *n.* • dinero (el)
How much money do you need?
¿Cuánto dinero necesitas?

monkey [MÄN ki] *n.* • mono (el)
It's fun to watch the monkeys.
Es divertido observar los monos.

month [MÄNTH] *n.* • mes (el)
June is my favorite month.
Junio es mi mes favorito.

monument [MAN yu ment] *n.* • monumento (el)
That monument is a popular tourist attraction.
Ese monumento es una atracción turística popular.

mood [MUD] *n.* • humor (el)
He is in a good mood.
Él está de buen humor.

moon [MUN] *n.* • luna (la)
We can see the moon in his telescope.
Podemos ver la luna con su telescopio.

mop [MAP] *n.* • trapeador (el)
Where is the kitchen mop?
¿Dónde está el trapeador de la cocina?

moral [MOR al] *adj.* • moral
moral (of a story) *n.* • moraleja (la)
The moral of the story is very obvious.
La moraleja del cuento es muy obvia.

more [MOR] *adv.* • más
We want to know more.
Queremos saber más.

morning [MORN ing] *n.* • mañana (la)
The sun is beautiful early in the morning.
El sol es hermoso temprano por la mañana.

mosquito [mäs KI to] *n.* • mosquito (el)
There are lots of mosquitoes in the summer.
Hay muchos mosquitos en el verano.

motor [MO tër] *n.* • motor (el)
motorboat *n.* • lancha (la)
motorcycle *n.* • motocicleta (la)
This car needs a larger motor.
Este coche necesita un motor más grande.

mother [MÄTH ër] *n.* • madre (la)
mother-in-law *n.* • suegra (la)
My mother is from Chicago.
Mi madre es de Chicago.

mountain [MAUN tän] *n.* • montaña (la)
My favorite mountains are the Andes
Mis montañas favoritas son los Andes.

mouth [MAUTH] *n.* • boca (la)
Open your mouth.
Abre la boca.

move, to (relocate) [MUV] *v.* • mudarse
move, to (change place) *v.* • mover
We are moving to the coast.
Nos mudamos a la costa.

We need to move this couch to the attic.
Tenemos que mover este sofá al ático.

movie [MUV i] *n.* • película (la)
That movie is very good!
¡Esa película es muy buena!

much [MÄCH] *adj.* • mucho, a
adv. • mucho
Is there much tourism in the winter?
¿Hay mucho turismo en el invierno?

mud [MÄD] *n.* • lodo (el), barro (el)
There's a lot of mud after the rain.
Hay mucho lodo después de la lluvia.

museum [myu ZI äm] *n.* • museo (el)
We're going to an art museum this afternoon.
Vamos a un museo de arte esta tarde.

music [MYU zic] *n.* • música (la)
musician *n.* • músico, a (el, la)
We listen to a lot of music.
Escuchamos mucha música.

His father is a musician too.
Su padre también es músico.

must [MÄST] *v.* • deber
You must study
Debes estudiar.

mustache [MÄS tash] *n.* • bigote (el)
He has a big mustache.
Él tiene un bigote grande.

my [MAI] *adj.* • mi
My book is blue.
Mi libro es azul.

mysterious [mis TIR iäs] *adj.* • misterioso, a
She is a mysterious person.
Ella es una persona misteriosa.

N

nail (finger) [NEIL] *n.* • uña (la)
nail (tool) *n.* • clavo (el)
My nails are not very long.
Mis uñas no son muy largas.

These nails are for the project.
Estos clavos son para el proyecto.

name [NEIM] *n.* • nombre (el)
He has an uncommon name.
Él tiene un nombre poco común.

napkin [NAP kin] *n.* • servilleta (la)
We need napkins for the table.
Necesitamos servilletas para la mesa.

narrow [NAR ro] *adj.* • estrecho, a
This street is very narrow.
Esta calle es muy estrecha.

nation [NEI shän] *n.* • nación (la)
The nation of Bolivia has no sea coast.
La nación de Bolivia no tiene costa.

national [na shän al] *adj.* • nacional
We listen to the national anthem.
Escuchamos el himno nacional.

nationality [na shän AL i ti] *n.* • nacionalidad (la)
What is Elena's nationality?
¿De qué nacionalidad es Elena?

natural [NACH e ral] *adj.* • natural
This is a place of great natural beauty.
Éste es un lugar de gran belleza natural.

nature [NEI chër] *n.* • naturaleza (la)
They like nature.
A ellos les gusta la naturaleza.

near [NIR] *prep.* • cerca de
His house is near the factory.
Su casa está cerca de la fábrica.

neck [NEC] *n.* • cuello (el)
necklace *n.* • collar (el)
Swans have long necks.
Los cisnes tienen cuellos largos.

I have a pearl necklace.
Tengo un collar de perlas.

need, to [NID] *v.* • necesitar
We need to sell the house before January.
Necesitamos vender la casa antes de enero.

needle [NI dl] *n.* • aguja (la)
Please buy a packet of needles at the store.
Por favor compra un paquete de agujas en la tienda.

neighbor [NEI bër] *n.* • vecino, a (el, la)
neighborhood *n.* • barrio (el)
Our neighbors are friendly.
Nuestros vecinos son amables.

neither [NI thër] *adj.* • ninguno, a
neither...nor *conj.* • ni...ni
Neither team has the advantage.
Ninguno de los equipos tiene la ventaja.

Neither she nor her husband can attend.
Ni ella ni su esposo pueden asistir.

nephew [NEF yu] *n.* • sobrino (el)
How many nephews do you have?
¿Cuántos sobrinos tienes?

nervous [NËR väs] *adj.* • nervioso, a
I'm so nervous!
¡Estoy tan nervioso!

nest [NEST] *n.* • nido (el)
We watch the bird build the nest.
Vemos al pájaro construir el nido.

never [NEV ër] *adv.* • nunca
I never eat cheese.
Nunca como queso.

new [NUZ] *adj.* • nuevo, a
That car is new.
Ese carro es nuevo.

news [NUZ] *n.* • noticias (las)
newspaper *n.* • periódico (el)
She always knows the news.
Ella siempre sabe las noticias.

next (in time) [NEXT] *adj.* • que viene, próximo, a
next (following) *adj.* • siguiente
We are going next Tuesday.
Vamos el martes que viene.

Answer the next question.
Contesta la siguiente pregunta.

nice [NAIS] *adj.* • simpático, a
The policeman is very nice.
El policía es muy agradable.

niece [NIS] *n.* • sobrina (la)
We have two nieces.
Tenemos dos sobrinas.

night [NAIT] *n.* • noche (la)
The night is dark when there is no moon.
La noche es oscura cuando no hay luna.

no [NO] *adv.* • no
No, I am not writing a letter.
No, no escribo una carta.

no one, nobody [NO wän] *pron.* • nadie
No one is here.
Nadie está aquí.

noise [NOYZ] *n.* • ruido (el)
Noise can be a problem.
El ruido puede ser un problema.

none [NÄN] *pron.* • ninguno, a
None of the books are red.
Ninguno de los libros es rojo.

noon [NUN] *n.* • mediodía (el)
Let's eat at noon.
Comamos al mediodía.

north [NORTH] *n.* • norte (el)
Canada is north of the U.S.
Canadá está al norte de los EE.UU.

nose [NOZ] *n.* • nariz (la)
Cyrano's nose is big.
La nariz de Cyrano es grande.

note [NOT] *n.* • nota (la)
  notebook *n.* • cuaderno (el)
I'm writing a note to Jane.
Escribo una nota a Jane.

nothing [NÄTH ing] *pron.* • nada
There is nothing on the table
No hay nada en la mesa.

novel [NAV äl] *n.* • novela (la)
This is an excellent novel.
Ésta es una novela excelente.

November [no VEM bër] *n.* • noviembre
November has 30 days.
Noviembre tiene 30 días.

now [NAU] *adv.* • ahora
nowadays *adv.* • hoy día
We want the results now.
Queremos los resultados ahora.

Nowadays everyone has a car.
Hoy día todo el mundo tiene coche.

number [NÄM bër] *n.* • número (el)
What's your phone number?
¿Cuál es tu número de teléfono?

nurse [NËRS] *n.* • enfermero, a (el, la)
My sister is a nurse.
Mi hermana es enfermera.

O

oatmeal [OT mil] *n.* • harina de avena (la)
We eat oatmeal for breakfast.
Comemos harina de avena para el desayuno.

obey, to [o BEI] *v.* • obedecer
He does not obey me.
Él no me obedece.

object, to [äb GECT] *v.* • protestar
object [AB gect] *n.* • objeto (el)
She objects to that comment.
Ella protesta ese comentario.

What is that object?
¿Qué es ese objeto?

obtain, to [äb TEIN] *v.* • obtener
I can obtain three tickets.
Puedo obtener tres boletos.

occupied [ÄC u paid] *adj.* • ocupado, a
This seat is occupied.
Este asiento está ocupado.

occur, to [ä KËR] *v.* • ocurrir
I'm cold; this always occurs when I go to the movies.
Tengo frío; siempre ocurre cuando voy al cine.

ocean [O shän] *n.* • océano (el)
The ocean still has many secrets.
El océano todavía tiene muchos secretos.

October [ac TO bër] *n.* • octubre
The twelfth of October is an important date.
El doce de octubre es una fecha importante.

odd [AD] *adj.* • extraño, a
What an odd person!
¡Qué persona tan extraña!

of [äv] *prep.* • de
He is a friend of Esteban's.
Es un amigo de Esteban.

of course [äv CORS] *intj.* • por supuesto
Of course we are going!
¡Por supesto que vamos!

offer, to [o fër] *v.* • ofrecer
offer *n.* • oferta (la)
He is offering me a good opportunity.
Me ofrece una buena oportunidad.

office [O fis] *n.* • oficina (la)
Her office is huge.
Su oficina es enorme.

often [OF än] *adv.* • frecuentemente; a menudo
They often eat in that restaurant.
Comen frecuentemente en ese restaurante.

oil [OYL] *n.* • aceite (el)
Please change the oil in the car.
Por favor, cambie el aceite en el automóvil.

O.K. [O KEI] *coll.* • **está bien, O.K.**
It is O.K. with me if you want to come.
Está bien conmigo si quieres venir.

old [OLD] *adj.* • viejo, a
old (ancient) *adj.* • antiguo, a
Who is that old man?
¿Quién es ese hombre viejo?

Greece has some very old buildings.
Grecia tiene unos edificios muy antiguos.

on [an] *prep.* • sobre, en
John puts the books on the table.
John pone los libros sobre la mesa.

once [WÄNS] *adv.* • una vez
She eats once a day.
Ella come una vez al día.

onion [ÄN yän] *n.* • cebolla (la)
We like onion soup.
Nos gusta la sopa de cebolla.

only [ON li] *adv.* • solamente, sólo
only child *n.* • hijo, a único, a (el, la)
I only work here.
Solamente trabajo aquí.

They visit only once a year.
Ellos visitan sólo una vez al año.

open, to [O pen] *v.* • abrir
opener *n.* • abrelatas (el)
open *adj.* • abierto, a
Can you open this window?
¿Puede abrir esta ventana?

The door is open.
La puerta está abierta.

or [OR] *conj.* • o
You can have apples or pears.
Puedes tener manzanas o peras.

orchestra [OR kes tra] *n.* • orquesta (la)
He plays trumpet in the orchestra.
Él toca la trompeta en la orquesta.

orchid [OR kid] *n.* • orquídea (la)
She grows orchids.
Ella cultiva orquídeas.

order, to (command) [OR dër] *v.* • mandar, ordenar
order (rule) *n.* • orden (la)
order (sales) *n.* • pedido (el)
The general orders the soldiers.
Él general manda a los soldados.

He disobeys the order.
Él desobedece la orden.

I have to place an order for 10 cassettes.
Tengo que hacer un pedido de diez casetes.

other [Ä thër] *adj.* • otro, a
We also visit other places.
Nosotros también visitamos otros lugares.

our [AUR] *adj.* • nuestro, a
Our town is quiet.
Nuestra ciudad es tranquila

out [AUT] *adv.* • fuera
Jorge is out of the office.
Jorge está fuera de la oficina.

outside [aut SAID] *adv.* • afuera
It is cold outside.
Hace frío afuera.

over there [ovër THER] *adv.* • allá, allí
Can you please put the chair over there?
¿Puede poner la silla allá, por favor?

owe, to [O] *v.* • deber
You owe me five dollars.
Me debes cinco dólares.

owl [AUL] *n.* • búho el; lechuza (la)
Owls live in the forest.
Los búhos viven en el bosque.

own, to [ON] *v.* • tener
own *adj.* • propio, a
He owns seven cars.
Él tiene siete coches.

This is my own desk.
Éste es mi propio escritorio.

P

pack, to [PA̲C] *v.* • hacer las maletas
You have to pack for the trip.
Tiene que hacer las maletas para el viaje.

package [PA̲C äg̲] *n.* • paquete (el)
What is in this package?
¿Qué hay en este paquete?

page [PEIG̲] *n.* • página (la)
This book has more than a thousand pages.
Este libro tiene más de mil páginas.

pail [PEIL] *n.* • cubo (el)
This pail of water is heavy.
Este cubo de agua es pesado.

pain [PEIN] *n.* • dolor (el)
Take aspirin for the pain.
Toma aspirina para el dolor.

paint, to [PEINT] *v.* • pintar
paint *v.* • pintura (la)
Nathan paints the house this weekend.
Nathan pinta la casa este fin de semana.

We need more paint to finish the job.
Necesitamos más pintura para terminar el trabajo.

painter [PEIN tër] *n.* • pintor, a (el, la)
We should hire a painter for the house.
Debemos contratar a un pintor para la casa.

painting [PEIN ti̲ng] *n.* • pintura (la)
The exhibition of Impressionist paintings is a success.
La exhibición de pinturas impresionistas es un éxito.

pair [PER] *n.* • par (el)
I want another pair of shoes.
Quiero otro par de zapatos.

pajamas [pä ga mäs] *n.* • pijama (el)
My new pajamas are silk.
Mi nuevo pijama es de seda.

palace [PAL äs] *n.* • palacio (el)
He lives in a crystal palace.
Él vive en un palacio de cristal.

pale [PEIL] *adj.* • pálido, a
He is too pale. He needs more sun.
Él está demasiado pálido. Necesita más sol.

pan [PAN] *n.* • cazuela (la)
frying pan *n.* • sartén (la)
We need an iron pan to cook.
Necesitamos una cazuela de hierro para cocinar.

pants [PANTS] *n.* • pantalones (los)
Diego needs new pants.
Diego necesita pantalones nuevos.

paper [PEI për] *n.* • papel (el)
paper (news) *n.* • periódico (el)
paper (sheet) *n.* • hoja de papel (la)
I want more paper.
Quiero más papel.

The paper arrives at 7 a.m.
El periódico llega a las siete de la mañana.

Can you lend me a sheet of paper?
¿Puedes prestarme una hoja de papel?

parachute [PA rä shut] *n.* • paracaídas (el)
I use my parachute when I jump from the plane.
Uso mi paracaídas cuando salto del avión.

parade [pä REID] *n.* • desfile (el)
March 17th is the St. Patrick's Day parade
El 17 de marzo es el desfile de San Patricio.

pardon, to [PAR dän] *v.* • **perdonar**
pardon me *coll.* • **perdóname**
The governor pardons the criminal.
El gobernador perdona al criminal.

Pardon me, may I get through?
Perdóname, ¿puedo pasar?

parents [PER änts] *n.* • padres (los)
His parents travel a lot.
Sus padres viajan mucho.

park, to [PARC] *v.* • **estacionar, aparcar**
parking lot *n.* • **estacionamiento (el)**
They park the car close to the house.
Ellos estacionan el coche cerca de la casa.

park [PARC] *n.* • parque (el)
The park is open until 10 p.m.
Él parque está abierto hasta las diez de la noche.

part (of an object) [PART] *n.* • parte (la)
part (in a play) *n.* • papel (el)
We need to replace this part.
Necesitamos reemplazar esta pieza.

He has a good part in the play.
Él tiene un buen papel en el drama.

party, to have a [PAR ti] *v.* • dar una fiesta
party *n.* • fiesta (la)
party (political) *n.* • partido (el)
Esperanza is having a party tomorrow.
Esperanza da una fiesta mañana.

The Democratic Party is winning the election.
El partido democrático gana la elección.

pass, to [PAS] *v.* • pasar
Please pass me the butter.
Por favor, pásame la mantequilla.

The car passes the truck.
El automóvil pasa el camión.

passenger [PA sen gër] *n.* • pasajero, a (el, la)
The train carries many passengers.
El tren lleva muchos pasajeros.

paste, to [PEIST] *v.* • pegar
Paste the photograph in the album.
Pega la fotografía en el álbum.

patience [PEI shäns] *n.* • paciencia (la)
She has patience with the children.
Ella tiene paciencia con los niños.

patient [PEI shänt] *adj.* • paciente
patient *n.* • paciente (el, la)
Teachers have to be patient.
Los maestros tienen que ser pacientes.

The hospital has a lot of patients.
El hospital tiene muchos pacientes.

paw [PO̲] *n.* • pata (la)
The cat has soft paws.
El gato tiene patas suaves.

pay, to [PEI] *v.* • pagar
pay attention, to *v.* • prestar atención
We pay ten dollars for the tickets.
Pagamos diez dólares por los boletos.

I know you are tired, but please pay attention.
Sé que estás cansado, pero por favor presta atención.

pea [PI] *n.* • guisante (el)
Linda doesn't like peas.
A Linda no le gustan los guisantes.

peach [PICH] *n.* • durazno (el); melocotón (el)
Peaches are delicious.
Los duraznos son deliciosos.

peanut [PI nät] *n.* • cacahuate (el)
The elephant likes peanuts.
Al elefante le gustan los cacahuates.

pear [PER] *n.* • pera (la)
We're eating pears for dessert.
Comemos peras de postre.

pen [PEN] *n.* • pluma (la)
pen (ballpoint) *n.* • bolígrafo (el)
pencil *n.* • lápiz (el)
Will you lend me a pen?
¿Me prestas un bolígrafo?

people [PI pl] *n.* • gente (la)
people (individuals) *n.* • personas (las)
people (nation) *n.* • pueblo (el)
Many people go to Florida in the winter.
Mucha gente va a Florida en el invierno.

There are 15 people in my class.
Hay quince personas en mi clase.

The American people vote in November.
El pueblo norteamericano vota en noviembre.

pepper (condiment) [PE për] *n.* • pimienta (la)
pepper (vegetable) *n.* • pimiento (el)
The salad needs salt and pepper.
La ensalada necesita sal y pimienta.

perhaps [për JAPS] *adv.* • tal vez
Perhaps you want to rest.
Tal vez tú quieres descansar.

permit, to [për MIT] *v.* • permitir
permit [PËR mit] *n.* • permiso (el)
permission *n.* • permiso (el)
Will you permit me to accompany you?
¿Me permites acompañarte?

I need my father's permission.
Necesito el permiso de mi papá.

person [PËR sän] *n.* • persona (la)
personal *adj.* • personal
Do you know this person?
¿Conoces a esta persona?

This is a personal phone call.
Ésta es una llamada personal.

pet [PET] *n.* • animal domesticado (el)
Many of my friends have pets.
Muchos de mis amigos tienen animales domesticados.

pharmacy [FAR ma si] *n.* • farmacia (la)
The pharmacy also sells shampoo.
La farmacia también vende champú.

photograph [FO to graf] *n* • foto (la), fotografía (la)
photographer *n.* • fotógrafo, a (el, la)
I put my photos in an album.
Pongo mis fotos en un álbum.

This photographer takes excellent pictures.
Este fotógrafo saca fotografías excelentes.

piano [pi A no] *n.* • piano (el)
grand piano *n.* • piano de cola (el)
He likes to play the piano.
A él le gusta tocar el piano.

pick, to (choose) [PIC] *v.* • escoger
pick up, to *v.* • recoger
Pick two shirts to take with you.
Escoge dos camisas para llevar contigo.

We're going to pick up Ellen at 5.
Vamos a recoger a Ellen a las cinco.

picture (painting) [PIC chër] *n.* • pintura (la)
(movie) *n.* • película (la)
(photo) *n.* • fotografía (la), foto (la)
(portrait) *n.* • retrato (el)
What a beautiful painting!
¡Qué pintura tan hermosa!

pie [PAI] *n.* • pastel (el)
Cherry pie is my favorite.
El pastel de cerezas es mi favorito.

piece (portion) [PIS] *n.* • pedazo (el)
piece (in a set) • pieza (la)
The broken mirror is in a thousand pieces.
El espejo roto está en mil pedazos.

We're missing one piece of the puzzle.
Nos falta una pieza del rompecabezas.

pillow [PIL lo] *n.* • almohada (la)
The pillow is soft.
La almohada es suave.

pilot [PAI lät] *n.* • piloto (el, la)
Martin is a commercial pilot.
Martín es un piloto comercial.

pin (ornament) [PIN] *n.* • broche (el)
pin (sewing) *n.* • alfiler (el)
That pin is very nice.
Ese broche es muy bonito.

Pins are useful in sewing.
Los alfileres son útiles para coser.

pink [PINC] *adj.* • rosado, a
My new dress is pink.
Mi vestido nuevo es rosado.

place [PLEIS] *n.* • lugar (el)
It's an interesting place.
Es un lugar interesante.

plan, to [PLAN] *v.* • planear
plan *n.* • plan (el)
We plan our trip.
Planeamos nuestro viaje.

John has a good plan.
John tiene un buen plan.

planet [PLAN et] *n.* • planeta (el)
Earth is the third planet of the solar system.
La Tierra es el tercer planeta del sistema solar.

plant, to [PLANT] *v.* • plantar
plant *n.* • planta (la)
We plant flowers in the spring.
Plantamos flores en la primavera.

plate [PLEIT] *n.* • plato (el)
Please put the plates on the table.
Por favor pon los platos en la mesa.

play, to (a game) [PLEI] *v.* • jugar (a)
play, to (an instrument) *v.* • tocar
play (theater) *n.* • obra (la)
Tom plays basketball.
Tom juega al baloncesto.

Elisa plays the piano.
Elisa toca el piano.

pleasant [PLE zänt] *adj.* • agradable
He has a pleasant personality.
Él tiene una personalidad agradable.

please, to (to be agreeable) [PLIZ] *v.* • agradar
please, to (to satisfy) *v.* • satisfacer
please *coll.* • por favor
Your work pleases me, Ana.
Tu trabajo me agrada, Ana.

It's difficult to please the teacher.
Es difícil satisfacer a la maestra.

Please sit down.
Siéntense por favor.

pleasure [PLEZ ër] *n.* • placer (el)
It is a pleasure to meet you.
Es un placer conocerte.

plum [PLÄM] *n.* • ciruela (la)
When plums are dried they are prunes.
Cuando las ciruelas se secan son ciruelas pasas.

plus [PLÄS] *prep.* • más
Two plus one is three.
Dos más uno son tres.

pocket [PAK et] *n.* • bolsillo (el)
This shirt has no pockets.
Esta camisa no tiene bolsillos.

poem [PO äm] *n.* • poema (el)
She writes beautiful poems.
Ella escribe poemas hermosos.

police (force) [pä LIS] *n.* • policía (la)
police (officer) *n.* • policía (el, la)
We should call the police.
Debemos llamar a la policía.

The police officer is very friendly.
El policía es muy amable.

polite [pä LAIT] *adj.* • cortés
Bill is very polite.
Bill es muy cortés.

pool [PUL] *n.* • piscina (la)
Our house has a pool.
Nuestra casa tiene piscina.

poor [PUR] *adj.* • pobre
poor *n.* • pobre (el, la)
The man is poor and has no money.
El hombre es pobre y no tiene dinero.

The poor need better opportunities.
Los pobres necesitan mejores oportunidades.

pop [PAP] *n.* • refresco (el)
I like to drink cold pop on hot days.
Me gusta tomar un refresco frío en los días calurosos.

pop, to [PAP] *v.* • estallar
We pop balloons with a pin.
Estallamos globos con un alfiler.

popular • [PAP yu lër] *adj.* • popular
popularity *n.* • popularidad (la)
He is popular in town.
Él es popular en el pueblo.

There is a popularity contest.
Hay un concurso de popularidad.

population [pap yu LEI shän] *n.* • población (la)
The world's population is almost five billion.
La población mundial es casi cinco mil millones.

possible [PÄ si bl] *adj.* • posible
It is possible to start a fire with two sticks.
Es posible prender fuego con dos palos.

post office [POST O fis] *n.* • correo (el)
post card *n.* • tarjeta postal (la)
postman *n.* • cartero (el)
I'm going to buy stamps at the post office.
Voy a comprar estampillas en el correo.

He receives a post card from a friend.
Él recibe una tarjeta postal de un amigo.

potato [pä TEI to] *n.* • papa (la), patata (la)
Potatoes are one of my favorite foods.
Las papas son una de mis comidas favoritas.

pour, to [POR] *v.* • echar (*liquid*); servir (*to serve someone*)
She is pouring the water.
Ella echa el agua.

We pour tea for our guests.
Servimos té a nuestros invitados.

prefer, to [pri FËR] *v.* • preferir
He prefers to do it without help.
Él prefiere hacerlo sin ayuda.

present [PRE zänt] *n.* • regalo (el)
be present, to *v.* • estar presente
Her birthday present is a wristwatch.
Su regalo de cumpleaños es un reloj de pulsera.

We are all present at the meeting.
Todos estamos presentes en la junta.

president [PRE zi dent] *n.* • presidente, a (el, la)
He is the president of his company.
Él es presidente de su compañia.

pretty [PRI ti] *adj.* • bonito, a
That girl is very pretty.
Esa niña es muy bonita.

prince [PRINS] *n.* • príncipe (el)
The prince hopes to become a king.
El príncipe espera hacerse rey.

princess [PRIN ses] *n.* • princesa (la)
The princess works with the poor.
La princesa trabaja con los pobres.

principal [PRIN si päl] *n* • director, a (el, la)
The parents talk with the principal.
Los padres hablan con el director.

program [PRO gram] *n.* • programa (el)
programmer *n.* • programador, a (el, la)
I like this program.
Me gusta este programa.

The computer programmer likes his work.
Al programador le gusta su trabajo.

promise, to [PRA mis] *v.* • prometer
promise *n.* • promesa (la)
I promise to arrive on time.
Prometo llegar a tiempo.

He makes a promise.
Él hace una promesa.

proud [PRAUD] *adj.* • orgulloso, a
She is proud of herself.
Ella está orgullosa de sí misma.

pull, to [PÜL] *v.* • jalar; tirar
Just pull the door.
Sólo jala la puerta.

pumpkin [PÄMP kin] *n.* • calabaza (la)
I like pumpkin pie.
Me gusta el pastel de calabaza.

punish, to [PÄ nish] *v.* • castigar
They are punishing the criminal.
Ellos castigan al criminal.

pupil [PYU pil] *n.* • alumno, a (el, la)
There are twenty pupils in this class.
Hay veinte alumnos en esta clase.

puppy [PÄ pi] *n.* • cachorro, a (el, la)
What a cute puppy!
¡Qué cachorro tan mono!

purple [PËR pl] *adj.* • morado, a
Eggplant is purple.
La berenjena es morada.

purse [PËRS] *n.* • bolsa (la)
change purse *n.* • monedero (el)
The money is in my purse.
El dinero está en mi bolsa.

push, to • [PÜSH] *v.* • empujar
Please push the door.
Por favor, empuja la puerta.

put, to [PÜT] *v.* • poner
put on, to *v.* • ponerse
I put flowers in a vase.
Pongo flores en un florero.

I put on my clothes.
Me pongo la ropa.

Q

quantity [KWAN ti̲ ti] *n.* • cantidad (la)
They prepare food in great quantities for their family.
Ellos preparan comida en grandes cantidades para su familia.

quarrel, to [KWO̲ rel] *v.* • pelear, discutir
quarrel *n.* • pelea (la), discusión (la)
They quarrel a lot.
Ellos pelean mucho.

quarter [KWO̲R tër] *n.* • cuarto (el)
Kevin wants a quarter of the pie.
Kevin quiere un cuarto del pastel.

They meet at quarter after eight.
Ellos se encuentran a los ocho y cuarto.

queen [KUIN] *n.* • reina (la)
The queen has three daughters.
La reina tiene tres hijas.

question, to [KWES chän] *v.* • preguntar
question *n.* • pregunta (la)
Are you asking if they accept credit cards?
¿Preguntas si aceptan tarjetas de crédito?

Do you have any questions?
¿Tienen ustedes preguntas?

quickly [KWIK li] *adv.* • rápido, rápidamente
They need to finish quickly.
Ellos necesitan terminar rápidamente.

quiet (calm) [KWAI et] *adj.* • tranquilo, a
quiet (silent) *adj.* • callado, a
Sandy is a quiet person.
Sandy es una persona tranquila.

quit, to [KWIT] *v.* • dejar, abandonar
The principal wants to quit his job.
El director quiere dejar su trabajo.

R

race [REIS] *n.* • carrera (la)
The race starts at 7 a.m.
La carrera empieza a las siete de la mañana.

racket [RAK et] *n.* • raqueta (la)
She cannot find her racket.
Ella no puede encontrar su raqueta.

radiator [REI di ei tër] *n.* • radiador (el)
The radiator needs to be repaired.
Hay que arreglar el radiador.

radio [REI dio] *n.* • radio (la)
She has a portable radio.
Ella tiene una radio portátil.

radish [RA dish] *n.* • rábano (el)
Radishes are hot.
Los rábanos son picantes.

rag [RAG] *n.* • trapo (el)
The dust rag is in the closet.
El trapo para quitar polvo está en el armario.

railroad [REIL rod] *n.* • ferrocarril (el)
The railroad is close to the house.
El ferrocarril está cerca de la casa.

rain [REIN] *n.* • lluvia (la)
There is a lot of rain in April.
Hay mucha lluvia en abril.

rainbow [REIN bo] *n.* • arco iris (el)
The rainbow appears when it rains.
El arco iris aparece cuando llueve.

raincoat [REIN cot] *n.* • impermeable (el)
Susan buys a new raincoat every year.
Susan compra un impermeable nuevo cada año.

rain forest [REIN FOR est] *n.* • selva tropical (la)
There are many flowers in the rain forest.
Hay muchas flores en la selva tropical.

raise, to [REIS] *v.* • levantar
Raise your hand when you have the answer.
Levanta la mano cuando tengas la respuesta.

rare [RER] *adj.* • raro, a; poco común
It is rare to see a rainbow.
Es raro ver un arco iris.

razor [REI sër] *n.* • navaja de afeitar (la)
The razor is sharp.
La navaja de afeitar es afilada.

read, to [RID] *v.* • leer
Nancy likes to read in the library.
A Nancy le gusta leer en la biblioteca.

ready [RE di] *adj.* • listo, a
Are you ready to go?
¿Estás lista para ir?

reason [RI sän] *n.* • razón (la)
I am sure there is a reason.
Estoy seguro que hay una razón.

receive, to [RI siv] *v.* • recibir
Debbie receives a gift for her birthday.
Debbie recibe un regalo para su cumpleaños.

record, to [ri KORD] *n.* • grabar
record [REC ërd] *n.* • disco (el)
I want to record that song.
Quiero grabar esa canción.

That record is very good.
Ese disco es muy bueno.

record player [REK ërd PLEI ër] *n.* • tocadiscos (el)
The record player is broken.
El tocadiscos está roto.

recorder (tape) [ri COR dër] *n.* • grabadora (la)
Where is the recorder?
¿Dónde está la grabadora?

rectangle [REC tang gl] *n.* • rectángulo (el)
The painting is a rectangle.
La pintura es un rectángulo.

red [RED] *adj.* • rojo, a
Mrs. Smith likes to wear red jackets.
A la Sra. Smith le gusta llevar chaquetas rojas.

refrigerator [ri FRIG ër ei tër] *n.* • nevera (la), refrigerador (el)
The refrigerator is empty.
La nevera está vacía.

relative [REL a tiv] *n.* • pariente (el, la)
Do you have many relatives?
¿Tienes muchos parientes?

remember, to [ri MEM bër] *v.* • recordar
Jane always remembers my birthday.
Jane siempre recuerda mi cumpleaños.

repair, to [ri PER] *v.* • reparar, arreglar
The mechanic repairs the car.
El mecánico repara el coche.

repeat, to [ri PIT] *v.* • repetir
Please repeat the question.
Repite la pregunta, por favor.

rescue, to [RES cyu] *v.* • rescatar
rescue *n.* • rescate (el)
The firemen rescue the cat.
Los bomberos rescatan el gato.

rest, to [REST] *v.* • descansar
I need to rest.
Necesito descansar.

restaurant [RES tä rant] *n.* • restaurante (el)
Where can we find a good restaurant?
¿Dónde podemos encontrar un buen restaurante?

return, to [ri TËRN] *v.* • regresar, volver
He will return tomorrow.
Regresa mañana.

ribbon [RI̲B bän] *n.* • cinta (la)
There are a lot of yellow ribbons on the trees.
Hay muchas cintas amarillas en los árboles.

rice [RAIS] *n.* • arroz (el)
Sylvester likes rice.
A Sylvester le gusta el arroz .

rich [RI̲CH] *adj.* • rico, a
Ralph wants to be rich.
Ralph quiere ser rico.

ride, to [RAID] *v.* • montar
Bob likes to ride his bike.
A Bob le gusta montar en bicicleta.

ridiculous [ri̲ DI̲ cyu läs] *adj.* • ridículo, a
He wears a ridiculous hat.
Él usa un sombrero ridículo.

right [RAIT] *adj.* • derecho, a
right (correct) *adj.* • correcto, a
My right foot hurts.
Me duele el pie derecho.

John has the right answer.
John tiene la respuesta correcta.

ring (jewelry) [RI̲NG] *n.* • anillo (el)
She does not want an engagement ring.
Ella no quiere un anillo de compromiso.

ripe [RAIP] *adj.* • maduro, a
Those bananas are not ripe.
Esos plátanos no están maduros.

river [RI̲ vër] *n.* • río (el)
The boat is in the river.
La lancha está en el río.

road (highway) [ROD] *n.* • carretera (la)
(street) *n.* • calle (la)
(route) *n.* • camino (el)
There is a good restaurant on the highway.
Hay un buen restaurante en la carretera.

rob, to [RAB] *v.* • robar
robber, thief *n.* • ladrón (el)
The thieves rob a bank.
Los ladrones roban un banco.

rock [RAC] *n.* • roca (la)
The geologist collects rocks.
El geólogo colecciona rocas.

roll up, to [ROL] *v.* • enrollar
Please roll up the maps.
Enrolla los mapas, por favor.

roller skates [ROL lër SKEITS] *n.* • patines de ruedas (los)
Pepita wants roller skates for Christmas.
Pepita quiere patines de ruedas para la Navidad.

roof [RUF] *n.* • techo (el)
The roof is covered with snow.
El techo está cubierto de nieve.

room [RUM] *n.* • cuarto (el)
This house has seven rooms.
Esta casa tiene siete cuartos.

rope [ROP] *n.* • cuerda (la)
This is a strong rope.
Ésta es una cuerda fuerte.

rose [ROS] *n.* • rosa (la)
She receives roses from Fred.
Ella recibe rosas de Fred.

round [RAUND] *adj.* • redondo, a
roundtrip *n.* • viaje de ida y vuelta (el)
He has a round face.
Él tiene la cara redonda.

row [RO] *n.* • fila (la)
There are fifty rows in this theater.
Hay cincuenta filas en este teatro.

rubber [RÄB bër] *n.* • goma (la)
The boy has a rubber ball.
El niño tiene una pelota de goma.

rug [RÄG] *n.* • alfombra (la)
Oriental rugs are beautiful.
Las alfombras orientales son hermosas.

ruler [RU lër] *n.* • regla (la)
I need a ruler for math class.
Necesito una regla para la clase de matemáticas.

run, to [RÄN] *v.* • correr
run away, to *v.* • huir
The child runs in the park.
La niña corre en el parque.

The robbers run away.
Los ladrones huyen.

S

sack [SAC] *n.* • saco (el)
There is a sack race on Saturday.
Hay una carrera de sacos el sábado.

sad [SAD] *adj.* • triste
Why are you sad?
¿Por qué estás triste?

safe [SEIF] *adj.* • seguro, a
safe and sound *coll.* • sano y salvo
I put my money in a safe place.
Pongo mi dinero en un lugar seguro.

salad [SAL äd] *n.* • ensalada (la)
salad bowl *n.* • ensaladera (la)
This salad is delicious.
Esta ensalada está deliciosa.

salesperson [SEILS për sän] *n.* • vendedor, a (el, la)
The salesman visits on Mondays.
El vendedor visita los lunes.

salt [SOLT] *n.* • sal (la)
The soup needs salt.
La sopa necesita sal.

same [SEIM] *adj.* • mismo, a
Please buy the same brand.
Compra la misma marca por favor.

sand [SAND] *n.* • arena (la)
Some beaches have white sand.
Algunas playas tienen arena blanca.

sandwich [SAND wich] *n.* • bocadillo (el), sándwich (el)
Do you want a ham and cheese sandwich?
¿Quieres un bocadillo de jamón y queso?

Saturday [SAT ër dei] *n.* • sábado (el)
The party is Saturday.
La fiesta es el sábado.

save, to (money) [SEIV] *v.* • ahorrar
save, to (a person) *v.* • salvar
They are saving money for a trip.
Ellos ahorran dinero para un viaje.

The fireman is saving the child's life.
El bombero le salva la vida al niño.

say, to [SEI] *v.* • decir
What is he saying?
¿Qué dice?

scarf [SCARF] *n.* • bufanda (la)
We have a scarf for my mother.
Tenemos una bufanda para mi mamá.

schedule [SCEDG yul] *n.* • programa (el)
schedule (timetable) *n.* • horario (el)
The schedule is on the bulletin board.
El programa está en el tablero de anuncios.

I don't have a train schedule.
No tengo un horario de trenes.

school [SCUL] *n.* • escuela (la)
adj. • escolar
My cousin attends a public school.
Mi primo asiste a una escuela pública

We study a lot during the school year.
Estudiamos mucho durante el año escolar.

science [SAI äns] *n.* • ciencia (la)
Physics is an exact science.
La física es una ciencia exacta.

scientist [SAI än tist] *n.* • científico, a (el, la)
The scientist works on an experiment.
El cientifico trabaja en un experimento.

scissors [SIZ ërs] *n.* • tijeras (las)
Where are the scissors?
¿Dónde están las tijeras?

scold, to [SCOLD] *v.* • regañar
The mother scolds her son.
La madre regaña a su hijo.

sea [SI] *n.* • mar (el)
There are many sailboats on the sea.
Hay muchos veleros en el mar

season [SI zän] *n.* • estación (la), temporada (la)
The four seasons are spring, summer, fall and winter.
Las cuatro estaciones son primavera, verano, otoño e invierno.

The soccer season starts in September.
La temporada de fútbol empieza en septiembre.

seat, to [SIT] *v.* • sentar
sit down, to; to be seated *v.* • sentarse
seat *n.* • asiento (el)
seat belt *n.* • cinturón de seguridad (el)
seated *adj.* • sentado, a
The maid seats the guests.
La criada sienta a los invitados.

Please be seated.
Siéntese, por favor.

second [SE cänd] *adj.* • segundo, a
n. • segundo (el)
The second prize is a stereo.
El segundo premio es un estéreo.

A minute has sixty seconds.
Un minuto tiene sesenta segundos.

secret [SI cret] *adj.* • secreto, a
secret *n.* • secreto (el)
The project is a secret.
El proyecto es un secreto.

secretary [SEC ra ter i] *n.* • secretario, a (el, la)
The secretary works at that desk.
El secretario trabaja en ese escritorio.

see, to [SI] *v.* • ver
see you later *coll.* • ¡hasta luego!
see you soon *coll.* • ¡hasta pronto!
see you tomorrow *coll.* • ¡hasta mañana!
They see the paintings at the museum.
Ellos ven las pinturas en el museo.

seem, to [SIM] *v.* • parecer
It seems the cat is hungry.
Parece que el gato tiene hambre.

seesaw [SI so] *n.* • subibaja (el)
There is a seesaw at the park.
Hay un subibaja en el parque.

sell, to [SEL] *v.* • vender
He sells vacuum cleaners.
Él vende aspiradoras.

send, to [SEND] *v.* • mandar
send, to (mail) *v.* • enviar
My father frequently sends flowers to my mother.
Mi padre frecuentemente manda flores a mi madre.

I send a letter to my sister.
Envío una carta a mi hermana.

sentence [SEN täns] *n.* • oración (la)
Paul has to write ten sentences in Spanish.
Paul tiene que escribir diez oraciones en español.

September [sep TEM bër] *n.* • septiembre
Her birthday is in September.
Su cumpleaños es en septiembre.

serious [SIR i äs] *adj.* • serio, a
This is a serious matter.
Éste es un asunto serio.

set, to (put) [SET] *v.* • poner
set the table, to *v.* • poner la mesa
Pablo sets the book on the desk.
Pablo pone el libro en el escritorio.

Jane sets the table.
Jane pone la mesa.

several [SEV ër äl] *adj.* • **varios, as**
There are several dresses she likes.
Hay varios vestidos que le gustan a ella.

sew, to [SO] *v.* • **coser**
She sews very well.
Ella cose muy bien.

shadow [SHA do] *n.* • sombra (la)
Can you see your shadow?
¿Puedes ver tu sombra?

shake, to [SHEIC] *v.* • **temblar**
shake hands, to *v.* • **darse la mano**
The soldiers shake with fear.
Los soldados tiemblan de miedo.

They shake hands before the match.
Ellos se dan la mano antes del partido.

shampoo [sham PU] *n.* • **champú (el)**
She uses a special shampoo.
Ella usa un champú especial.

share, to [SHER] *v.* • **compartir**
They share their lunch.
Ellas comparten el almuerzo.

she [SHI] *pron.* • ella
She is a nice person.
Ella es una persona amable.

sheet (cloth) [SHIT] *n.* • **sábana (la)**
sheet (paper) *n.* • **hoja (la)**
The clean sheets are in the closet.
Las sábanas limpias están en el armario.

This notebook has one hundred sheets.
Este cuaderno tiene cien hojas.

shell [SHEL] *n.* • concha (la)
They look for shells at the beach.
Ellos buscan conchas en la playa.

ship, to [SHIP] *v.* • enviar
ship *n.* barco (el)
He ships the package.
Él envía el paquete.

The ship is at the port.
El barco está en el puerto.

shirt [SHËRT] *n.* • camisa (la)
He wears a nice shirt.
Él lleva una camisa bonita.

shoe [SHU] *n.* • zapato (el)
shoe store *n.* • zapatería (la)
Imelda likes shoes.
A Imelda le gustan los zapatos.

There are several shoe stores downtown.
Hay varias zapaterías en el centro de la ciudad.

shop, to [SHAP] *v.* • ir de compras
shop *n.* • tienda (la)
They go shopping on Saturdays.
Ellos van de compras los sábados.

She goes to the shop.
Ella va a la tienda.

short (height) [SHORT] *adj.* • bajo, a
short (length) *adj.* • corto, a
My mother is short.
Mi madre es baja.

I like short stories.
Me gustan los cuentos cortos.

shovel [SHÄV el] *n.* • pala (la)
The shovel is in the garage.
La pala está en el garaje.

show, to [SHO] *v.* • mostrar, enseñar
His mother shows us the family pictures.
Su mamá nos muestra las fotos de la familia.

shower, to [SHAU wër] *v.* • ducharse
shower *n.* • ducha (la)
He showers before going out.
Él se ducha antes de salir.

The bathroom has a new shower.
El baño tiene una ducha nueva.

shy [SHAI] *adj.* • tímido, a
Connie is a shy person.
Connie es una persona tímida.

sick [SI̲C] *adj.* • enfermo, a
Are you sick?
¿Estás enfermo?

sidewalk [SAID woc] *n.* • acera (la)
The sidewalk is covered with snow.
La acera está cubierta de nieve.

silver [SI̲L vër] *n.* • plata (la)
She likes silver jewelry.
A ella le gustan las joyas de plata.

similar [SI̲M i̲ lër] *adj.* • similar, parecido, a
That is a similar style.
Ése es un estilo similar.

simple [SI̲M pel] *adj.* • sencillo, a
It's very simple.
Es muy sencillo.

sing, to [SING] *v.* • cantar
singer *n.* • cantante (el, la)
The family sings at the party.
La familia canta en la fiesta.

sister [SIS tër] *n.* • hermana (la)
sister-in-law *n.* • cuñada (la)
My sister lives in California.
Mi hermana vive en California.

sit down, to [SIT daun] *v.* • sentarse
The public sits down after the national anthem.
El público se sienta después del himno nacional.

skate, to [SCEIT] *v.* • patinar
skate *n.* • patín (el)
We like to skate in the park.
Nos gusta patinar en el parque.

skin [SCIN] *n.* • piel (la)
skin (complexion) *n.* • cutis (el)
This cream is for sensitive skin.
Esta crema es para la piel sensible.

skirt [SCËRT] *n.* • falda (la)
The skirt is red.
La falda es roja.

sky [SCAI] *n.* • cielo (el)
skyscraper *n.* • rascacielos (el)
The sky is blue.
El cielo es azul.

The skyscraper is a tall building.
El rascacielos es un edificio alto.

sled [SLED] *n.* • trineo (el)
The children play with their sleds.
Los niños juegan con sus trineos.

sleep, to [SLIP] *v.* • dormir
sleeping bag *n.* • bolsa de dormir (la)
Susan is sleeping now.
Susan duerme ahora.

slip, to [SLIP] *v.* • resbalarse
Be careful! You can slip and fall.
¡Cuidado! Puedes resbalarte y caerte.

slow [SLO] *adj.* • lento, a
slow down! *coll.* • ¡más despacio!
The traffic is slow.
El tráfico es lento.

small [SMOL] *adj.* • pequeño, a
The room is small.
El cuarto es pequeño.

smell, to [SMEL] *v.* • oler
smell *n.* • olor (el), aroma (el)
The roses smell good.
Las rosas huelen bien.

What is that smell?
¿Qué es ese olor?

smile, to [SMAIL] *v.* • sonreírse
smile *n.* • sonrisa (la)
They smile in the picture.
Ellos se sonríen en la foto.

His smile is charming.
Su sonrisa es encantadora.

snack [SNAC] *n.* • bocado (el)
The cafeteria has some good snacks.
La cafetería tiene unos bocados buenos.

snake [SNEIC] *n.* • serpiente (la), víbora (la)
That snake is not poisonous.
Esa serpiente no es venenosa.

sneeze, to [SNIZ] *v.* • estornudar
sneeze *n.* • estornudo (el)
David sneezes when he is near cats.
David estornuda cuando está cerca de los gatos.

snow, to [SNO] *v.* nevar
snow *n.* • nieve (la)
It snows in winter.
Nieva en el invierno.

There is always snow on that mountain.
Siempre hay nieve en esa montaña.

so [SO] *adv.* • tan
so much, so many *adj.* • tanto, a; os, as
so-so *coll.* • así, así
He is so nice.
Él es tan amable.

Juan has so much money!
¡Juan tiene tanto dinero!

Julia has so many friends!
¡Julia tiene tantas amigas!

soap [sop] *n.* • jabón (el)
soap (laundry) *n.* • detergente (el)
The soap does not have perfume.
El jabón no tiene perfume.

The laundry soap is in the box.
El detergente está en la caja.

soccer [SAC cẽr] *n.* • fútbol (el)
My brother plays soccer.
Mi hermano juega al fútbol.

sock [SAC] *n.* • calcetín (el)
The socks are in the washing machine.
Los calcetines están en la lavadora.

sofa [SO fä] *n.* • sofá (el)
The sofa is comfortable.
El sofá es cómodo.

soft [SO̱FT] *adj.* • suave
soft drink *n.* • refresco (el)
Cotton is soft.
El algodón es suave.

They want a soft drink.
Ellos quieren un refresco.

soldier [SOL gër] *n.* • soldado (el)
The soldiers return tomorrow.
Los soldados regresan mañana.

some [SÄM] *adj.* • algún, alguno, a
somebody *pron.* • alguien
someone *pron.* • alguien
something *n.* • algo
sometimes *adv.* • algunas veces
I want to visit Spain some day.
Quiero visitar España algún día.

Somebody wants to be your friend.
Alguien quiere ser tu amigo.

I have something in my hand.
Tengo algo en la mano.

Sometimes we speak Spanish.
Algunas veces hablamos español.

son [SÄN] *n.* • hijo, el
son-in-law *n.* • yerno, el
Her sons are all married.
Todos sus hijos están casados

song [SONG] *n.* • canción (la)
That is a beautiful song!
¡Ésa es una canción hermosa!

soon [SUN] *adv.* • pronto
They're coming soon.
Vienen pronto.

soup [SUP] *n.* • sopa (la)
They like tomato soup.
Les gusta la sopa de tomate.

south [SAUTH] *n.* • sur (el)
They visit their relatives in the South.
Ellos visitan a sus parientes en el sur.

Spanish [SPAN ish] *adj.* • español, a
n. • español (el)
Miss González is Spanish.
La señorita González es española.

We learn Spanish at school.
Aprendemos español en la escuela.

speak, to [SPIC] *v.* • hablar
speaker *n.* • conferencista (el, la)
Paul is speaking to the teacher.
Paul le habla al profesor.

spectator [SPEC tei tër] *n.* • espectador, a (el, la)
I prefer to be a spectator; I don't like to play sports.
Prefiero ser espectador; no me gusta hacer deporte.

spend, to (money) [SPEND] *v.* • gastar
spend, to (time) *v.* • pasar
She spends her money on books.
Ella gasta su dinero en libros.

They spend their vacation in Nevada.
Ellos pasan sus vacaciones en Nevada.

spider [SPAI dër] *n.* • araña (la)
The spider eats other insects.
La araña come otros insectos.

spill, to [SPIL] *v.* • derramar
The child spills his milk.
El niño derrama su leche.

spoon [SPUN] *n.* • cuchara (la)
spoonful *n.* • cucharada (la)
We need spoons for dessert.
Necesitamos cucharas para el postre.

sport [SPORT] *n.* • deporte (el)
There are lots of different sports at the Olympic Games.
Hay muchos deportes diferentes en los Juegos Olímpicos.

spring [SPRING] *n.* • primavera (la)
Flowers bloom in spring.
Las flores florecen en la primavera.

square (town) [SKWER] *n.* • plaza (la)
square (shape) *n.* • cuadrado (el)
The concert is in the main square.
El concierto es en la plaza principal.

A square has four sides.
Un cuadrado tiene cuatro lados.

stair (step) [STER] *n.* • escalón (el)
staircase, stairs *n.* • escalera (la)
Paco is sitting on the stair.
Paco está sentado en el escalón.

They are building a new staircase.
Construyen una escalera nueva.

stamp [STAMP] *n.* • estampilla (la)
The post office sells stamps.
La oficina de correos vende estampillas.

stamp, to [STAMP] *v.* • patear
He stamps his foot.
Él patea el pie.

stand, to [STAND] *v.* • estar de pie
stand (up), to *v.* • levantarse
stand in line, to *v.* • hacer cola
My mother stands all day.
Mi madre está de pie todo el día.

Please stand up.
Levántenso, por favor.

They stand in line to get tickets.
Ellos hacen cola para conseguir boletos.

star [STAR] *n.* • estrella (la)
It's cloudy; we can't see the stars.
Está nublado; no podemos ver las estrellas.

start, to [START] *v.* • comenzar, empezar
start, to (a machine) *v.* • arrancar
They start the project today.
Ellos comienzan el proyecto hoy.

The car does not start today.
El automóvil no arranca hoy.

state [STEIT] *n.* • estado (el)
Alaska is the biggest state in the country.
Alaska es el estado más grande del país.

station [STEI shän] *n.* • estación (la)
The train station is downtown.
La estación de tren está en el centro.

stay, to [STEI] *v.* • quedarse
stay, to (on a trip) *v.* • alojarse
She stays at home because she is sick.
Ella se queda en casa porque está enferma.

We're staying at the Plaza Hotel.
Nos alojamos en el Hotel Plaza.

steal, to [STIL] *v.* • robar
The robbers steal the money.
Los ladrones roban el dinero.

step (walking) [STEP] *n.* • paso (el)
step (of stairs) *n.* • escalón (el)
Do you have a picture of her first step?
¿Tienes una foto de su primer paso?

The stairs have twelve steps.
La escalera tiene doce escalones.

stepbrother [STEP brä thër] *n.* • hermanastro (el)
stepfather *n.* • padrastro (el)
stepmother *n.* • madrastra (la)
stepsister *n.* • hermanastra (la)
She has three stepbrothers.
Ella tiene tres hermanastros.

stick [STIC] *n.* • palo (el)
There are some sticks in the work room.
Hay unos palos en el taller.

still [STIL] *adv.* • todavía
I still do not understand.
Todavía no entiendo.

stingy [STIN gi] *adj.* • tacaño, a
He is very stingy.
Él es muy tacaño.

stocking [STAK ing] *n.* • media (la)
The stockings are in the closet.
Las medias están en el armario.

stomach [STÄM äc] *n.* • estómago (el)
Cows have four stomachs.
Los vacas tienen cuatro estómagos.

stone [STON] *n.* • piedra (la)
These stones come from Hawaii.
Estas piedras vienen de Hawai.

stop, to [STAP] *v.* • detener, parar
stop *n.* • parada (la)
They are stopping all cars at the border.
Detienen todos los coches en la frontera.

The stop is at the corner.
La parada está en la esquina.

store [STOR] *n.* • tienda (la)
This is an interesting store.
Ésta es una tienda interesante.

storm [STORM] *n.* • tormenta (la)
The storm is coming from the north.
La tormenta viene del norte.

story (tale) [STO ri] *n.* • cuento (el); historia (la)
story (floor of a building) *n.* • piso (el)
Jorge likes to read short stories.
A Jorge le gusta leer cuentos.

They live on the third story.
Viven en el tercer piso.

stove [STOV] *n.* • estufa (la)
The food is on the stove.
La comida está en la estufa.

straight [STREIT] *adj.* • derecho, a
straight (hair) *adj.* • lacio, a
straight ahead *adv.* • enfrente
There is only one straight fork!
¡Hay sólo un tenedor derecho!

All her children have straight hair.
Todos sus hijos tienen el pelo lacio.

The sign is straight ahead.
El letrero está enfrente.

strange [STREING] *adj.* • extraño, a; raro, a
He is strange.
Él es extraño.

strawberry [STRO bër ri] *n.* • fresa (la)
The cake has strawberries.
El pastel tiene fresas.

street [STRIT] *n.* • calle (la)
street lamp *n.* • farol (el)
They live on Elm Street.
Ellos viven en la calle Elm.

string [STRING] *n.* • cuerda (la)
string (necklace) *n.* • collar (el)
They need a string to tie the newspapers.
Necesitan una cuerda para atar los periódicos.

She wants a string of pearls.
Ella quiere un collar de perlas.

strong [STRONG] *adj.* • fuerte
Conan is a strong man.
Conan es un hombre fuerte.

student [STU dent] *n.* • estudiante (el, la)
The students don't have school tomorrow.
Los estudiantes no tienen clases mañana.

study, to [STÄD i] *v.* • estudiar
study *n.* • estudio (el)
They study for their tests.
Ellos estudian para sus exámenes.

The study is upstairs.
El estudio está arriba.

stumble, to [STÄM bel] *v.* • tropezar
Ellen always stumbles on that step.
Ellen siempre tropieza en ese escalón.

subway [SÄB wei] *n.* • metro (el)
Small towns do not have subways.
Los pueblos pequeños no tienen metro.

succeed, to [säx SID] *v.* • tener éxito
success *n.* • éxito (el)
The expedition succeeds.
La expedición tiene éxito.

His success is unexpected.
Su éxito es inesperado.

suddenly [SÄD den li] *adv.* • de repente
They suddenly decide to leave.
Deciden salir de repente.

sugar [SHÜ gër] *n.* • azúcar (el)
She drinks coffee without sugar.
Ella toma café sin azúcar.

suit [SUT] *n.* • traje (el)
The tailor makes suits.
El sastre hace trajes.

suitcase [SUT keis] *n.* • maleta (la)
We have to pack the suitcases today.
Tenemos que hacer las maletas hoy.

summer [SÄM mër] *n.* • verano (el)
We swim during the summer.
Nosotros nadamos durante el verano.

sun [SÄN] *n.* • sol (el)
sunbath *n.* • baño de sol (el)
sunrise *n.* • amanecer (el)
sunset *n.* • atardecer (el)
Where are our seats? Sun or shade?
¿Dónde están nuestros asientos? ¿Sol o sombra?

Sunday [SÄN dei] *n.* • domingo (el)
The store is closed on Sundays.
La tienda está cerrada los domingos.

supermarket [SU për mar ket] *n.* • supermercado (el)
They do not sell shoes at the supermarket.
No venden zapatos en el supermercado.

surprise [sër PRAIZ] *n* • sorpresa (la)
The gift is a surprise.
El regalo es una sorpresa.

sweater [SWET ër] *n.* • suéter (el)
This is a wool sweater.
Éste es un suéter de lana.

sweep, to [SWIP] *v.* • barrer
Please sweep the floor.
Por favor barre el piso.

sweet [SWIT] *adj.* • dulce
n. • dulce (el)
The sweets are in the box.
Los dulces están en la caja.

swim, to [SWIM] *v.* • nadar
swimmer *n.* • nadador, a (el, la)
swimming *n.* • natación (la)
They like to swim in the sea.
Les gusta nadar en el mar.

T

T-shirt [TI shërt] *n.* • camiseta (la)
These T-shirts are at the store.
Estas camisetas están en la tienda.

table [TEIBL] *n.* • mesa (la)
The table is in the dining room.
La mesa está en el comedor.

tablecloth [TEIBL cloth] *n.* • mantel (el)
My grandmother is embroidering a tablecloth.
Mi abuela borda un mantel.

tail [TEIL] *n.* • cola (la).
These cats have short tails.
Estos gatos tienen colas cortas.

tailor [TEI lër] *n.* • sastre (el)
The tailor makes suits.
El sastre hace trajes.

take, to [TEIC] *v.* • tomar
to take along • llevar
to take a bath • bañarse
to take a trip • hacer un viaje
to take a walk • dar un paseo
to take effect • tener efecto
to take off (remove) • quitar
to take out • sacar
to take over • hacerse cargo de
to take photos • sacar fotos
Please take a book and sit down.
Toma un libro y siéntate, por favor.

I'm going to take along my umbrella.
Voy a llevar mi paraguas.

talk, to [TOK] *v.* • hablar
The students need to talk to the principal.
Los estudiantes necesitan hablar con el director.

tall [TOL] *adj.* • alto, a
There are some tall buildings in the city.
Hay algunos edificios altos en la ciudad.

tan, to [TAN] *v.* • broncearse, tostarse
tan (skin) *adj.* • bronceado, a, tostado, a
tan (color for things) *adj.* • color tostado
Children tan easily.
Los niños se broncean fácilmente.

The jacket is tan.
La chaqueta es de color tostado.

tank [TANC] *n.* • tanque (el)
tank (fish) *n.* • acuario (el)
tank (gas) *n.* • tanque de gasolina (el)
My brother drives a tank in the army.
Mi hermano conduce un tanque en el ejército.

The fish tank is very pretty.
El acuario es muy bonito.

tape, to [TEIP] *v.* • grabar
tape recorder *n.* • grabadora (la)
tape (adhesive) *n.* • cinta adhesiva (la)
Do you want to tape your voice?
¿Quieres grabar tu voz?

taste, to (try) [TEIST] *v.* • probar
taste, to (have a flavor) *v.* • saber, tener sabor
Do you want to taste the salad?
¿Quieres probar la ensalada?

This food tastes great!
¡Esta comida sabe bien!

tattletale [TAT tl teil] *n.* • chismoso, a (el, la)
Darío is a tattletale.
Darío es un chismoso.

taxi [TAX i] *n.* • taxi (el)
taxi driver *n.* • taxista (el, la)
We are waiting for a taxi.
Esperamos un taxi.

tea [TI] *n.* • té (el)
Do you want coffee or tea?
¿Quieres café o té?

teach, to [TICH] *v.* • enseñar
She is teaching biology.
Ella enseña biología.

teacher [TICH ër] *n.* • maestro, a (el, la)
The teacher arrives early.
La maestra llega temprano.

team [TIM] *n.* • equipo (el)
The team wins.
El equipo gana.

tear [TIR] *n.* • lágrima (la)
His tears are false.
Sus lágrimas son falsas.

tear, to [TER] *v.* • romper
He is tearing the papers.
Él rompe los papeles.

teeth [TITH] *n.* • dientes (los)
The baby has three teeth.
El bebé tiene tres dientes.

telephone [TEL ä fon] *n.* • teléfono (el)
(tele)phone book *n.* • guía telefónica (la)
(tele)phone booth *n.* • cabina de teléfono (la)
(tele)phone number *n.* • número de teléfono (el)
I need a public telephone to make a call.
Necesito un teléfono público para hacer una llamada.

television [TEL ä vi̲ shän] *n.* • televisión (la)
  television set *n.* • televisor (el)
What is the name of that television program?
¿Cómo se llama ese programa de televisión?

The T.V. set is not in the kitchen.
El televisor no está en la cocina.

tell, to [TEL] *v.* • decir, contar
Are you going to tell the truth?
¿Vas a decir la verdad?

Grandmother tells interesting stories.
La abuela cuenta historias interesantes.

tennis [TEN ni̲s] *n.* • tenis (el)
I cannot play tennis.
Yo no puedo jugar al tenis.

tent [TENT] *n.* • tienda de campaña; tienda (la)
The tent has a hole.
La tienda de campaña tiene un agujero.

terrible [TER ri̲ bäl] *adj.* • terrible
Tornadoes are terrible.
Los tornados son terribles.

test [TEST] *n.* • examen (el)
The test is tomorrow.
El examen es mañana.

thank, to [THANC] *v.* • agradecer
  thank you *coll.* • gracias
The actors thank the public.
Los actores agradecen al público.

Thank you for the flowers.
Gracias por las flores.

that [THAT] *adj.* • ese, a
that one *pron.* • ése, a
That man is my history teacher.
Ese señor es mi maestro de historia.

That one is my history teacher.
Ése es mi maestro de historia.

the [THÄ] *art.* • el, la, los, las
The employees are with the boss.
Los empleados están con el jefe.

The girls are with the teacher.
Las chicas están con la maestra.

theater [THI ä tër] *n.* • teatro (el)
The theater is downtown.
El teatro está en el centro.

their [THER] *adj.* • su, sus
Susan and Joe lend their cars to their children.
Susan y Joe prestan sus coches a sus hijos.

then (in that case) [THEN] *adv.* • entonces
then (after) *adv.* • luego
You can't go? Then we won't either.
¿No puedes ir? Entonces no vamos tampoco.

I have to clean my room, and then I can go with you.
Tengo que limpiar mi cuarto y luego puedo ir contigo.

there [THER] *adv.* • allí, allá
The house is there on the corner.
La casa está allí, en la esquina.

there is [THER is] *v.* • hay
there are *v.* • hay
There is a man at the door.
Hay un señor a la puerta.

There are three men at the door.
Hay tres señores a la puerta.

these [THIZ] *adj.* • estos, as
pron. • éstos, as
These shoes are for the dance.
Estos zapatos son para el baile.

These are for walking.
Éstos son para caminar.

they [THEI] *pron.* • ellos, as
Who are they?
¿Quiénes son ellos?

thick [THIC] *adj.* • espeso, a
Beavers have thick fur.
Los castores tienen el pelo muy espeso.

thief [THIF] *n.* • ladrón (el)
The thief in the story has a good heart.
El ladrón del cuento tiene un buen corazón.

thin [THIN] *adj.* • delgado, a
He is very thin.
Él es muy delgado.

thing [THING] *n.* • cosa (la)
What are those things?
¿Qué son esas cosas?

think, to [THINC] *v.* • pensar, creer
think about, to *v.* • pensar en
think of, to (opinion) *v.* • pensar de
I'm thinking about my boyfriend.
Pienso en mi novio.

What do you think of my boyfriend?
¿Qué piensas de mi novio?

thirsty, to be [THËRS ti] *v.* • tener sed
There is lemonade if you are thirsty.
Hay limonada si tienes sed.

this [THIS] *adj.* • este, a
this one *pron.* • éste, a
I want this book.
Quiero este libro.

I want this one.
Quiero éste.

throat [THROT] *n.* • garganta (la)
My throat is sore.
Me duele la garganta.

through [THRU] *prep.* • por
John is coming through the door now.
John entra por la puerta ahora.

throw, to [THRO] *v.* • tirar
throw away, to *v.* • tirar
Jaime likes to throw stones at the garbage can.
A Jaime le gusta tirar piedras al cubo de basura.

Can you throw this away?
¿Puedes tirar esto?

thunder [THĂN dër] *n.* • trueno (el)
He is scared of thunder.
Él tiene miedo a los truenos.

Thursday [THËRS dei] *n.* • jueves (el)
The lady goes shopping on Thursdays.
La señora va de compras los jueves.

ticket (transport) [TI̲K et] *n.* • boleto (el), billete (el)
ticket (movies, theater, etc.) *n.* • entrada (la), boleto (el)
Do you have tickets for the concert?
¿Tienes boletos para el concierto?

tight [TAIT] *adj.* • apretado, a
I don't like those tight shoes!
¡No me gustan esos zapatos apretados!

time [TAIM] *n.* • tiempo (el)
time of day *n.* hora (la)
They always arrive on time.
Ellos siempre llegan a tiempo.

What time is it?
¿Qué hora es?

tip [TI̲P] *n.* • propina (la)
The tip is fifteen percent.
La propina es quince por ciento.

tire [TAIR] *n.* • llanta (la)
The car needs new tires.
El automóvil necesita nuevas llantas.

tired [TAIRD] *adj.* • cansado, a
She is tired today.
Ella está cansada hoy.

to [TU] *prep.* • a, para
Please give this to Kay.
Por favor dále esto a Kay.

The package is for you.
El paquete es para ti.

toast, to (to heat bread) [TOST] *v.* • tostar
toast, (to drink to the health of) *v.* • brindar
pan tostado (el), tostada (la)
toast (bread) *n.* toast (salute) *n.* brindis
There is toast and jelly.
Hay pan tostado y mermelada.

The guests toast the bride and groom.
Los invitados brindan por los novios.

I need to prepare a toast.
Necesito preparar un brindis.

toaster [TOST ër] *n.* • tostadora (la)
The toaster is broken.
La tostadora está descompuesta.

today [tu DEI] *adv.* • hoy
She can't come today.
Ella no puede venir hoy.

together [tu GETH ër] *adv.* • juntos, as
Why don't we go to the party together?
¿Por qué no vamos a la fiesta juntos?

tomato [tä MEI to] *n.* • tomate (el)
Are there fresh tomatoes in the refrigerator?
¿Hay tomates frescos en el refrigerador?

tomorrow [tä MAR ro] *adv.* • mañana
The results are going to be ready tomorrow.
Los resultados van a estar listos mañana.

tongue [TÄNG] *n.* • lengua (la)
You shouldn't stick out your tongue.
No debes sacar la lengua.

tonight [tu NAIT] *adv.* • esta noche
Erica is going to the movies tonight.
Erica va al cine esta noche.

too [TU] *adv.* • también
too much; too many *adj.* • demasiado, a; os, as
too much *adv.* • demasiado
Her cousins are coming too.
Sus primos vienen también.

Pepe eats too much.
Pepe come demasiado.

There are too many chairs in the classroom.
Hay demasiadas sillas en el salón de clase.

tooth [TUTH] *n.* • diente (el)
toothbrush *n.* • cepillo de dientes (el)
toothpaste *n.* • pasta de dientes (la)
The toothbrush and toothpaste are in the bathroom.
El cepillo y la pasta de dientes están en el baño.

My grandfather has false teeth.
Mi abuelo tiene dientes postizos.

touch, to [TÄCH] *v.* • tocar
The museum has a sign that says "Please do not touch."
El museo tiene un letrero que dice "Favor de no tocar".

tourist [TUR ist] *n.* • turista (el, la)
Acapulco has many tourists.
Acapulco tiene muchos turistas.

towards [TORDS] *prep.* • hacia
She drives towards the city.
Ella maneja hacia la ciudad.

towel [TAUL] *n.* • toalla (la)
towel rack *n.* • toallero (el)
The towels are on the towel rack.
Las toallas están en el toallero.

tower [TAU ër] *n.* • torre (la)
The castle has several towers.
El castillo tiene varias torres.

town [TAUN] *n.* • pueblo (el)
town square *n.* • plaza (la)
This town has sixty thousand inhabitants.
Este pueblo tiene sesenta mil habitantes.

The festivities are at the town square.
Las festividades son en la plaza.

toy [TOY] *n.* • juguete (el)
Her favorite toy is that car.
Su juguete favorito es ese automóvil.

track [TRAC] *n.* • pista (la)
The team runs on the track.
El equipo corre en la pista.

tractor [TRAC tër] *n.* • tractor (el)
The farmer uses a tractor.
El granjero usa un tractor.

traffic [TRA fic] *n.* • tráfico (el), tránsito (el)
traffic jam *n.* • embotellamiento (el)
traffic light *n.* • semáforo (el)
The traffic is terrible; we need a traffic light here.
El tráfico es terrible; necesitamos un semáforo aquí.

The traffic jams are usually at 5:30 p.m.
Los embotellamientos son usualmente a las 5:30 p.m.

trail [TREIL] *n.* • sendero (el)
The bicycle trail is beautiful.
El sendero para bicicletas es hermoso.

train [TREIN] *n.* • tren (el)
train station *n.* • estación de trenes (la)
We wait for the train in the train station.
Esperamos el tren en la estación de trenes.

travel, to [TRA vel] *v.* • viajar
She wants to travel around the world.
Ella quiere viajar alrededor del mundo.

traveler [TRAV ä lër] *n.* • viajero, a (el, la)
The travelers are tired.
Los viajeros están cansados.

tree [TRI] *n.* • árbol (el)
We plant a tree in the garden.
Plantamos un árbol en el jardín.

triangle [TRAI ang gäl] *n.* • triángulo (el)
A triangle has three sides.
Un triángulo tiene tres lados.

truck [TRÄC] *n.* • camión (el)
That truck is very heavy.
Ese camión es muy pesado.

true [TRU] *adj.* • verdadero, a
It is true. *coll.* • Es verdad.
It is a true story.
Es una historia verdadera.

trunk (chest) [TRÄNC] *n.* • baúl (el)
The blankets are in the cedar trunk.
Las mantas están en el baúl de cedro.

truth [TRUTH] *n.* • verdad (la)
She tells the truth.
Ella dice la verdad.

try, to (attempt) [TRAI] *v.* • tratar de
try, to (taste) *v.* • probar
I want to try to cook Mexican food.
Quiero tratar de cocinar comida mexicana.

Do you want to try the soup?
¿Quieres probar la sopa?

Tuesday [TUS dei] *n.* • martes (el)
They are going to be here on Tuesday.
Ellas van a estar aquí el martes.

turkey [TËR ki] *n.* • guajolote (el); pavo (el)
There is turkey for dinner.
Hay pavo para la cena.

turn, to (direction) [TËRN] *v.* • doblar
turn off, to *v.* • apagar
turn on, to *v.* • prender
Turn to the right.
Dobla a la derecha.

Please turn off the TV.
Por favor apaga el televisor.

twice [TWAIS] *adv.* • dos veces
She called twice.
Ella llamó dos veces.

type, to [TAIP] *v.* • escribir a máquina
I am learning to type.
Aprendo escribir a máquina.

type [TAIP] *n.* • tipo (el)
There are many types of cheese.
Hay muchos tipos de queso.

typewriter [TAIP rai tër] *n.* • máquina de escribir (la)
The typewriter needs a new ribbon.
La máquina de escribir necesita una cinta nueva.

typist [TAIP ist] *n.* • mecanógrafo, a (el, la)
The typist is going to have the papers ready tomorrow.
El mecanógrafo va a tener listos los papeles mañana.

The typist helps the students.
La mecanógrafa ayuda a los estudiantes.

U

ugly [ÄG li] *adj.* • feo, a
That is an ugly dress!
¡Ése es un vestido feo!

umbrella (for rain) [äm BREL lä] *n.* • paraguas (el)
umbrella (for sun), parasol *n.* • sombrilla (la), parasol (el)
Bring your umbrella.
Trae tu paraguas.

Do you have a parasol?
¿Tienes una sombrilla?

uncle [ÄNG cäl] *n.* • tío (el)
My uncle lives in Mexico.
Mi tío vive en México.

uncomfortable [än CÄM fër tä bl] *adj.* • incómodo, a
The seats in the theater are uncomfortable.
Los asientos en el teatro son incómodos.

under [ÄN dër] *prep.* • debajo de
The ball is under the table.
La pelota está debajo de la mesa.

understand, to [än dër STAND] *v.* • entender, comprender
She understands Spanish.
Ella comprende español.

unhappy [än JAP pi] *adj.* • infeliz
Bob is very unhappy.
Bob está muy infeliz.

unique [yu NIC] *adj.* • único, a
His art is unique.
Su arte es único.

united [yu NAI ted] *adj.* • unido, a
United Nations *n.* • Naciones Unidas (las)
United States of America *n.* • Estados Unidos de América (los)
Our class is visiting the United Nations.
Nuestra clase visita las Naciones Unidas.

My grandmother is not from the United States.
Mi abuela no es de los Estados Unidos.

university [yu ni VËR si ti] *n.* • universidad (la)
My sister attends the state university.
Mi hermana asiste a la universidad estatal.

until [än TIL] *adv.* • hasta
They want to stay until tomorrow.
Ellos quieren quedarse hasta mañana.

unusual [än YU shu äl] *adj.* • poco común, raro, a
It is an unusual situation.
Es una situación poco común.

upstairs [äp STERS] *adv.* • arriba
The bedrooms are upstairs.
Los dormitorios están arriba.

use, to [YUS] *v.* • usar
May I use your pencil?
¿Puedo usar tu lápiz?

useful [YUS fäl] *adj.* • útil
It is useful to carry a map in the car.
Es útil llevar un mapa en el coche.

useless [YUS les] *adj.* • inútil
It is useless to talk to him.
Es inútil hablar con él.

V

vase [VEIS] *n.* • florero (el)
The vase is from Spain.
El florero es de España.

very [VE ri] *adv.* • muy
She is very brave.
Ella es muy valiente.

visit, to [VI zit] *v.* • visitar
Tomorrow we'll visit our grandparents.
Mañana vamos a visitar a nuestros abuelos.

W

waist [WEIST] *n.* • cintura (la)
She does exercises for her waist.
Ella hace ejercicios para la cintura.

wait for, to [WEIT for] *v.* • esperar
We are waiting for the bus.
Esperamos el autobús.

waiter [WEIT ër] *n.* • mesero (el), camarero (el)
waitress *n.* • mesera (la), camarera (la)
The waiter is kind.
El mesero es amable.

wake up, to [WEIC äp] *v.* • despertarse
The baby wakes up during the night.
El bebé se despierta durante la noche.

walk, to [WQC] *v.* • caminar
Barbara walks two miles every day.
Barbara camina dos millas todos los días.

wall [WQL] *n.* • pared (la)
There is a map on the wall.
Hay un mapa en la pared.

wallet [WQL let] *n.* • cartera (la), billetera (la)
He has a leather wallet.
Él tiene una billetera de cuero.

want, to [WANT] *v.* • querer
Martha wants to travel.
Martha quiere viajar.

war [WQR] *n.* • guerra (la)
Nobody likes war.
A nadie le gusta la guerra.

warm [WQRM] *adj.* • caliente
The food is warm.
La comida está caliente.

wash, to [WQSH] *v.* • lavar
wash oneself, to *v.* • lavarse
washing machine *n.* • lavadora (la)
The clothes are ready to wash.
La ropa está lista para lavar.

The washing machine is new.
La lavadora es nueva.

watch, to [WACH] *v.* • mirar
Are they watching T.V.?
¿Miran la televisión?

watch [WACH] *n.* • reloj (el), reloj de pulsera (el)
Ángela has a collection of watches.
Ángela tiene una colección de relojes.

water [WQ tër] *n.* • agua (el) (f.)
We should drink eight glasses of water a day.
Debemos beber ocho vasos de agua al día.

waterfall [WQ ter fql] *n.* • catarata (la)
There are lots of waterfalls in the mountains.
Hay muchas cataratas en las montañas.

watermelon [WQ tër me län] *n.* • sandía (la)
Watermelon is her favorite fruit.
La sandía es su fruta favorita.

wave [WEIV] *n.* • ola (la)
They play with the waves at the beach.
Ellos juegan con las olas en la playa.

we [WI] *pron.* • nosotros, as
We are studying Spanish.
Nosotros estudiamos español.

weak [WIC] *adj.* • débil
She is weak after her illness.
Ella está débil después de su enfermedad.

wear, to [WER] *v.* • usar, llevar
That rock group wears unusual clothes.
Ese grupo de rock usa ropa poco común.

I'm going to wear my new coat.
Voy a llevar mi abrigo nuevo.

weather [WE thër] *n.* • tiempo (el)
The weather is nice
Hace buen tiempo.

wedding [WED ding] *n.* • boda (la)
They are going to have a small wedding.
Ellos van a tener una boda pequeña.

Wednesday [WENS dei] *n.* • miércoles (el)
I don't have class on Wednesdays.
No tengo clase los miércoles.

week [WIC] *n.* • semana (la)
weekend *n.* • fin de semana (el)
The year has fifty-two weeks.
El año tiene cincuenta y dos semanas.

Do you want to go to the movies this weekend?
¿Quieres ir al cine este fin de semana?

welcome, to [WEL cäm] *v.* • dar la bienvenida a
welcome! *coll.* • ¡bienvenido, a!
She welcomes the guests.
Ella da la bienvenida a los invitados.

well [WEL] *adv.* • bien
Jessie sings very well.
Jessie canta muy bien.

west [WEST] *n.* • oeste (el)
San Diego is west of Phoenix.
San Diego está al oeste de Phoenix.

wet [WET] *adj.* • húmedo, a
wet blanket *coll.* • aguafiestas (el, la)
This towel is wet.
Esta toalla está húmeda.

He is a wet blanket.
Él es un aguafiestas.

wheat [WIT] *n.* • trigo (el)
The farmer harvests the wheat.
El granjero cosecha el trigo.

wheel [WIL] *n.* • rueda (la)
wheel (steering) *n.* • volante (el)
That cart needs new wheels.
Esa carreta necesita ruedas nuevas.

There is a problem with the steering wheel.
Hay un problema con el volante.

white [WAIT] *adj.* • blanco, a
The bride wears a white dress.
La novia usa un vestido blanco.

whole [JOL] *adj.* • entero, a
The whole world waits for news of the war.
El mundo entero espera noticias de la guerra.

wide [WAID] *adj.* • ancho, a
Fifth Avenue is a wide avenue.
La Quinta Avenida es una avenida ancha.

wife [WAIF] *n.* • esposa (la)
Paul's wife is an economist.
La esposa de Paul es economista.

wild [WAILD] *adj.* • salvaje
Tigers are wild animals.
Los tigres son animales salvajes.

win, to [WIN] *v.* • ganar
They want to win the contest.
Ellos quieren ganar el concurso.

wind [WIND] *n.* • viento (el)
The wind is coming from the east.
El viento es del este.

window [WIN do] *n.* • ventana (la)
His house has big windows.
Su casa tiene ventanas grandes.

windshield [WIND shild] *n.* • parabrisas (el)
The car needs a new windshield.
El automóvil necesita un parabrisas nuevo.

wine [WAIN] *n.* • vino (el)
This wine is from 1987.
Este vino es de 1987.

wing [WING] *n.* • ala (el) (f.)
The plane has huge wings.
El avión tiene alas enormes.

winter [WIN tër] *n.* • invierno (el)
Winter starts in December.
El invierno empieza en diciembre.

wise [WAIS] *adj.* • sabio, a
Her grandmother is a wise woman.
Su abuela es una mujer sabia.

wish, to [WISH] *v.* • desear
wish *n.* • deseo (el)
They wish you happy holidays.
Ellos te desean unas fiestas felices.

Cinderella's wish is to go to the party.
El deseo de Cenicienta es ir a la fiesta.

with [WITH] *prep.* • con.
Are you coming with us?
¿Vienes con nosotros?

without [with AUT] *prep.* • sin
They are going without us.
Ellos van sin nosotros.

wolf [WÜLF] *n.* • lobo, a (el, la)
Wolves are intelligent animals.
Los lobos son animales inteligentes.

woman [WÜ män] *n.* • mujer (la)
That woman is the president of the company.
Esa mujer es presidente de la compañía.

wonderful [WÄN dër fäl] *adj.* • maravilloso, a
He is a wonderful teacher.
Él es un maestro maravilloso.

wood [WÜD] *n.* • madera (la)
That sculpture is made of wood.
Esa escultura es de madera.

work, to [WËRC] *v.* • trabajar
work, to (machine) *v.* • funcionar
work *n.* • trabajo (el)
My mother works at the hospital.
Mi mamá trabaja en el hospital.

This machine does not work.
Esta máquina no funciona.

Pablo is looking for work.
Pablo busca trabajo.

worker [WËRC ër] *n.* • trabajador, a (el, la)
The workers have a union.
Los trabajadores tienen un sindicato.

world [WËRLD] *n.* mundo (el)
How many countries are there in the world?
¿Cuántos países hay en el mundo?

wrap, to [RAP] *v.* • envolver
wrap *n.* • envoltura (la)
Please wrap the gifts.
Por favor, envuelve los regalos.

She makes her own wrapping paper.
Ella hace su propio papel de envoltura.

write, to [RAIT] *v.* • escribir
She likes to write poetry.
A ella le gusta escribir poesía.

Y

year [YIR] *n.* • año (el)
There are twelve months in a year.
Hay doce meses en un año.

yell, to [YEL] *v.* • gritar
The crowd yells at the referee.
El público le grita al árbitro.

yellow [YEL lo] *adj.* • amarillo, a
She likes yellow roses.
A ella le gustan las rosas amarillas.

yes [YES] *adv.* • sí
Yes, I have a driver's license.
Sí, tengo licencia de manejar.

yesterday [YES tër dei] *adv.* • ayer
How do you say "yesterday" in French?
¿Cómo se dice "ayer" en francés?

yet [YET] *adv.* • todavía
The newspaper is not here yet.
El periódico no está aquí todavía.

young [YÄng] *adj.* • joven
The boss is a young man.
El jefe es un hombre joven.

Z

zebra [ZI brä] *n.* • cebra (la)
The zebra is an African animal.
La cebra es un animal africano.

zone [ZON] *n.* • zona (la)
The city is divided into three zones.
La ciudad está dividida en tres zonas.

zoo [ZU] *n.* • zoo (el), jardín zoológico (el)
There are very interesting animals at the zoo.
Hay animales muy interesantes en el zoo.

Appendices/*Apéndices*

Spanish Names—*Nombres*

Masculine Names—*Nombres masculinos*

Adolph	*Adolfo*	Hugh, Hugo	*Hugo*
Augustin	*Agustín*	Ignatius	*Ignacio*
Albert	*Alberto*	Isidore	*Isidoro*
Alexander	*Alejandro*	James	*Jaime*
Alfred	*Alfredo*	James	*Diego*
Andrew	*Andrés*	Jeremy	*Jeremías*
Angel	*Ángel*	Jerome	*Jerónimo*
Anthony	*Antonio*	Joseph	*José*
Arnold	*Arnaldo*	Joseph, Joe	*Pepe*
Arthur	*Arturo*	Joshua	*Josué*
Basil	*Basilio*	John	*Juan*
Benjamin	*Benito*	Jack, Johnny	*Juanito*
Bernard	*Bernardo*	Julius, Jules	*Julio*
Charles	*Carlos*	Leo, Leon	*León*
Cecil	*Cecilio*	Leonard	*Leonardo*
Claude	*Claudio*	Lawrence	*Lorenzo*
Clement	*Clemente*	Lucas, Luke	*Lucas*
Christopher	*Cristóbal*	Louis	*Luis*
Daniel	*Daniel*	Mark	*Marcos*
David	*David*	Martin	*Martín*
Dominick	*Domingo*	Matthew, Matt	*Mateo*
Donald	*Donaldo*	Michael, Mike	*Miguel*
Edmund	*Edmundo*	Nathan	*Natán*
Edward	*Eduardo*	Nicholas	*Nicolás*
Emil	*Emilio*	Oscar	*Óscar*
Emmanuel	*Manuel*	Paul	*Pablo*
Ernest	*Ernesto*	Patrick	*Patricio*
Eugene	*Eugenio*	Peter	*Pedro*
Fabian	*Fabián*	Phillip	*Felipe*
Frank	*Paco, Pancho*	Ralph	*Rafael*
Frederick	*Federico*	Raymond	*Ramón*
Ferdinand	*Fernando*	Raoul	*Raúl*
Francis	*Francisco*	Richard, Rick	*Ricardo*
Gabriel	*Gabriel*	Robert	*Roberto*
Gerard	*Gerardo*	Rudolph	*Rodolfo*
George	*Jorge*	Roderick, Rod	*Rodrigo*
Gilbert	*Gilberto*	Roger	*Rogelio*
Gregory	*Gregorio*	Roland	*Rolando*
Gustaf, Gus	*Gustavo*	Reuben	*Rubén*
Henry	*Enrique*	Samuel	*Samuel*
Herbert	*Heriberto*	Saul	*Saúl*
Horace	*Horacio*	Simon	*Simón*

Masculine Names—*Nombres masculinos* (continued)

Stephen, Steven	*Esteban*	Virgil	*Virgilio*
Timothy, Tim	*Timoteo*	Wilfred	*Wilfredo*
Thomas, Tom	*Tomás*	William	*Guillermo*
Vincent	*Vicente*	Xavier	*Javier*
Victor	*Víctor*		

Feminine Names—*Nombres femeninos*

Adele	*Adela, Adelita*	Esther	*Éster*
Alberta	*Alberta*	Eugenia	*Eugenia*
Alexandra	*Alejandra*	Eve, Eva	*Eva*
Alice	*Alicia*	Frederica	*Federica*
Amelia	*Amalia*	Frances	*Francisca*
Ann, Anne	*Ana*	Gloria	*Gloria*
Andrea	*Andrea*	Grace	*Graciela*
Angela	*Ángela*	Anges, Inez	*Inés*
Anita	*Anita*	Irene	*Irene, Irena*
Antonia	*Antonia*	Elizabeth	*Isabel*
Barbara	*Bárbara*	Josephine	*Josefina*
Beatrice	*Beatriz*	Jean, Joan	*Juana*
Bernadine	*Bernardina*	Judith, Judy	*Judit*
Bertha	*Berta*	Julia	*Julia*
Blanche	*Blanca*	Laura	*Laura*
Carla	*Carla*	Eleanor	*Leonor*
Charlotte	*Carlota*	Lydia	*Lidia*
Carmen	*Carmen*	Linda	*Linda*
Caroline	*Carolina*	Lola	*Lola*
Kathleen	*Catalina*	Lucy	*Lucía*
Catherine	*Catarina*	Lucinda	*Lucinda*
Cecile	*Cecilia*	Louise, Lois	*Luisa*
Claire	*Clara*	Magdalene	*Magdalena*
Claudia	*Claudia*	Margaret	*Margarita*
Constance	*Constancia*	Mary, Maria	*María*
Corinne	*Corina*	Mary Ann	*Mariana*
Christine	*Cristina*	Martha	*Marta*
Deborah	*Débora*	Matilda	*Matilde*
Diana, Diane	*Diana*	Mercedes	*Mercedes*
Dolores	*Dolores*	Minerva	*Minerva*
Elaine	*Elena*	Olga	*Olga*
Lisa, Elise	*Elisa*	Patricia	*Patricia*
Elsa	*Elsa*	Paula	*Paula*
Emma	*Ema*	Prudence	*Prudencia*
Emily	*Emilia*	Rachel	*Raquel*
Henrietta	*Enriqueta*	Rebecca	*Rebeca*
Hope	*Esperanza*	Roberta	*Roberta*
Estelle, Stella	*Estela*	Rose	*Rosa*

Feminine Names—*Nombres Femeninos* (continued)

Rosalie	*Rosalía*	Theresa	*Teresa*
Sara, Sarah	*Sara*	Toni	*Tonia*
Sylvia	*Silvia*	Victoria	*Victoria*
Sophie	*Sofía*	Violet	*Violeta*
Susan	*Susana*	Virginia	*Virginia*

Feminine Names—*Nombres femeninos* (continued)

parents	*los padres*
mom, mother	*la mamá, la madre*
dad, father	*el papá, el padre*
son, daughter	*el hijo, la hija*
brother, sister	*el hermano, la hermana*
grandmother, grandfather	*el abuelo, la abuela*
grandchild	*el nieto, la nieta*
uncle, aunt	*el tío, la tía*
nephew, niece	*el sobrino, la sobrina*
cousin	*el primo, la prima*
father-in-law, mother-in-law	*el suegro, la suegra*
brother-in-law, sister-in-law	*el cuñado, la cuñada*
stepfather	*el padrastro*
stepmother	*la madrastra*
stepchild	*el hijastro, la hijastra*
stepbrother, stepsister	*el hermanastro, la hermanastra*
godmother	*la madrina*
godfather	*el padrino*
godchild	*el ahijado, la ahijada*

The Body—*El cuerpo*

ankle	*el tobillo*	head	*la cabeza*
arm	*el brazo*	hips	*las caderas*
back	*la espalda*	lip	*el labio*
cheek	*la mejilla*	mouth	*la boca*
chin	*la barbilla*	neck	*el cuello*
face	*la cara*	shoulder	*el hombro*
finger	*el dedo*	toe	*el dedo, del pie*
hair	*el cabello*	tongue	*la lengua*
hand	*la mano*	wrist	*la muñeca*

Countries	***Países***	**Nationalities**	***Nacionalidades***
Argentina	*Argentina*	Argentine	*argentino(-a)*
Australia	*Australia*	Australian	*australiano(-a)*
Brazil	*Brasil*	Brazilian	*brasileño(-a)*
Bolivia	*Bolivia*	Bolivian	*boliviano(-a)*
Canada	*Canadá*	Canadian	*canadiense*
Chile	*Chile*	Chilean	*chileno(-a)*
China	*China*	Chinese	*chino(-a)*
Colombia	*Colombia*	Colombian	*colombiano(-a)*
Costa Rica	*Costa Rica*	Costa Rican	*costarricense*
Cuba	*Cuba*	Cuban	*cubano(-a)*
Dominican Republic	*República Dominicana*	Dominican	*dominicano(-a)*
Ecuador	*Ecuador*	Ecuadorian	*ecuatoriano(-a)*
Egypt	*Egipto*	Egyptian	*égipcio(-a)*
El Salvador	*El Salvador*	Salvadorian	*salvadoreño(-a)*
England	*Inglaterra*	English	*inglés(-esa)*
France	*Francia*	French	*francés(-esa)*
Germany	*Alemania*	German	*alemán(-ana)*
Great Britain	*Gran Bretaña*	British	*británico(-a)*
Guatemala	*Guatemala*	Guatemalan	*guatemalteco(-a)*
Holland	*Holanda*	Dutch	*holandés(-esa)*
Honduras	*Honduras*	Honduran	*hondureño(-a)*
Italy	*Italia*	Italian	*italiano(-a)*
Japan	*Japón*	Japanese	*japonés(-esa)*
Korea	*Corea*	Korean	*coreano(-a)*
Mexico	*México*	Mexican	*mexicano(-a)*
Nicaragua	*Nicaragua*	Nicaraguan	*nicaragüense*
Panama	*Panamá*	Panamanian	*panameño(-a)*
Paraguay	*Paraguay*	Paraguayan	*paraguayo(-a)*
Peru	*Perú*	Peruvian	*peruano(-a)*
Portugal	*Portugal*	Portuguese	*portugués(-esa)*
Russia	*Rusia*	Russian	*ruso(-a)*
Spain	*España*	Spanish	*español(-a)*
United States	*Estados Unidos*	American	*americano(-a)*
Uruguay	*Uruguay*	Uruguayan	*uruguayo(-a)*
Venezuela	*Venezuela*	Venezuelan	*venezolano(-a)*

Foods—*La comida*

bread	*el pan*	cream	*la crema*
broccoli	*el bróculi*	fish	*el pescado*
butter	*la mantequilla*	french fries	*las papas fritas*
cake	*la torta*	ham	*el jamón*
celery	*el apio*	hamburger	*la hamburguesa*
chicken	*el pollo*	ice cream	*el helado*
coffee	*el café*	jam	*la mermelada*

Foods—*La comida* (continued)

ketchup	*la salsa de tomate*	sandwich	*el bocadillo, el sándwich*
meat	*la carne*	sausage	*la salchicha*
mushroom	*el hongo*	soft drink	*el refresco*
mustard	*la mostaza*	soup	*la sopa*
noodles	*los fideos*	steak	*el bistec*
omelet	*la tortilla*	sugar	*el azúcar*
pepper (spice)	*la pimienta*	tea	*el té*
rice	*el arroz*	toast	*el pan tostado*
salad	*la ensalada*		
salt	*la sal*		

Sports—*Los deportes*

baseball	*el béisbol*
baketball	*el baloncesto*
boxing	*el boxeo*
cycling	*el ciclismo*
car racing	*las carreras de coches*
cross-country skiing	*el esquí nórdico*
downhill skiing	*el esquí alpino*
football	*el fútbol americano*
gymnastics	*la gimnasia*
hockey	*el hockey*
horseback riding	*la equitación*
jogging	*el jogging*
running	*el correr*
sailing	*la vela*
skating	*el patinaje*
soccer	*el fútbol*
swimming	*la natación*
tennis	*el tenis*
volleyball	*el voleibol*
weight lifting	*el levantamiento de pesos*

At the Zoo—*En el jardín zoológico*

alligator	*el caimán*	giraffe	*la jirafa*
bear	*el oso*	gorilla	*el gorila*
bear cub	*el cachorro de oso*	hippopotamus	*el hipopótamo*
camel	*el camello*	jaguar	*el jaguar*
deer	*el ciervo*	leopard	*el leopardo*
eagle	*el águila*	lizard	*el lagarto*
elephant	*el elefante*	ostrich	*el avestruz*
flamingo	*el flamenco*	panda	*el panda*
fox	*el zorro*	parrot	*el loro*

At the Zoo—*En el jardín zoológico* (continued)

parrot	*el loro*	tiger	*el tigre*
peacock	*el pavo real*	tiger cub	*el cachorro de tigre*
penguin	*el pingüino*	turtle	*la tortuga*
polar bear	*el oso polar*	walrus	*la morsa*
rhinoceros	*el rinoceronte*	wolf	*el lobo*
seal	*la foca*		

Months of the Year—*Meses del año*

January	*enero*	July	*julio*
February	*febrero*	August	*agosto*
March	*marzo*	September	*septiembre*
April	*abril*	October	*octubre*
May	*mayo*	November	*noviembre*
June	*junio*	December	*diciembre*

Days of the Week—*Días de la semana*

Monday	*lunes*	Friday	*viernes*
Tuesday	*martes*	Saturday	*sábado*
Wednesday	*miércoles*	Sunday	*domingo*
Thursday	*jueves*		

Numbers—*Números*

0	zero	*cero*
1	one	*uno*
2	two	*dos*
3	three	*tres*
4	four	*cuatro*
5	five	*cinco*
6	six	*seis*
7	seven	*siete*
8	eight	*ocho*
9	nine	*nueve*
10	ten	*diez*
11	eleven	*once*
12	twelve	*doce*
13	thirteen	*trece*
14	fourteen	*catorce*
15	fifteen	*quince*
16	sixteen	*dieciséis*
17	seventeen	*diecisiete*
18	eighteen	*dieciocho*

Numbers—*Números* (continued)

19	nineteen	*diecinueve*
20	twenty	*veinte*
30	thirty	*treinta*
40	forty	*cuarenta*
50	fifty	*cincuenta*
60	sixty	*sesenta*
70	seventy	*setenta*
80	eighty	*ochenta*
90	ninety	*noventa*
100	one hundred	*cien (ciento)*
200	two hundred	*doscientos*
500	five hundred	*quinientos*
1000	one thousand	*mil*
2000	two thousand	*dos mil*

Temperature—La temperatura

	Fahrenheit	*Centigrade / centígrados*
Water freezes *El agua se congela*	32°	0°
Water boils *El agua hierve*	212°	100°

Temperature Chart
Tabla de temperaturas

F	C
110°	43°
100°	37.8°
90°	32.2°
80°	26.7°
70°	21.1°
60°	15.5°
50°	10°
40°	4.4°
32°	0°
20°	–6.7°
10°	–12.2°
0°	–17.8°
–10°	–23.3°
–20°	–28.9°

To convert Centrigrade into Fahrenheit:
Para convertir los grados centígrados en grados Fahrenheit:

$$(C° \times 9/5) + 32 = F°$$

To convert Fahrenheit into Centigrade:
Para convertir los grados Fahrenheit en grados centígrados:

$$(F° - 32) \times 5 / 9 = F°$$

Weights and Measures—*Pesos y medidas*

acre (ac)/*acre*
centimeter (cm)/*centímetro*
foot (ft)/*pie*
gallon (gal)/*galón*
gram (g)/*gramo*
hectare (ha)/*hectárea*
inch (in)/*pulgada*
kilogram (kg)/*kilogramo*
kilometer (km)/*kilómetro*
liter (l)/*litro*
meter (m)/*metro*
metric ton (t)/*tonelada métrica*
mile (mi)/*milla*
millimeter (mm)/*milímetro*
ounce (oz)/*onza*
pound (lb)/*libra*
short ton/*tonelada corta*

Weights and Measures—*Pesos y medidas* (continued)

LINEAR/ *LINEAR*	1 in	=	2.54	cm		
	1 ft	=	30.48	cm		
	1 yd	=	.914	m		
	1 mi	=	1.610	km		
	1 mm	=	.03987	in		
	1 cm	=	.3937	in		
	1 m	=	3.2808	ft	= 1.0936	yd
	1 km	=	.621	mi		
WEIGHT/ *PESO*	1 oz	=	28.3495	grams		
	1 lb	=	.4536	kg		
	1 short ton	=	907.18	kg		
	1 g	=	.035	oz		
	1 kg	=	2.204	lb		
	1 t	=	1.1023	short ton		
VOLUME/ *VOLÚMEN*	1 oz	=	29.58	ml		
	1 qt	=	.9464	l		
	1 gal	=	3.7854	l		
	1 cubic in	=	16.39	cubic cm		
	1 cubic ft	=	.0283	cubic m		
	1 cubic yd	=	.7646	cubic m		
	1 ml	=	.0348	oz		
	1 l	=	1.0567	qt		
	1 l	=	.2642	gal		
	1 cubic cm	=	.0610	cubic in		
	1 cubic m	=	35.315	cubic ft		
	1 cubic m	=	1.3080	cubic yd		
AREA/ *ÁREA*	1 ac	=	.4047	ha		
	1 ha	=	2.4711	ac		

NORTH AMERICA / AMÉRICA DEL NORTE
Bering Straits
Bering Sea
ARCTIC OCEAN
GREENLAND
Alaska
Yukon River
Anchorage
VICTORIA ISLAND
Great Bear Lake
Baffin Bay
BAFFIN ISLAND
Juneau
MacKenzie River
Great Slave Lake
PACIFIC OCEAN / OCÉANO PACÍFICO
QUEEN CHARLOTTE ISLAND
CANADA
Hudson Bay
VANCOUVER ISLAND
Edmonton
Nelson River
Vancouver
Calgary
Seattle
Lake Winnipeg
Regina
Portland
Winnipeg
OCÉANO ATLÁNTICO
NEWFOUNDLAND
Snake River
Superior
GREAT LAKES
Quebec
Gulf of St. Lawrence
San Francisco
UNITED STATES OF AMERICA
Missouri River
Huron
Montreal
Michigan
Ottawa
St. Lawrence River
Halifax
Colorado River
Denver
Toronto
NOVA SCOTIA
Los Angeles
Detroit
Ontario
Boston
San Diego
Platte River
Chicago
Erie
New York
Phoenix
Albuquerque
Philadelphia
BAJA CALIFORNIA
Oklahoma City
St. Louis
Washington, D.C.
El Paso
Arkansas River
Mississippi River
ATLANTIC OCEAN /
MEXICO
Río Bravo del Norte
Dallas
Red River
Atlanta
Houston
New Orleans
Monterrey
San Antonio
Tampa
Gulf of Mexico / Golfo de México
Miami
Guadalajara
México, D.F
CUBA
ISLA ESPAÑOLA
PUERTO RICO
JAMAICA
Caribbean Sea / Mar Caribe
CENTRAL AMERICA
SOUTH AMERICA
Hawaii
KAUAI
OAHU
MOLOKAI
MAUI
HAWAII
Honolulu
PACIFIC OCEAN

CENTRAL AMERICA / CENTRO AMÉRICA

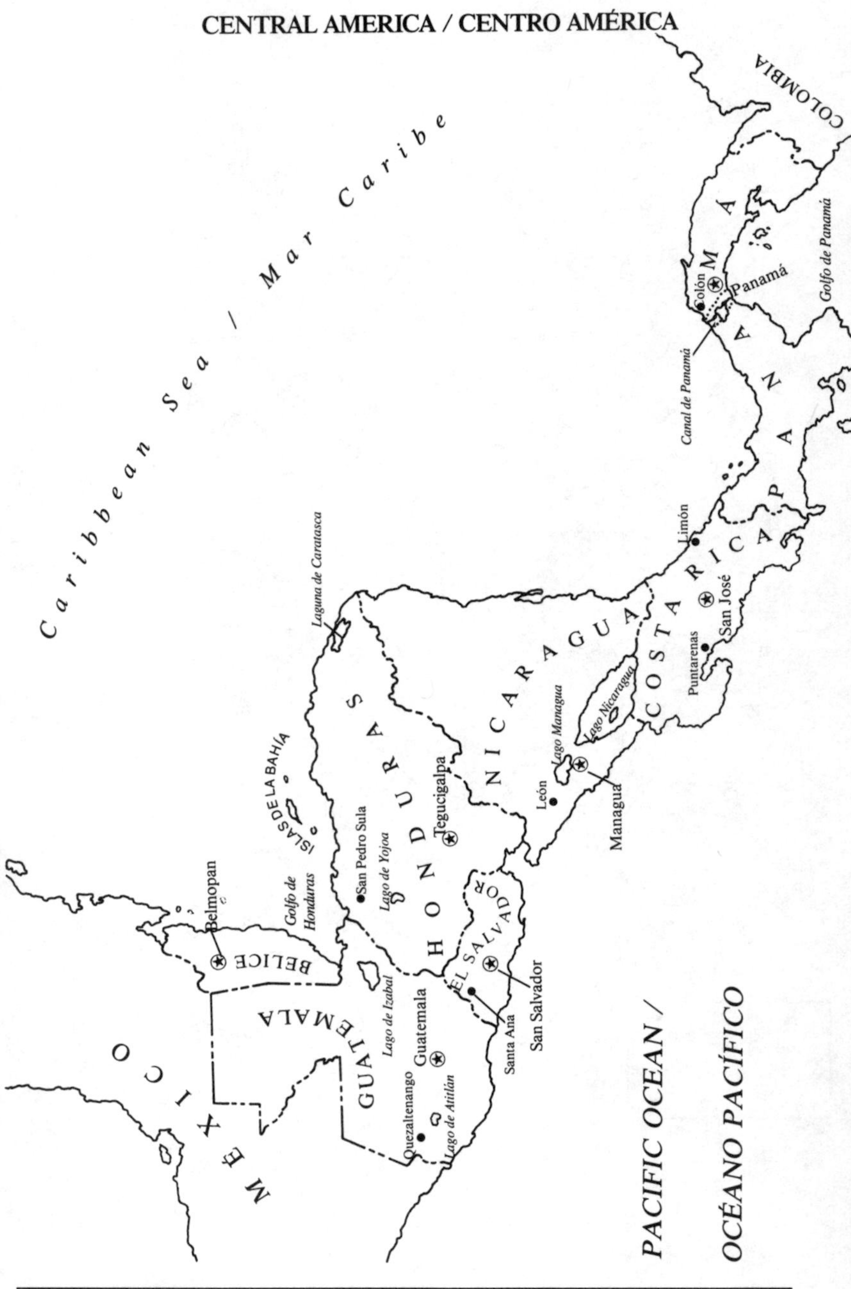

MEXICO / MÉXICO
UNITED STATES / ESTADOS UNIDOS
Gulf of Mexico / Golfo de México
Bahía de Campeche
PENÍNSULA DE YUCATÁN
BELICE
GUATEMALA
Cozumel
Mérida
Campeche
Matamoros
Reynosa
Monterrey
Nuevo Laredo
Río Grande / Río Bravo del Norte
San Luis Potosí
Querétaro
México, D.F.
Veracruz
Puebla
Cuernavaca
Oaxaca
Acapulco
Guadalajara
Morelia
Manzanillo
Puerto Vallarta
Durango
Mazatlán
Chihuahua
Ciudad Juárez
MÉXICO
Nogales
Hermosillo
Tijuana
Mexicali
BAJA CALIFORNIA
PACIFIC OCEAN / OCÉANO PACÍFICO

WEST INDIES / INDIAS OCCIDENTALES
Gulf of Mexico / Golfo de México
FLORIDA
Miami
Key West
Straits of Florida
ANDROS ISLAND
Nassau
BAHAMAS
La Habana
CUBA
ISLA DE LOS PINOS
Camagüey
CAYMAN ISLANDS
Santiago de Cuba
Guantánamo
ATLANTIC OCEAN / OCÉANO ATLÁNTICO
HAITÍ
Cap Haïtien
DOMINICANA
REPÚBLICA
Santiago
ISLA ESPAÑOLA
Port-au-Prince
Santo Domingo
JAMAICA
Kingston
GREATER ANTILLES
PUERTO RICO
San Juan
Ponce
Mayagüez
VIRGIN ISLANDS
ST. CROIX
LEEWARD ISLANDS
WINDWARD ISLANDS
GUADELOUPE
DOMINICA
MARTINIQUE
SAINT LUCIA
ST. VINCENT
BARBADOS
GRENADA
Port of Spain
TRINIDAD AND TOBAGO
LESSER ANTILLES
ARUBA
CURAÇAO
HONDURAS
NICARAGUA
COSTA RICA
PANAMÁ
CENTRAL AMERICA
COLOMBIA
VENEZUELA

SOUTH AMERICA / AMÉRICA DEL SUR
Caribbean Sea/ Mar Caribe
ATLANTIC OCEAN / OCÉANO ATLÁNTICO
CENTROAMÉRICA
PANAMÁ
Barranquilla
Medellín
Cali
Bogotá
COLOMBIA
Maracaibo
Valencia
Caracas
Barquisimeto
Río Orinoco
VENEZUELA
Río Magdalena
Cauca
Port of Spain
Georgetown
GUYANA
Paramaribo
Cayenne
FRENCH GUIANA
ARCHIPIÉLAGO DE COLÓN
Quito
ECUADOR
Guayaquil
Cuenca
Iquitos
Río Negro
Río Amazonas
BRASIL
Fortaleza
Recife
Brasilia
PERÚ
Lima
Callao
Cuzco
La Paz
BOLIVIA
Cochabamba
Santa Cruz
Lago de Poopó
Sucre
Potosí
PARAGUAY
Concepción
Paraná
Belo Horizonte
Asunción
São Paulo
Rio de Janeiro
PACIFIC OCEAN / OCÉANO PACÍFICO
CHILE
ARGENTINA
San Miguel de Tucumán
Porto Alegre
Córdoba
Santa Fe
Valparaíso
Santiago
Mendoza
Rosario
URUGUAY
Buenos Aires
Montevideo
La Plata
ATLANTIC OCEAN / OCÉANO ATLÁNTICO
FALKLAND ISLANDS / ISLAS MALVINAS
Estrecho de Magallanes
TIERRA DEL FUEGO
Cabo de Hornos

SPAIN AND PORTUGAL / ESPAÑA Y PORTUGAL

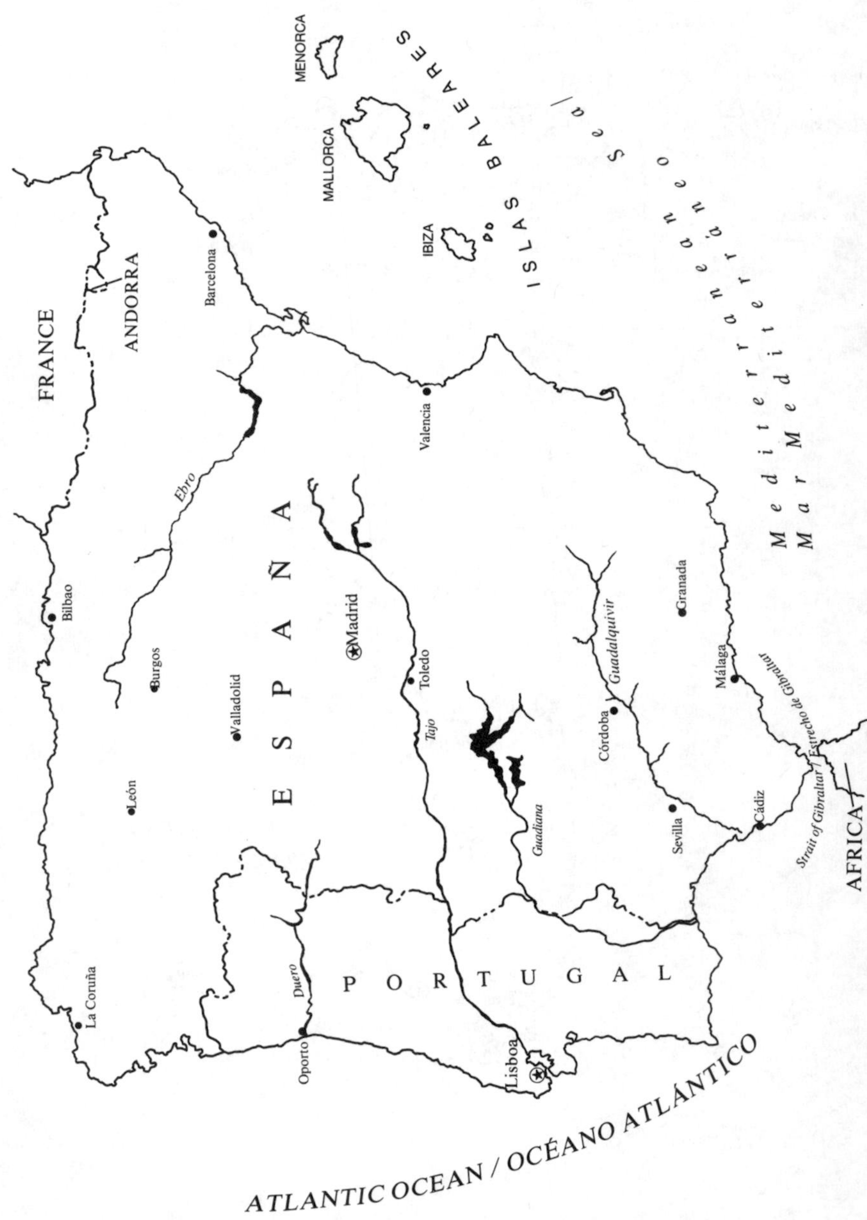